and
league.
k

# UNDERSTANDING BLINDNESS

An Integrative Approach

# UNDERSTANDING BLINDNESS

## An Integrative Approach

MARK HOLLINS

University of North Carolina
at Chapel Hill

LAWRENCE ERLBAUM ASSOCIATES, PUBLISHERS
1989 Hillsdale, New Jersey Hove and London

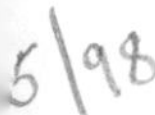

Lawrence Erlbaum Associates, Inc., Publishers
365 Broadway
Hillsdale, New Jersey 07642



**Library of Congress Cataloging-in-Publication Data**

Hollins, Mark.
Understanding blindness: a multidisciplinary approach / Mark Hollins; with a chapter by Eleanor H. L. Leung.
p. cm.
Bibliography: p.
Includes index.
ISBN 0-89859-952-0
1. Blindness. 2. Blindness—Psychological aspects. I. Leung, Eleanor H. L. II. Title.
[DNLM: 1. Blindness. WW 276 H741u]
RE91.H65 1989
617.7'12—dc19
DNLM/DLC
for Library of Congress 89-1584
CIP

Printed in the United States of America
10 9 8 7 6 5 4 3 2 1

# CONTENTS

# PREFACE

Much is known about blindness, but the field is divided into specialties. Experts in these different areas are widely dispersed among university departments, rehabilitation agencies,and school systems, with the result that people in one specialty area often know little about developments in other areas. It is hoped that the present work will be useful in reducing this isolation, by presenting, within a single volume, basic information derived from different approaches to the subject of blindness. Individuals who are already familiar with material in some of the chapters can gain added perspective on the field as a whole by reading about aspects of blindness outside their specialty area.

This book is also intended as a text for courses at the advanced undergraduate or graduate level, especially in departments of psychology, special education, and rehabilitation. In order to make the book accessible to students in a variety of fields, I have written it for readers with no particular technical background; terms are defined and technical concepts explained when they are introduced.

The role played by scientific research in increasing our understanding of blindness is emphasized throughout the book. Whenever possible I have backed statements up by reference to empirical studies, rather than to simple assertions on the part of other writers, however authoritative. Methods as well as results of experiments are described, in order to afford readers an opportunity to judge the persuasiveness of the evidence for themselves.

It is a pleasure to acknowledge the essential contributions that my wife, Eleanor Leung, has made to the writing of this book. In addition to bringing her rich understanding of infant and child development to bear on the final chapter, of which she is the primary author, she has, through sound advice and steady encouragement, greatly helped in the writing of the other chapters as well.

We are both extremely grateful to David H. Warren, who critically read the manuscript and offered many valuable suggestions. The book benefited greatly from his balanced judgment and profound knowledge of the blindness literature. I also wish to thank an anonymous second reviewer, who offered helpful advice on Chapters 5 and 6.

My training in the field of visual perception, both normal and abnormal, was a major point of origin for my interest in blindness: The importance of many of the issues discussed in this book was first pointed out to me by my teachers, Lorrin Riggs, Mitchell Glickstein, and Mathew Alpern. I am grateful for their friendship and mentoring. Other friends and colleagues whose perspectives sharpened my thinking about blindness include Grant Dahlstrom, Morty Heller, Jim Kessler, Bob Lambert, Slater Newman, Mario Perroni, and Tom Wallsten.

Finally, I wish to thank my editors at Lawrence Erlbaum Associates, Jack Burton, Jane Zalenski, and Hollis Heimbouch, whose encouragement and helpfulness have played a major role in bringing this project to fruition.

*Mark Hollins*

# 1 BLINDNESS AND THE EYE

## DEFINITIONS OF BLINDNESS

This book is about blindness. It might seem that there is little to say about this subject, without delving into medical details, that the average person does not know. Blind people are, after all, just like the rest of us except that they cannot see. What more is there to tell? The answer is, a lot. Recent scientific investigations have begun to answer questions about blindness that have been asked for centuries, such as "Do congenitally blind people have mental images? How are they sometimes able to detect an object without touching it? Is the visual part of the brain doing anything in a blind person?" On a more practical level, recent technological advances offer great promise to blind people, for example, by making it possible for them to read print, not just braille, without assistance. The role that public attitudes can play in helping blind people to fulfill their aspirations is better understood now than in the past. And new studies of blind infants and children have turned up important new principles regarding their development. Many of these recent developments rest on a foundation of earlier knowledge, and one goal of the book is to explain how new findings have both changed and added to our previous level of understanding. Before we begin, however, we must define blindness, or rather explain that there are multiple definitions, for much confusion has been caused in the past by the fact that this term is interpreted differently by different people.

The confusion arises because there are degrees of blindness, with some blind people able to see nothing, while others can see a little, and still others can see quite a bit—enough to recognize another person by his or her bearing or gait, for example. The 52,000 individuals in this country who are totally insensitive to light are in fact outnumbered about nine to one by others who, although they are ordinarily considered blind, have some residual vision (National Society to Prevent Blindness, 1980). About equal in number to the totally blind are those who can tell whether they are in a bright or dark environment, but cannot say, without turning their head, from which direction the light comes; they have *light perception*. Still others are able to point out the source of light, say a window in an otherwise dark room, but cannot make out any details or shapes; this basic visual ability is called *projection*.

Although individuals with light perception and projection are not totally blind, they are blind in the sense that they can make little use of their vision. And even persons who have still more vision, so that they can see faint or hazy shapes, but can make out no details, may be considered blind for some purposes. But how blurred should vision have to be before this term is applied? Any answer to this question must be arbitrary, for all degrees of visual impairment exist, from total blindness to just a slight blurring of vision. For statistical and legal purposes, however, it is useful to have a cutoff point which separates those who are *legally blind* from those with a lesser visual impairment, or none at all.

The definition of legal blindness involves measurements of acuity, that is, the visual system's ability to perceive detail. This is typically measured with an eyechart, placed 20 feet from the person being tested. The average person with unimpaired vision can just read letters of a certain size at this distance, and is said to have 20/20 vision. A person who cannot read these letters, but is just able to make out others of twice that size, has 20/40 vision, which is to say that he or she can just read at 20 feet letters that someone with unimpaired vision could distinguish at a distance of 40 feet from the chart. The worse the person's acuity, the larger the denominator. Someone who, even when wearing glasses, has an acuity of 20/200 or worse—that is, 10 times poorer than that of a person with good vision—is legally blind.

It is possible, however, to have good acuity and still not get much practical use from vision, if the field of vision is very restricted. In certain conditions, such as retinitis pigmentosa, to be discussed later, an individual may be able to see straight ahead, but not off to the sides. This failure of peripheral vision can be quantified by a diagnostic procedure called *perimetry*, in which the patient stares fixedly at a small mark, while the person administering the test moves a spot of light from place to place in the visual field. This examination is usually carried out using a half-sphere, about 60 cm in diameter, into which the patient looks. The inside of this perimeter is painted white and is diffusely illuminated; the additional moving spot of light can be shined onto the inner surface of the sphere from a small projector located just above and behind the patient's shoulder. An overhead view of a perimeter is shown in Fig. 1.1.

A person who cannot see the moving light in a certain region has a scotoma, or blind spot, in that region of the visual field. The size of a scotoma is expressed in terms of degrees of arc subtended at the center of the sphere, where the patient's eye is located. The same units of measurement are used to specify the size of a small sighted area that is surrounded by blind regions. Normally the eye's visual field is almost 180 degrees from side to side, but in some cases of *tunnel vision* only an island of sight a few degrees in diameter may exist (see Fig. 1.2). Anyone whose visual field is less than 20 degrees in diameter qualifies as being legally blind, regardless of the acuity in the small region of the field that remains.

Thus a person may be legally blind either because of low acuity or because of a restricted visual field. The two eyes may of course differ in acuity, or in size of the visual field, and legal blindness exists only when both eyes are sufficiently impaired to meet the criterion.

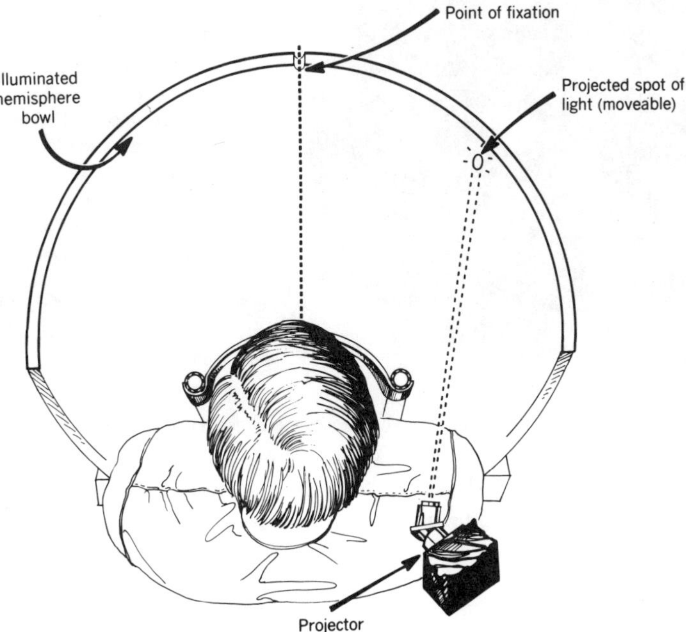


FIGURE 1.1. A perimeter. The patient stares at the point of fixation within the diffusely illuminated bowl, while a small spot of light is moved about to detect blind regions within the visual field. (Reprinted by permission from D. R. Anderson, *Perimetry With and Without Automation*, 2nd edition, St. Louis, 1987, The C. V. Mosby Co.)

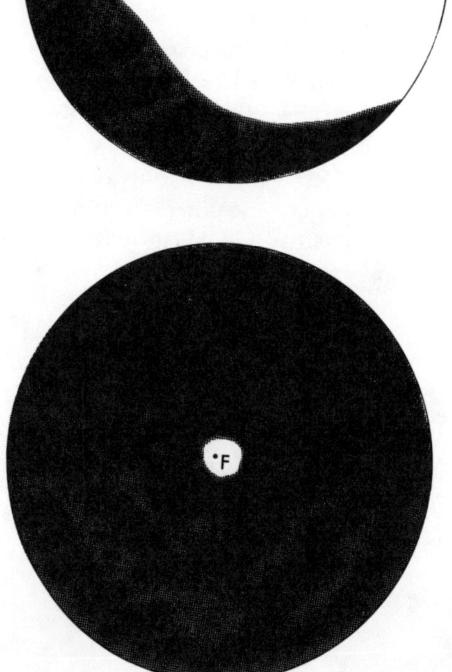


FIGURE 1.2. Visual fields determined with a perimeter. In both cases the large circle represents the edge of the perimeter. Throughout testing, the patient looks fixedly at a dark spot (F) in the center of the bowl. The white area is the visual field, that is, the region within which the subject can detect visual stimuli. The upper drawing shows the visual field of a normal right eye; the lower figure shows the small visual field of someone with tunnel vision.

There are some who say that the legal definition of blindness is too encompassing, because it includes many people who can still get a lot of use from sight: It would be a disservice to categorize these people as blind if that caused some of them to give up on trying to use their remaining vision. An alternative term, *low vision*, is now sometimes used to describe individuals who have a serious visual impairment, but nevertheless still have some useful vision (Colenbrander, 1976). Thus some people who are legally blind, and some who are not, would be considered to fall into this broad category. Perhaps the best course to follow is to use both terms, but in different ways: "legal blindness" for statistical and governmental purposes, where an unambiguous method of categorization is needed, and "low vision" for medical and optometric purposes, and in everyday life, where the emphasis should be on making the best of residual vision. This book is concerned primarily with people who are totally blind or have light perception only, rather than with those who have low vision. In this initial chapter, however, information on the prevalence of blindness will be presented in terms of legal blindness, for that is the form in which the most systematic data are available.

## PREVALENCE OF BLINDNESS

How many people in the United States are legally blind? This is difficult to determine, for there is no nationwide registry of blind people. Some data do exist at the federal level, but they are very incomplete. For example, the Social Security Administration has records indicating the visual status of Social Security recipients. What fraction these may represent of the total blind population of the country, however, is unknown. In 1962, a group of nine states decided to cooperate, with federal financial support, in an attempt to standardize, and improve, the collection of statistical information about blindness. This undertaking became known as the Model Reporting Area project, the idea being that its methods would serve as a model for the rest of the country. In fact, seven other states did join the MRA within a decade, and a systematic record of blind people in those states, using uniform criteria not just to define blindness, but to specify its cause, came into being (Kahn & Moorhead, 1973). In 1971, however, the MRA project was terminated by the federal government as a cost-cutting measure.

In short, there is currently no way to determine with certainty the number of cases of blindness in the country. However, the National Society to Prevent Blindness, a private, non-profit organization, has for many years combined information from several sources in order to arrive at overall statistical estimates. For its most recent comprehensive estimates, published in 1980 (National Society to Prevent Blindness, 1980), the Society used the last available data from the Model Reporting Area to ascertain the rate of blindness per 100,000 persons, for each MRA state. Since the MRA data indicate how the rate varies as a function of the age, sex, and other demographic characteristics of the population, it was possible to estimate the rates of blindness in non-MRA states as well, based on their demographic makeup. (For example, the rate of blindness is higher in the elderly than in young people. Therefore, a state with a large elderly population, such as Florida, would be expected to have a higher rate of blindness than a state with a small elderly population.) The Society then combined these rates with 1978 data on the size of the population, obtained from the Bureau of the Census, to arrive at estimates of the prevalence of blindness as of that year. The numbers given here are drawn from their report.

There are roughly half a million legally blind people in the United States. For those under the age of twenty, 55 out of every 100,000 are blind; but for those 65 and over, the rate is more than 1,100 per 100,000, so that people in this age group make up more than half the blind population. In between those two extremes there is a gradual increase with age in the prevalence of blindness. This is a result of three factors, one of which is purely statistical: An elderly person has been exposed to life's vicissitudes longer, and the chances of his or her having suffered an irreversible loss of vision at some time are therefore greater than they are for a young person. A second factor is that even a healthy eye undergoes changes with advancing age, such as a yellowing of the lens and constriction of the pupil, which gradually reduce visual ability; any additional loss of sight through trauma or disease is thus more likely to push the person over the threshold of severe visual impairment. Third and most importantly, however, some blinding diseases, such as macular degeneration, strike much more often in elderly people than in the young. Later in this chapter, the most common causes of blindness will be discussed, and information about their frequency will be given.

Such statistics on the prevalence and causes of blindness are useful in that they help to guide long-term planning, both in and out of government. For example, the National Eye Institute, the agency that oversees federally sponsored research on medical aspects of blindness, takes the prevalence of various blinding diseases into account, along with other factors, in setting research priorities. Data on the prevalence of blindness are also important in the private sector, where research on the development of sensory aids for blind people, such as computer terminals that "talk" or use braille, requires a knowledge of the potential market for such devices.

So far only blindness in the United States has been discussed. Estimates of the prevalence of blindness worldwide are much more difficult to make. While many countries collect data on the prevalence of blindness, they often use different definitions. Thus legal blindness in some countries (as in the United States) is acuity of 20/200 or worse or a severe restriction of the visual field, while in other countries it is defined in a more everyday context, such as the inability to count the examiner's fingers at a certain distance, or even as the inability to earn a living using vision. It is seldom possible to convert statistics obtained using one criterion to what they would have been if another criterion had been employed. Another difficulty is that some countries have a well-organized system of reporting, while others do not. Even if they use the same definition of blindness, it is not certain that their data are comparable. Despite these difficulties, the World Health Organization (1979/1980) has been able to piece together data from many sources to reach an overall estimate: Approximately 40 million persons worldwide are, by the U.S. definition, legally blind.

This figure is so large because of the prevalence, in many poor nations, of infectious and nutritional diseases that are rare in the developed countries. For example, there are some 2 million persons (Dawson, Jones, & Tarizzo,

1981) who have lost their sight because of trachoma, an infectious disease, but only about 1,000 of them are in the United States (National Society to Prevent Blindness, 1980).

In the rest of this chapter we will examine trachoma and other common causes of blindness, both in this country and elsewhere, discussing the ways in which they affect the eyes, and the subjective visual experiences that they produce in a person who is losing sight. It is first necessary, however, to describe the structure of the normal eye.

## STRUCTURE OF THE EYE

The eye is very nearly a sphere, about 2.5 cm in diameter, with an additional bulge called the *cornea* on the front (see Fig. 1.3). The white of the eye, or *sclera*, is a tough outer layer which gives the eyeball its shape and protects the soft inner tissues. The sclera also prevents light from entering anywhere except at the front, where the transparent cornea provides a window. Light passing through the cornea must then pass through a smaller aperture, the *pupil*, and traverse the eye's *lens*, if it is eventually to reach the back of the eye, where a layer of neural tissue, the *retina*, lies like a carpet on the inner surface of the globe.

Two humors, or liquids, fill up the eye, occupying the spaces between successive structures. The *aqueous humor* is in the front part of the eye, occupying the region behind the cornea and in front of the lens. It is therefore

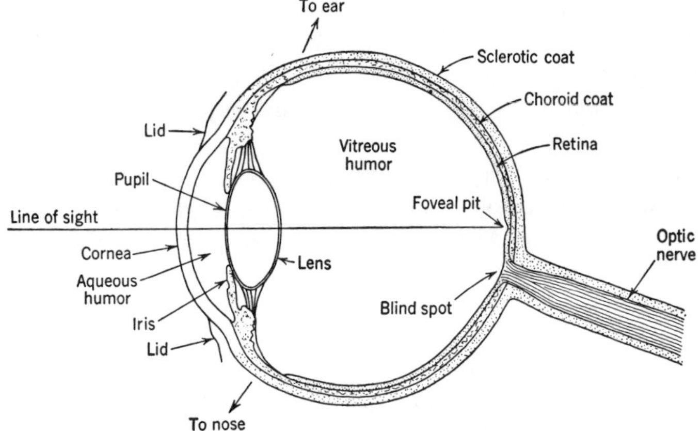


FIGURE 1.3. Cross-section of the eye, seen from above. Because there are no receptors where the optic nerve leaves the eye, this region is called the blind spot. The foveal pit is a small depression in the center of the macula, within which vision is especially acute. (From *Color in Business, Science, and Industry*, 2nd edition, by D. B. Judd and G. Wyszecki, 1963, New York: Wiley. Copyright 1963 by John Wiley & Sons, Inc. Reprinted by permission.)

both in front of and behind the *iris*, a ring of muscle which surrounds the pupil and gives the eye its characteristic brown, blue, or green color. The aqueous humor is a watery liquid, resembling lymph; it carries oxygen and nutrients to the cornea and lens, which, being transparent, contain no blood vessels.

Behind the lens, and filling somewhat more than the back half of the eye, is the *vitreous humor*, a gelatinous substance which presses out against the sclera and so helps the eye to maintain its proper shape.

The retina itself is a complicated structure, with a variety of types of cells. Some of these, the *receptors*, absorb light and use it to trigger electrical events which are the first step in the neural transmission of information to the brain. Of all the cell types in the visual system, only these can be directly influenced by light. Receptors are of two types: the cones, which are active in moderately lit or bright surroundings, and which allow color and detail vision; and the rods, which function in dim light, such as moonlight, and mediate only crude, black and white vision. Cones are most numerous in a centrally located region of the retina, 3 mm in diameter, called the *macula*, which is used for reading and other tasks requiring good acuity.

Receptors of both types convey their messages to other retinal cells, the bipolars, which in turn pass the information along to ganglion cells (see Fig. 1.4). Surprisingly, the retina is oriented in a way that seems backwards, for the receptors, which light must reach, are on the back of the retina, farthest from the vitreous. Light therefore passes without effect through the nearly transparent ganglion and bipolar cells before reaching the rods and cones. This puzzling arrangement is explained by the fact that the receptors, with their high level of metabolic activity, must be located close to the *choroid*, an opaque layer of vascular tissue sandwiched between the retina and the sclera. This tissue is a rich source of the nutrients and oxygen required by the rods and cones, and is in addition a route by which waste products, produced in large amounts by the receptors, can be removed from the eye. Separating the choroid from the receptors, and serving to control the flow of metabolites between them, is a one-cell-thick layer called the *pigment epithelium*. One of its functions is to decompose and digest chunks of waste matter that periodically break off from the receptors. The pigment epithelium also serves to reduce glare-producing scattered light within the eye, by absorbing photons that get past the receptors.

Thus neural messages, after arising in the receptors, travel forward through the retina until they arrive at the ganglion cells. These each have a thin extension called an axon, which is capable of relaying nerve impulses to the brain. The axons of all the eye's ganglion cells run across the front of the retina to a common spot, the *optic disk*, where they turn toward the back of the eye, and, passing out of it as a group, become the *optic nerve*. The optic nerve passes through the layers of fat and connective tissue which form a

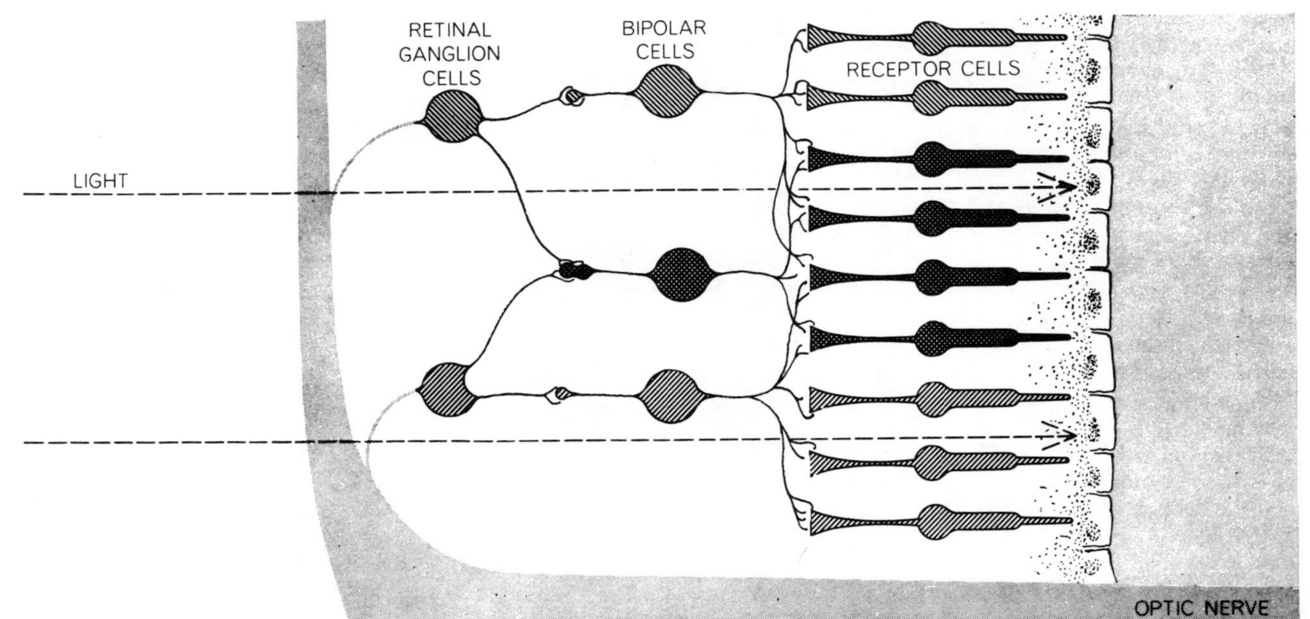


FIGURE 1.4. Schematic diagram of the structure of the retina, showing three types of cells: the receptors, which absorb light and produce an electrical response; the bipolar cells, which convey these neural messages from the receptors to the front of the retina; and the ganglion cells, which transmit the information to the brain along their axons, the optic nerve fibers. Immediately behind the receptors (to their right in the figure) are the cells of the pigment epithelium, which convey nutrients to the receptors, and remove their waste products. (From "The Visual Cortex of the Brain," by D. H. Hubel. Copyright © 1963 by Scientific American, Inc. All rights reserved. Reprinted by permission.)

cushion behind the eye, and leave the eye socket through a hole in the back, entering the cranium. Its destinations within the brain are a subject that will be taken up in the following chapter. Our more immediate concern is to discuss some of the more common injuries and disease processes which can seriously interfere with the functioning of the eye, and so cause blindness.

## CAUSES OF BLINDNESS

In this part of the chapter we will consider a number of the most common blinding eye diseases. While most of these diseases tend to strike in adulthood, some, such as retinitis pigmentosa, often begin in childhood or adolescence; others, such as retrolental fibroplasia, damage the eye during infancy; and still others, such as glaucoma and cataract, may occur even before birth. A person who was born without sight is *congenitally blind*, while one who lost his or her sight at some later time is said to be *adventitiously blinded.* As will be made clear in later chapters, this distinction is important, for the individual's perceptions, mental imagery, and attitudes toward blindness itself depend in part on whether he or she was sighted during the early years of life.

In the following sections, the leading causes of blindness are discussed, not in order of the age groups at which they strike, but rather, according to the part of the eye that is primarily involved. The first to be considered are those which prevent light from passing through the cornea; next will be those conditions affecting the lens and vitreous humor; finally, diseases of the retina will be discussed.

### Opacities of the Ocular Media

The various structures and substances through which light must pass on its way to the retina—that is, the cornea, aqueous humor, lens, and vitreous humor—must of course be transparent, or nearly so, if the person is to see well. Anything that clouds or scars any of these media therefore interferes with vision.

Many people have an opacity, typically a white, cloudy zone, on the cornea. This can have a variety of causes, local infection being one of the most common. Some microorganisms that cause sores or blisters on other parts of the body, such as the herpes viruses, can attack the cornea as well, sometimes leaving opaque scars when the infection subsides. Trauma to the cornea, such as wounds from a foreign object, or burns inflicted by spattered chemicals, also frequently cause scarring and opacity. If the clouding of the cornea becomes severe and widespread enough, the person can become blind to patterns of light, although in all but the severest cases light perception is retained.

The prognosis for restoring sight is good in many cases of corneal opacity, because a corneal transplant is often possible. In this surgical procedure, an opthalmologist removes the opaque cornea of the patient, and sews in its place a transparent cornea obtained earlier from the eye of a deceased donor. Because a cornea—even a healthy one—has a very slow metabolism, and is not in direct contact with the antibody-containing bloodstream, the problem of tissue rejection is not so difficult as in the case of, say, a kidney transplant, and the new cornea is usually accepted by the patient's body. After a recovery period, the patient's vision in many cases returns to more or less what it was before the opacity developed.

A particular type of corneal opacity, caused by a combination of infection and mechanical trauma, is the disease process called *trachoma* (Dawson et al., 1981), mentioned earlier. This condition is rare in the United States and other countries with a high standard of living, but is widespread in the Third World, particularly in a band of countries extending from Northern Africa through the Middle East and India, and into Southeast Asia. A bacterium-like microorganism, *Chlamydia trachomatis*, infects the eyes, producing as initial symptoms watery eyes, aversion to light, and a feeling of ocular discomfort. The conjunctiva, a mucous membrane lining the insides of the eyelids and the front of the eye itself, becomes swollen. Small lumps develop, leaving scars behind them when they subside. The upper eyelid is particularly likely to become deformed from swelling and scarring, and to turn under, so that the eyelashes, instead of being directed outward, are aimed at the eye and constantly rake across the cornea. Already irritated by the infection itself, and now abraded by the eyelashes as well, the cornea becomes scarred and opaque, thus preventing sight. The infection is spread from eye to eye by contaminated towels, personal contact, or, most often, by flies which feed on discharge from the eyes. The condition can be treated by administering antibiotic drops or ointment directly to the eye to eradicate the infection, and following up with surgery on the eyelids, if necessary, to reorient the lashes away from the eye. Corneal transplantation may be indicated in severe cases; but trachoma is as much an economic as a medical problem, and a person living in a poor, rural village far from a doctor's office is not a good candidate for an operation that requires careful medical follow-up. Improvement of living conditions in the countries involved is the most promising large-scale way of attacking the disease.

Corneal opacity is also one of the ways in which another disease, *onchocerciasis*, causes blindness. This parasitic infection by nematode worms of the species *Onchocerca volvulus* affects some 20 million persons in tropical Africa, the Middle East, and Latin America, often causing severe visual impairment. The disease begins when immature worms, called microfilariae, are introduced into a person's bloodstream through the bite of an infected blackfly. Since these flies need aerated water to reproduce, the disease is most prevalent near fast-flowing rivers, and so it is often called "river blindness."

Once in the bloodstream, the microfilariae migrate throughout the body, congregating in especially large numbers in the skin and the eyes. An ophthalmologist viewing the eyes of a heavily infected individual with a slit lamp can see many of the worms, about a third of a millimeter in length, wriggling about in the aqueous and vitreous humors, and even within the cornea. More serious than the tissue damage done by the worms themselves are the severe inflammatory and immune responses triggered by their presence. When prolonged, these reactions cause pathological tissue changes in several parts of the eye: the cornea becomes white and opaque; the iris exudes a heavily pigmented discharge that can spread across the front surface of the lens, thus setting up a second barrier to the passage of light; and the retina is damaged by scarring and other processes (Buck, 1974).

To battle onchocerciasis, the World Health Organization in 1975 began a program of aerial insecticide spraying of rivers in West Africa, the most severely affected region in the world. By killing the flies that carry the disease, the WHO program seeks to prevent it from spreading from one person to another. The spraying campaign has been very successful (Walsh, 1986), but the files have gradually developed resistance to one insecticide after another, showing that additional strategies are needed to combat the disease. Fortunately, it has recently been discovered that ivermectin, a veterinary drug used to kill parasitic worms in animals, is also effective against onchocerciasis microfilariae (Cupp et al., 1986; Greene et al., 1985); and Merck & Co., the drug's manufacturer, plans to make it available at no charge to countries that agree to use it in accordance with international standards (Walsh, 1987).

Still another blinding condition common in developing countries is *xerophthalmia*, a disease of the cornea and retina that results from vitamin A deficiency. The first symptom of the disease is night blindness, a loss of visual sensitivity in dim illumination. This is attributable to the fact that vitamin A, after modification by the body, constitutes a necessary part of each visual pigment molecule in the receptor cells of the retina. This vitamin A derivative is constantly being used up as a result of visual stimulation, so that the eye requires a continuous supply. Should body reserves of the vitamin (primarily in the liver) be exhausted, the ability of the receptor cells to function will gradually decrease.

Often more noticeable than the retinal effects of the disease, however, is the damage it does to the cornea (Sommer, 1982). The term xerophthalmia literally means "dry eye," and an early sign is a dry, granular appearance. Later, foamy, opaque plaques may develop, along with pits in the cornea. Eventually the cornea as a whole starts to deteriorate, seeming to melt away, until only a thin opaque membrane remains. If treated early with vitamin A, the corneal changes can be largely reversed, but if the condition has advanced to its severest stages, the person will remain blind.

It is tragic that this disease remains widespread—with some hundreds of thousands of persons, many of them children, developing corneal symptoms each year—despite the fact that its cause is well understood, and the substance necessary for its prevention is inexpensive.

Opacities can occur in other ocular structures besides the cornea. In fact, opacities of the lens, called *cataracts*, are one of the leading causes of legal blindness in this country, accounting for nearly 14% of all cases (National Society to Prevent Blindness, 1980). Cataracts can form at any age, but they usually develop either prenatally, or in old age. While they can be caused by external factors, such as X rays, electrical shock, or wounds, they generally result from some breakdown of the elaborate metabolic processes that keep the lens transparent. For example, the lens has a lower water content than surrounding tissues, and a malfunction of the ionic regulatory mechanisms that keep it that way will allow too much water to be absorbed. Another metabolic cause is diabetes mellitus, a disease in which abnormal amounts of glucose are supplied to the lens (and other parts of the body). However caused, cataracts produce a gradual fogging of the person's vision, just as in the case of corneal opacity.

Surgical intervention is possible in the case of many cataract patients. The ophthalmologist removes the cloudy lens, often through a slit made at the side of the cornea, and may substitute an artificial, plastic lens before sewing the eye up again. There are several varieties of artificial lens from which the doctor can choose: Some are designed to go in front of the iris, but those which go behind the iris, in the position previously occupied by the patient's own lens, are now more widely used. Some doctors prefer not to implant a substitute lens, fearing that it may cause irritation; they rely instead on glasses or contact lens to supply focusing power. A recent survey of several hundred ophthalmologists, however, found that 89% now use implanted lens in more than half of their cataract patients (Dowling & Bahr, 1985).

In the case of an infant born with cataracts, there is now good evidence that they should be removed soon after birth, within 2 months if possible (Gelbart, Hoyt, Jastrebski, & Marg, 1982; Parks, 1982), in order to maximize the chances of normal vision later in life. The research that has led to this conclusion is described in Chapter 2.

Finally, opacities may form in the vitreous humor, blocking out the light on the last leg of its journey to the retina. Most often, such opacities are caused by blood leaking into the interior of the eye from diseased blood vessels located in the retina. This can occur in diabetic retinopathy, a condition discussed later in the chapter.

Surgical treatment of vitreal opacities is difficult, but possible in many cases. If leaky blood vessels are responsible, their hemorrhaging must first be stopped, and this can sometimes be done with a fine laser beam directed into the eye from the front. Aimed at a leak, the laser literally melts the vessels that it strikes, cauterizing them so that they no longer bleed. Once this is accomplished, the surgeon may attempt to remove blood or other opacities from the vitreous mechanically, sucking or scraping them out, and replacing the lost substance with artificial vitreous. These procedures are complicated, however, and success is not so sure as in the case of cataract or corneal transplant operations.

## Glaucoma

Glaucoma is a blinding disease that involves the ocular media without their becoming opaque. More than 13% of the country's blind population have this condition (National Society to Prevent Blindness, 1980), making it second only to cataract as a cause of blindness. Glaucoma is a complicated disease, caused by events occurring in the front part of the eye, but resulting in injury to the optic nerve and retina. The eye, it will be recalled, is held in shape by the pressure, exerted from within, of the aqueous and vitreous humors. In glaucoma this intraocular pressure increases enough to cause damage.

The increased pressure is usually due to a malfunction in the system that controls the amount of aqueous humor in the eye. This fluid is normally in a state of constant turnover, some of it draining out of the eye while new droplets enter. The aqueous humor is produced by a flabby ring of tissue called the ciliary process, which lies behind the iris (see Fig. 1.5); from here it flows forward through the pupil, and then toward the sides again, between the cornea and the iris. On reaching the angle between these two structures, the humor passes slowly through a spongy meshwork, and into a drainage ring, the canal of Schlemm, which lies just beyond. The normal rate of turnover in this system is about 2 drops per hour (Cole, 1978, p. 50). In some individuals, however, the angle formed between the iris and the cornea is too narrow, so that the aqueous humor has inadequate access to the drainage apparatus. In other cases, particles of solid matter, such as tiny flakes of pigment from the rear surface of the iris, may be swept into the meshwork and stop it up; while in still other individuals metabolic problems may cause the meshwork to become fibrous and lose its spongy, porous character. The result in any case is that aqueous humor is bottled up inside the eye, exerting pressure in all directions.

An ophthalmologist can measure the pressure with a device called a tonometer, which exerts a gentle inward force on the cornea and measures the resulting deformation of the corneal surface. In one widely used version, a flat surface is pressed against the eye until a corneal zone 3 mm in diameter has been flattened by it; the pressure that had to be used to bring about this

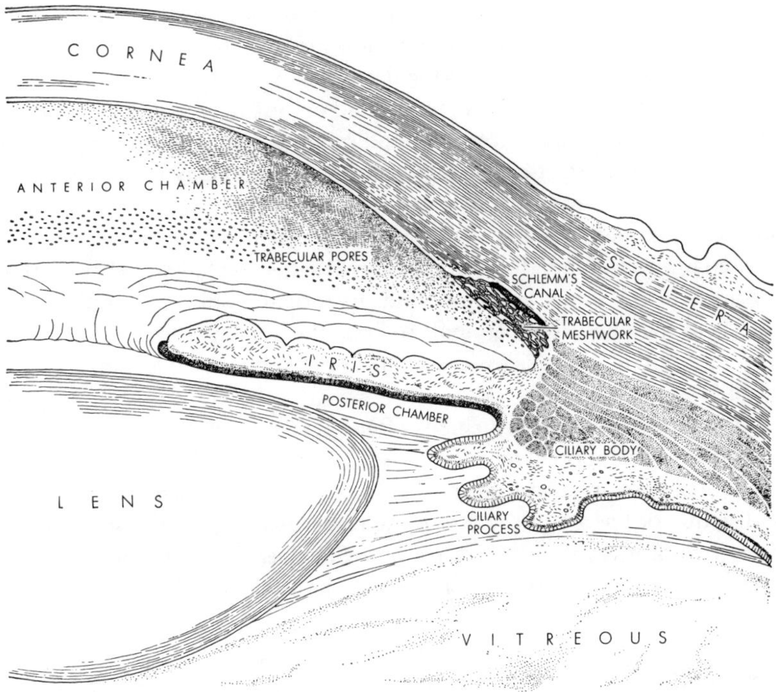


FIGURE 1.5. Structures involved in the circulation of aqueous humor are shown in this diagram of the anterior part of the eye. Aqueous humor fills the space between the cornea and the lens. It is secreted by the ciliary process, behind the iris, and absorbed into the trabecular meshwork in front of the iris. (From "Glaucoma," by S. Lerman. Copyright © 1959 by Scientific American, Inc. All rights reserved. Reprinted by permission.)

deformation is then noted. In another version, a tiny jet of air directed against the cornea substitutes for the flat probe. In either case the deformation of the cornea is only temporary, disappearing once the measuring instrument is removed. A local anesthetic is often administered before tonometry to prevent discomfort.

If intraocular pressure rises high enough, it causes damage to structures in the back of the eye, particularly the optic nerve. This bundle of nerve fibers, each the axon of one of the eye's million ganglion cells, leaves the eye through a perforated region of the sclera called the lamina cribrosa. This delicate, latticed region is more vulnerable than the solid areas of the sclera to deformation resulting from elevated intraocular pressure. In glaucoma, the head of the optic nerve and the lamina cribrosa are pushed backward, with resulting injury to the axons, which are easily harmed by stretching or compression. The deformation of the optic disk can usually be seen by a doctor examining the retina with an ophthalmoscope, for the disk's normal appearance, resembling somewhat a shallow moon crater, is altered, with the central depression, or cup, becoming deeper, larger or irregular.

The destruction of optic nerve fibers, and of the ganglion cells from which they originate, causes characteristic blind spots, or scotomas, in the patient's field of view. These start out small in most cases, and may go unnoticed in everyday life, but they can be detected by systematically exploring the visual field with a perimeter, as described earlier. If the glaucoma goes untreated, or is treated unsuccessfully, the scotomas may enlarge and fuse together, so that large areas of the visual field are blind. Eventually, only the center of the visual field may be left functional, so that the person sees things straight ahead, but not off to the sides—a condition called *tunnel vision*. Finally, even central vision may be lost.

In treating glaucoma, medicine is often given to modify the dynamics of the aqueous circulation. This is commonly in the form of eyedrops designed to slow the secretion of aqueous humor into the eye, to constrict the pupil so that the humor has a clearer path to the trabecular meshwork, or to modify the meshwork itself. If medicines prove ineffective, the doctor will consider surgery aimed at mechanically facilitating the drainage of aqueous humor from the eye.

There are many people with high intraocular pressure who show no cupping of the optic disk and no scotomas. Although these individuals, called "glaucoma suspects", do not yet have the disease, they are at risk with respect to it. Often the ophthalmologist will prescribe eyedrops or other medicine to such patients as a preventive measure. Why some people are more able than others to tolerate elevated pressure is not known.

Glaucoma is an insidious disease because it has a slow, and therefore imperceptible, onset in many people. The scotomas may go unnoticed until they have grown large and joined together to eliminate peripheral vision. While sudden vision losses may, if treated promptly, be partly restored, most people who lose vision because of glaucoma do not recover it.

### Detached Retina

While glaucoma usually produces blindness slowly, another retinal problem, detachment, often produces it suddenly. Detachment means that the retina tears loose from the choroid, the vascular and nutritive tissue that lies between it and the sclera. This sometimes results from a traumatic injury, such as a blow to the eye which causes sudden deformation of the globe. In other cases, however, there is no obvious precipitating event, and no clear explanation for why the retina becomes detached. One person who became totally blind as a result of detached retinas in both eyes described the first detachment as resembling "a jet black curtain" descending across the field of view, the second as a sudden clouding accompanied by "bright blue fireworks" (Chevigny, 1946, pp. 8 & 15).

The loss of sight accompanying retinal detachment is caused by the fact that the back surface of the retina depends for its blood supply on the choroid, and when these two tissues separate, the rods and cones asphyxiate. Surgical treatment can in many cases succeed in reattaching the retina, but it should be performed soon after detachment, for experiments on animals show that pathological changes in the receptor layer of the retina begin within an hour of detachment, and about half the receptors have died after 2 weeks (Erickson, Fisher, Anderson, Stern, & Borgula, 1983).

### Retrolental Fibroplasia (Retinopathy of Prematurity)

One retinal disease process that can lead to a completely detached retina in infancy, and thus to total blindness, is retrolental fibroplasia. The first cases of this disease were not reported until the early 1940s, when it was seen in a small number of premature babies; but the number of cases multiplied rapidly during that decade. Ironically, the onset of this epidemic coincided with many technical advances in the medical treatment of newborns. By the early 1950s, some scientists began to suspect that the widespread practice of giving oxygen to premature infants was responsible for the condition. To answer this question definitively, many hospitals took part in a *controlled clinical trial*, in which some premature babies were given the generous exposure to oxygen considered medically appropriate at the time, while others were given oxygen only when it was clearly needed. The babies were assigned randomly to one condition or the other. The results of the study showed clearly that oxygen was a causal factor, for retrolental fibroplasia was much more common in the high-oxygen group of babies (Kinsey, 1956). Physicians and hospitals were more conservative after this in giving oxygen to newborns, and the prevalence of the blinding condition dropped dramatically during the 1950s. Retrolental fibroplasia still occurs, however, in part because considerable exposure to oxygen is sometimes needed to save a premature baby's life.

The condition may not become detectable until weeks after the baby has been taken off oxygen. The first sign is an abnormal proliferation of blood vessels on the front surface of the retina, visible to a physician looking into the eye with an ophthalmoscope. Some of the vessels simply grow across the surface of the retina, but others leave the retina and spread into the vitreous humor. The retina gradually loses its attachment to the choroid and becomes detached. Once this occurs, the retina drifts slowly forward through the vitreous humor and adheres to the rear surface of the lens. Now riddled with vascular tissue, it forms an opaque, white backing for the lens which can often be seen on casual inspection of the infant's eye. The condition has generally developed fully by the end of the first 6 months of life.

The term retrolental fibroplasia refers to the white, fibrous structure behind the lens that forms in these most serious cases of the disease. However, the term is less appropriate as a description of the early stages of the disease, or of cases which do not proceed to full detachment of the retina. For this reason an alternative name (Heath, 1950), *retinopathy of prematurity*, has come into wide use (McCormick, 1977).

How does oxygen cause this condition? The answer is not entirely clear, but a basic, underlying factor is that the normal development of retinal blood vessels in newborns is stimulated by the retina's growing need for oxygen. In infants supplied with excessive amounts of oxygen for a long period of time, the retinal vessels do not form as extensive a network as they normally would, and in fact wither away (Ashton, 1966), perhaps because the retina can easily obtain all the oxygen it needs from the well-established blood vessels in the choroid. When the infant is later taken off supplementary oxygen, however, the spindly network of retinal vessels is not sufficient to supply the retina's requirements. The asphyxiation of the retina stimulates a dramatic, and for some reason uncontrolled, growth of the vessels, and the process that in severe cases leads to retrolental fibroplasia has begun. Although this rough outline of the disease process is now understood, many puzzles about the genesis and prevention of retinopathy of prematurity have still not been solved, and deserve further investigation (Silverman, 1980). This is especially true at the present time, because the disease, in the opinion of many ophthalmologists, is becoming increasingly common once again (Kolata, 1986). Conditions other than oxygen, such as high levels of ambient lighting in hospital nurseries (Glass et al., 1985), have been implicated as additional risk factors, but none has yet been tested in a fully controlled study.

## Diabetic Retinopathy

Diabetes mellitus is a common disease of the pancreas that disrupts the body's glucose metabolism; usually the disease can be controlled, although not cured, by periodic injections of insulin, the hormone that the diabetic pancreas is unable to secrete in sufficient quantities. Unfortunately, many diabetics, even though they follow the instructions of their doctor with regard to diet and medication, eventually experience a deterioration of vision caused by damage to the retina. This condition, called *diabetic retinopathy*, accounts for 6.6% of the blind population of this country; it is the leading cause of new cases of blindness for people between the ages of 20 and 74 (National Society to Prevent Blindness, 1980).

Diabetic retinopathy occurs when blood vessels contained within the retina, or coursing across its front surface, begin to degenerate. Their walls become abnormally permeable, permitting constituents of the blood which are normally retained to leak into the retinal tissues. These exudates harden and remain lodged within the retina, where they cut down on the transmission of light, and press on retinal cells, interfering with their function. As the deterioration of the blood vessels proceeds, whole blood often hemorrhages into the retina, or into the vitreous humor. This process may eventually damage the entire retina, causing a total loss of sight; but it often begins in a restricted, doughnut-shaped region surrounding but not including the macula. Thus there may be a ring of blindness surrounding central vision, with vision in the far periphery also being intact.

Although there is no cure for diabetic retinopathy, it is possible in some patients to slow the loss of sight by using a thin laser beam, directed into the eye through the pupil, to coagulate and seal off leaking blood vessels. As mentioned earlier, vitreal surgery may be of benefit if a large amount of blood has seeped into the vitreous humor.

## Macular Degeneration

The macula is the central region of the retina, containing the highest concentration of cones. Because acuity is best here, the macula is the most important retinal region for such activities as reading or sewing. Yet, ironically, it is the retinal region most vulnerable to the harmful effects of certain drugs and toxic substances, and to a type of deterioration that often accompanies the aging process. Combined, these forms of macular degeneration make up the leading cause of new cases of blindness in the country, for without the use of the macula, a person's acuity is usually low enough for the definition of legal blindness to be met.

The type that commonly strikes in old age, called *senile macular degeneration*, is the most widespread. It occurs because the one-cell-thick pigment epithelium, located just behind the retina and closely attached to the receptor cells, is not able to carry out its functions.

It will be recalled that one of the roles of the normal pigment epithelium is the removal of waste generated by the retinal receptors. In a healthy retina, the light-catching part of the receptors, which is closest to the pigment epithelium (see Fig. 1.4), grows outward from the base, like a hair; and to balance this growth, the rearmost tips of the receptors periodically break off and are digested by the pigment epithelium (Young, 1976).

In senile macular degeneration, however, the pigment epithelium loses its ability to dispose of this debris. Some of its constituents accumulate in the epithelial cells in the form of a yellow sludge, lipofuscin, and lumps of a similar material build up behind the epithelium, separating it from its blood supply in the choroid. These lumps distort the pigment epithelium and may cause it to tear, allowing serum or perhaps even whole blood to leak into the retina from the highly vascular choroid.

Little can be done to arrest these changes in most cases. It might seem that laser surgery, to seal off the leaks, would be indicated; but in fact the heat from the laser, if directed at or near the macula, might further harm the tissue it is designed to save. To determine whether the benefits of laser treatment outweigh the risks, a controlled clinical trial is now under way under the sponsorship of the National Eye Institute, but definitive conclusions are not likely to be reached for several years.

Fortunately, senile macular degeneration is usually limited to the retinal region for which it is named, so that total blindness does not result. A tendency to senile macular degeneration runs in families, and it is more common in people with blue, green, or gray irises than in those with darker eyes (Weiter, Delori, Wing, & Fitch, 1985); but beyond these hints, little is known about its ultimate cause. It has been suggested that a lifetime of exposure to often excessive light may hasten the deterioration with age of the retina and pigment epithelium, but this possibility requires further testing (Marmor, 1982).

## Other Blindness of Retinal Origin

There are many other retinal problems which can lead to a loss of sight. Often there is an inherited tendency for the optic nerve to atrophy early in life. This is, in fact, second only to prenatal cataract as a cause of legal blindness in children and adolescents (National Society to Prevent Blindness, 1980). There are several types of optic nerve atrophy, which vary in terms of their mode of genetic transmission, the trait being dominant in some varieties and recessive in others. The visual symptoms and age at which the degeneration occurs also vary from one form of the disease to another (Smith, Pokorny, & Ernest, 1977). Optic nerve fibers serving the macula seem to be the most vulnerable, for a common symptom, once the disease has run its course, is a large central scotoma. This deterioration of macular vision is accompanied by a drop in visual acuity. Outside this central region, however, vision may be roughly normal, although perception of colors is often disturbed.

*Retinitis pigmentosa* is another inherited disease that leads to blindness, usually in adolescence or young adulthood. It is named for the clumps of dark pigment that can be seen with an ophthalmoscope in the retina of someone with this condition. While the cause of retinitis pigmentosa has not been definitively established, one promising theory is that it results from a breakdown in the normal process by which the receptor cells are periodically rejuvenated, described earlier. In order for this process to work properly, the growth of the receptors from the base must be exactly balanced by the removal of their tips. In a person with retinitis pigmentosa, however, the pigment epithelium may perform this destructive task at a rate slightly exceeding that at which new cellular material is formed (Ripps, 1981). Thus the receptors grow gradually shorter and shorter until they can no longer function.

This disease usually starts in the peripheral retina, rather than in the macula, and gradually spreads inward over the course of perhaps a decade. During this gradual loss of sight, the person may therefore have a period of tunnel vision, seeing straight ahead but not off to the sides. Later the central part of the field becomes a mosaic of blind and sighted regions, with objects appearing blurred and distorted, until finally sight may be lost altogether.

An artist with an advanced case of retinitis pigmentosa described his remaining vision in these terms:

> My field now, piecing together the odd bits here and there, is less than 5 degrees. Because the losses are a patchwork of dead or dying cells, my functional vision is difficult to understand. . . . In the full mosaic of cells, the dysfunctional ones are not black, nor are there sharp boundaries between them and the neighboring useful cells. Blindness isn't blackness; it is nothingness. I have, therefore, on my retina, a tiny amount of somethingness surrounded and influenced by a vast nothingness. There is a disorganization of the whole; everything is ill-fitting, jagged and incomplete. . . . Objects appear or vanish abruptly and inexplicably. Nothing makes spatial sense, so I put together visual clues based largely on memory and imagination. For me, perceived reality is spotty, appearing in a kind of charged, flickering motion.[1]

## PREVENTION OF BLINDNESS

As this chapter has made clear, the list of ways in which sight can be lost is formidable. Our discussion would be one-sided, however, if in concluding we did not also take note of ways to prevent blindness, for these, too, are powerful.

Prominent among them is scientific research. Many scientists, in all parts of the world, are actively engaged in studying eye diseases, and in testing drugs and other methods of treatment. This research has been remarkably successful: It has led to effective ways of combatting glaucoma, onchocerciasis, and other blinding conditions. But many challenges lie ahead. For example, more research is needed to gain a fuller understanding of diabetic retinopathy, macular degeneration, and retinopathy of prematurity, so that these conditions can be more effectively prevented. Ways of treating even inherited conditions, such as retinitis pigmentosa, may eventually be found as researchers learn more about the workings of the retina.

No amount of research, however, can eliminate the need for each person

---

[1]From *Ordinary Daylight* (p. 33) by A. Potok, 1980, New York: Holt, Rinehart, & Winston. Copyright 1980 by Andrew Potok. Reprinted by permission.

to protect his or her own eyesight. There are several things an individual can do in this regard. One is to receive periodic eye examinations, along with general medical care. Many cases of blindness, especially from glaucoma, can be prevented if the sight-threatening condition is detected at an early stage.

Another way in which individuals can help to preserve their own sight, and that of people around them, is to take commonsense precautions against eye injuries. Information on the causes of such injuries, obtained by the government from hospital emergency rooms (National Society to Prevent Blindness, 1980), suggests that the damage was avoidable in many cases. Pieces of metal, such as are thrown into the air when someone drills through metal in a home workshop, cause more eye wounds than any other type of object; wearing safety glasses would greatly reduce the risk of such an accident. Among children under 5, the most hazardous type of item is cigarettes, cigars, and pipes: A lit cigarette dangling from the hand of an adult is at eye level for young children. Children between the ages of 5 and 14 sustain many eye injuries playing baseball; a large number of these could be prevented if a helmet were worn.

Most injuries affect only one eye, and so do not cause the person to become blind. In some cases, however, a penetrating wound of one eye can cause internal structures in *both* eyes to become seriously inflamed, making the complete loss of sight a possibility; to prevent such involvement of the second or "sympathizing" eye, it may be necessary for an ophthalmologist to remove the injured eye. Staring at the sun or other intense light sources can, of course, damage both eyes at once, as can accidental poisoning from certain toxic substances. All told, injuries and poisonings account for the blindness of nearly 20,000 Americans (National Society to Prevent Blindness, 1980).

# 2 BLINDNESS AND THE BRAIN

The visual system consists not just of the eyes, but also of brain structures that process or transmit visual information. In this chapter we will discuss these visual pathways and areas within the brain, and explain how a person's vision is impaired when these central structures are damaged. We will also discuss the converse possibility: that blindness caused by an ocular problem—even a temporary one such as a congenital cataract—might cause permanent damage to visual areas of the brain. Before these issues can be addressed, however, it is necessary to describe the anatomy of the central visual pathways.

## VISUAL PATHWAYS IN THE BRAIN

It will be recalled from Chapter 1 that visual information leaves the eyes via the optic nerves. These pass from the eye sockets into the cranium, and travel diagonally backward along the bottom of the brain, until they meet (see Fig. 2.1). Their junction is called the *optic chiasm*, for it has the shape of the letter X when seen from below, with the optic nerves representing the two upper arms of the X, and two other fiber bundles, the *optic tracts*, forming the lower arms of the X.

The fibers of the optic tracts are merely extensions of those making up the optic nerves, but neither tract contains just fibers from one nerve. Rather, each optic tract contains some fibers that were in the left optic nerve, and some fibers that were in the right optic nerve. Specifically, fibers coming from

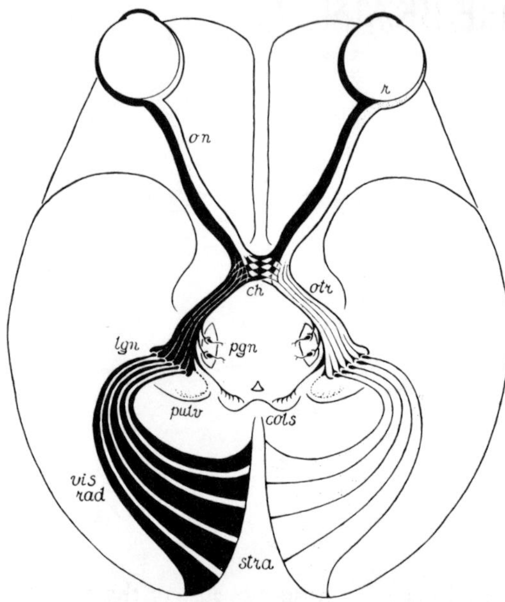


FIGURE 2.1. The central visual pathways. In this view of the brain from below, the optic nerves (on) can be seen to converge at the optic chiasm (ch). From the chiasm, the optic tracts (otr) carry visual information to the lateral geniculate nuclei (lgn), which in turn relay it to the primary visual cortex, also called the striate area (stra). Note that information from each retina's left half reaches the left half of the cortex, while information from the right hemiretinas travels to the right half of the cortex. Also shown are smaller numbers of fibers that terminate in the superior colliculus (cols), and in the pretectal area (pgn), which controls pupil size. (From *The Vertebrate Visual System* by S. Polyak, 1957, Chicago: University of Chicago Press. Copyright 1957 by the University of Chicago. Reprinted by permission.)

the left half of each retina all enter the left optic tract, while fibers coming from the right half of each retina leave the chiasm in the right optic tract. The functional significance of this rearrangement of fibers is that it brings together, within each optic tract, all available information concerning objects in the opposite half of the field of view. An object off to the observer's right, for example, will be imaged on, and thus seen with, the left half of *each* retina. Messages about this object will travel from the two eyes to the chiasm in separate optic nerves, but will be united at the chiasm and will continue their journey in just one optic tract (the left one in this case). Eventually the optic tracts enter the brain.

The brain can be divided into three large components. First and most basic is the *brainstem*, a structure roughly the size and shape of a lightbulb, which forms the core of the brain. Its narrow end, within the lower rear part of the skull, is attached to the spinal cord. About halfway along the brainstem, the cerebellum emerges from it, extending upward and backward. This, the brain's second major component, is involved in the control of movement and posture. Finally, growing upward from the brainstem near its front end, is the *cerebrum*, the largest of the brain's three divisions. Its outer covering is the cerebral cortex, about which much will be said later.

Optic tract fibers pass upward along the sides of the brainstem until they reach swellings or protuberances, one on each side, the *lateral geniculate nuclei of the thalamus.* The optic tracts enter these structures, and the tract fibers, which began in the retina, deliver their information to geniculate cells. These cells, in turn, relay the messages to the cerebral cortex in axons of their own, which travel in a curving, broad pathway called the optic radiation. Signals from the left and right halves of the visual field, which separated at the optic chiasm, remain on separate sides of the brain, for each optic tract goes only to the lateral geniculate nucleus on its own side, and the optic radiation from each geniculate goes only to the cortical hemisphere on the same side.

The *cerebral cortex* is the outermost layer of neural tissue over the cerebrum, and hence over most of the brain (see Fig. 2.2). Its surface area is very great, for the cortex dips down into many grooves and crevices in the brain. Anatomists divide it for convenience into four lobes, the frontal, temporal, parietal, and occipital. For our purposes the *occipital lobe*, at the back of the brain, is of the greatest interest, for it is this region that is most closely associated with vision.

Even within the occipital lobe, important subdivisions can be made. The fibers coming from the lateral geniculate nucleus do not spread out uniformly to all parts of the lobe, but instead go only to a particular region of it, the *primary visual cortex,* which is shown stippled in the figure. Neighboring regions of the occipital lobe obtain information when it is relayed to them by the primary visual cortex. These surrounding regions, collectively called *visual association cortex,* process this information further. From experiments with monkeys it is apparent that different regions of the visual association

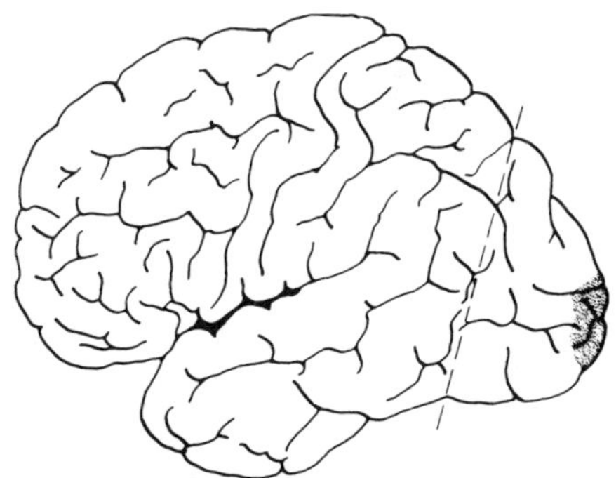

FIGURE 2.2. The human cerebral cortex, seen from the left. The part lying to the right of the dashed line is the occipital lobe; it is subdivided into primary visual cortex (stippled area), and visual association cortex. Both types of visual cortex extend onto the hemisphere's medial wall, which is not shown in this diagram.

cortex are concerned with different aspects of visual stimuli, such as their color, movement, three-dimensionality, and so on (Zeki, 1978). There may be a similar parcellation of function in the human brain (Livingstone & Hubel, 1987). For example, it has been demonstrated that a particular, small patch of visual association cortex is necessary for normal color perception: Individuals who have suffered damage to this region have abnormal color vision or none at all (Meadows, 1974; Pearlman, Birch, & Meadows, 1979). Other regions of visual association cortex within the occipital lobe of humans probably have other specific functions, but it is not yet certain how many such divisions there are.

In the parietal and temporal lobes are still other areas of association cortex, which integrate messages from the different senses, and participate in such tasks as the recognition of objects.

Not all optic tract fibers go to the lateral geniculate nucleus. A minority pass behind this structure and terminate instead in the *superior colliculi*, a pair of bumps on the upper surface of the brainstem, located between the attachments of the cerebrum and cerebellum. These structures are involved in the control of eye movements. In some lower mammals, the colliculi are important to the animal's ability to locate objects that it sees. For example, a hamster from which this structure has been surgically removed can detect the presence of a sunflower seed held by the experimenter, but does not know which way to turn to get the seed (Schneider, 1969). Whether the colliculi in people can play an analogous role in spatial behavior is a subject of controversy, as we shall see.

An even smaller number of optic tract fibers go to another brainstem structure, the pretectal region, that plays a role in adjusting the size of the pupil, constricting it in bright light but dilating it in the dark.

## EFFECTS OF CORTICAL LESIONS ON VISION

### The Map in Primary Visual Cortex

It was clear by the end of the 19th century that the occipital lobe of the cortex is important for vision, and that damage to this region of the brain causes abnormalities of visual perception, and in some cases total blindness. Further progress in understanding this relationship between anatomy and perception was achieved early in this century by careful study of war veterans who had suffered injury to the brain in combat (Glickstein, 1988). Sir Gordon Holmes, a British neurologist, was one of several scientists who made important contributions in this area by using perimetry (described in Chapter 1) to determine the extent of the visual field in patients with occipital lobe damage. Holmes (1919) compared these measurements with the location of the damaged area of the cortex, called the *lesion*, as estimated from the holes in the skull through which the bullet or shell fragment entered and left, or, in cases where the object remained inside the skull, from its position in X-ray photographs.

Holmes found that damage to the primary visual cortex always resulted in a region of blindness somewhere in the visual field, whereas damage to visual association cortex generally did not do so. The location of these scotomas depended on the specific region of the primary visual cortex that had been injured. For example, if the lesion was confined to the left hemisphere of the cortex, then the scotoma was in the right half of the patient's visual field, while lesions on the right caused scotomas on the left. This rule is understandable in terms of the anatomy presented earlier, for stimuli in the left half of the field of view are imaged on the right half of each retina, and so information about them is transmitted in the right optic tract to the right lateral geniculate nucleus, and then on to the right cortical hemisphere. The other rules described by Holmes are also consistent with the anatomical connections that transmit information from particular retinal regions to particular areas of the primary visual cortex. One important finding was that if the lesion was at the very back of the brain, then the scotoma was at the center of the visual field, and so prevented the patient from seeing an object that he attempted to look directly at. Figure 2.3 shows a patient from a later study (Teuber, Battersby, & Bender, 1960) who illustrates this principle. The dark area on the left of the X ray shows where a bullet, traveling from one side to the other, passed in and out of his skull near the back, destroying the occipital pole of the cortex. This produced a scotoma in the center of the visual field, shown in the lower part of the figure. Note that the scotoma was about the same whether plotted using the patient's left or right eye.

In fact Holmes consistently found that a scotoma caused by destruction of part of the primary visual cortex had roughly the same size and position whether measured with the patient's left or right eye. This shows that information about a given part of the visual field is delivered to the same region of cortex by both eyes: Signals from each eye produce a functional "map" of the visual field on the cortex, and the maps from the two eyes are in register. A scotoma that can only be measured in one eye, in contrast, generally indicates a lesion of that retina or optic nerve, rather than of the visual cortex.

Holmes's findings have been repeatedly confirmed in the years since they were reported: Destruction of any part of the visual cortex eliminates visual perception in a predictable region of the visual field (McAuley & Russell, 1979; Reivich et al., 1981; Teuber, Battersby, & Bender, 1960), and complete destruction of the visual cortex leaves the person with no visual sensations at all, except perhaps the ability to notice large changes in overall illumination (Brindley, Gautier-Smith, & Lewin, 1969).

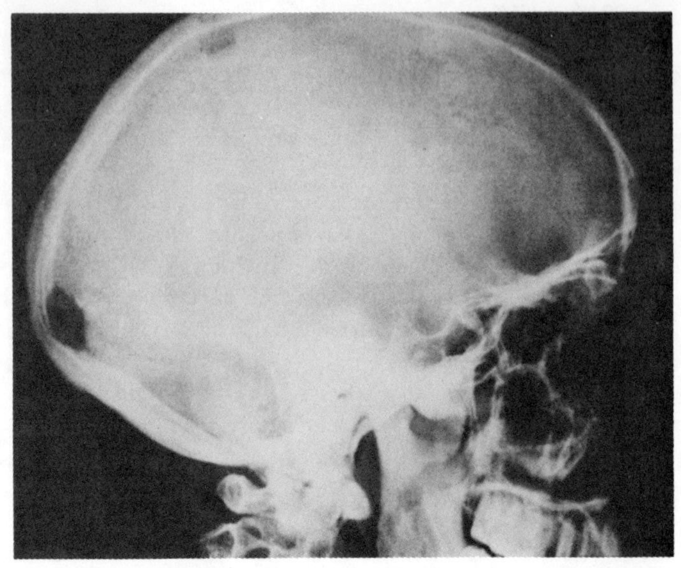

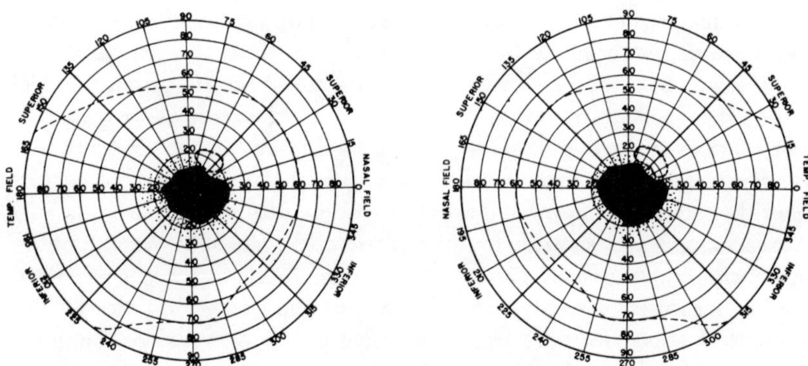


FIGURE 2.3. Relationship between the most posterior part of the visual cortex and the center of the visual field is seen in the case of this soldier wounded in World War II. A bullet traversed the skull from right to left near the occipital pole, destroying the posterior tip of the primary visual cortex. The dark region on the left of the X ray shows the cranial damage. The patient's visual fields, plotted below, contained a large central scotoma, eliminating macular vision. Surrounding this region of blindness was a larger area in which vision was poor (dotted region), but vision was normal in the periphery of his visual fields. Note that the scotoma is of approximately the same size and shape whether plotted using the left eye (left diagram) or the right eye (right diagram). (From *Visual Field Defects after Penetrating Missile Wounds of the Brain* by H.-L. Teuber, W. S. Battersby, and M. B. Bender, 1960, Cambridge, MA: Harvard University Press. Reprinted by permission.)

## Blindsight

Recently, however, the well-established doctrine that destruction of the primary visual cortex causes complete blindness has received a surprising challenge. A number of studies have turned up evidence that a person with a lesion of the primary visual cortex still has a lot of visual ability in the supposedly "blind" region, without realizing it (Bridgeman & Staggs, 1982; Perenin & Jeannerod, 1978; Pöppel, Held, & Frost, 1973; Weiskrantz, Warrington, Sanders, & Marshall, 1974). Such individuals report that they see nothing in the area of the visual field corresponding to the destroyed region of cortex, and say that it would be useless for them to attempt to point at a spot of light flashed in the blind region; but if the experimenter urges them to try anyway, their "guesses" turn out to be correct much more often than would be predicted by chance.

In some of these studies the cortical damage has been done by a stroke, and the site of the damage has been learned with computer tomography or other noninvasive methods. These techniques are invaluable from a clinical point of view, but unfortunately they cannot reveal with certainty whether a given patch of cortex has been totally destroyed, or only damaged, with some cells still functioning. Thus it is hard to know whether the residual vision of many of these patients, within their scotomas, is being mediated by other brain structures, or simply by a partly functioning visual cortex. The case reported by Weiskrantz and his colleagues, however, is one of several that get around this difficulty. Their patient, D.B., suffered from severe headaches, preceded by flashes of light in the left half of the visual field. Clinical tests showed that there was an arteriovenous malformation—a large, abnormal clump of blood vessels—embedded in and pressing against the right occipital lobe. This malformation was surgically removed, with a considerable amount of the right hemisphere's primary visual cortex having to be removed at the same time. Since a known amount of visual cortex was in this case actually cut away, there is no possibility that partially functioning cortex could mediate whatever residual vision might be found in D.B.'s scotoma.

Weiskrantz and his colleagues found that D.B. could in fact respond very well to visual stimuli in this supposedly blind region of the visual field, pointing at targets there and stating whether a given target was an X or an O. Acuity in the scotoma was an astonishingly good 20/40, as assessed by asking D.B. whether a round target contained stripes, or was uniformly filled with light. Throughout all tests, however, D.B. sincerely insisted that he saw nothing in his scotoma, and was simply guessing in all his responses.

These reports of "blindsight," to use Weiskrantz's term, are still being debated in the scientific literature. Some investigators remain skeptical, believing that light scattered within the eye onto retinal regions where vision is normal may be providing subtle cues that the subjects unintentionally use to formulate their responses; alternatively, light might be scattered into a visible area of the stimulus array before reaching the eye (Campion, Latto, & Smith, 1983). While this may be a valid criticism of some reports, other investigators have sought to minimize the effects of scattered light by presenting the test stimuli well within the blind region of the visual field, and intentionally flooding the part of the visual field in which vision is normal with intense light, so that additional scatter into this region would be unnoticeable. Moreover, in one case the entire primary visual cortex had been incapacitated by a stroke, making the person totally blind by ordinary criteria, so there was no normally sighted region into which light could be scattered (Perenin, Ruel, & Hecaen, 1980). The bulk of the evidence now points to the conclusion that blindsight is a genuine phenomenon, rather than an artifact of scattered light.

It is widely believed that the superior colliculus plays an important role in mediating blindsight, but no firm evidence on this point exists at the present time. The idea of a subcortical structure mediating a crude, unconscious type of perception is an important one, with implications for other areas of neuroscience and psychology. It deserves to be explored carefully.

For all its theoretical importance, however, blindsight is probably not of much practical significance. It might give a person whose visual cortex had been destroyed a "hunch" that he or she was approaching an obstacle, but the ability of such individuals to identify objects using their residual vision is very poor (Weiskrantz, 1980, 1987). This makes it doubtful that blindsight could make much of a contribution to everyday life.

## DOES THE CORTEX CHANGE AFTER EYESIGHT IS LOST?

Preceding sections have made it clear that vision is seriously impaired if the visual cortex is damaged by disease or injury. Let us now consider the converse question: How would visual cortex be affected by the loss of eyesight? If its sensory input were cut off by some disease of the eye, corneal opacity for example, would the visual cortex deteriorate, so that even surgical correction of the ocular problem would not enable the cortex to mediate vision as it had before? Or would it retain its functional capacity indefinitely? It turns out that the answer depends very much on the age at which vision is lost. If it is lost in adulthood, the visual cortex apparently changes very little, but if it is lost early in life, the visual cortex is drastically affected. The following sections explain the evidence for these statements.

### Electrical Activity

One way to study the activity of the human visual cortex is to record brain waves from the occipital region, by attaching disk electrodes to the scalp. When a visual stimulus is presented to a sighted subject, an electrical response consisting of one or more waves, and lasting perhaps half a second, occurs. Such a response is called an *evoked potential,* because it is "called forth" from the brain by a stimulus. It reflects the simultaneous activity of large numbers of cortical cells, primarily those in the region of brain underlying the electrode site. A type of stimulus widely used to produce evoked potentials is a checkerboard, or sometimes a stripe pattern, in which the dark areas become bright, and the bright areas dark, one or more times per second. Each alternation of the pattern evokes a new response, and successive responses can be electronically averaged by a computer to obtain a representative waveform in which much of the electrical "noise" has been averaged out.

A normal evoked potential in response to such a pattern can only occur if the visual cortex is functioning properly. This is shown by the fact that extensive damage to the occipital cortex, caused for example by a stroke that interrupts the blood supply, abolishes the pattern-evoked potential (Hess, Meienberg, & Ludin, 1982). Unfortunately, this test of the functional integrity of the cortex cannot be used in the case of a person whose eyesight is failing or gone, however, because in that case there is no way to deliver visual signals to the cortex.

Another way to address the problem is to record the spontaneous, rather than the evoked, activity of the cortex. Such *electroencephalograms* are widely used in medical diagnosis and research. One prominent feature of the electroencephalogram in sighted people is the alpha wave, a repetitive, roughly sinusoidal wave, with a frequency of about 10 cycles per second, which can be recorded from the occipital lobe. The alpha wave seems to have a special, if paradoxical, connection with the visual system, for it is largest in darkness or when the eyes are closed, and can be abolished by opening the eyes and looking at one's surroundings.

Novikova (1967/1974) has recorded electroencephalograms from large numbers of blind people, at an institute for the study of sensory deficits in Moscow. She has found that the alpha rhythm is absent from most people who have been totally blind for several months or more. Immediately after sight is lost, the person retains an alpha rhythm, but this declines slowly in amplitude over the course of a few months, finally disappearing. This disappearance of alpha suggests that in some way, the visual cortex changes as a result of blindness. The cause of the alpha rhythm is not well understood, but it probably reflects, in part, the intrinsic patterns of activity of resting cortical neurons. What, then, causes the disappearance of alpha when eyesight is lost? An overall reduction in the activity of visual-cortex neurons is one possibility, but another is that the neurons in the visual cortex fall out of synchrony with one another, firing as much as before, but staggered in time. A choice among these and other possibilities cannot be made on the basis of existing data.

Whatever the underlying change in the brains of Novikova's subjects, it was reversible, for that minority of patients who were able to have their sight restored through an operation (say, for the removal of cataracts) regained their alpha rhythm shortly after sight was regained. This was true even in cases where the individual had been without sight for several years. This is an important finding, for it suggests that the visual cortex of a man or woman who becomes blind retains much, if not all, of its functional integrity despite a lack of visual input. The same conclusion is implied by the common clinical observation that a person who develops cataracts as an adult, and delays having them removed for many months, nevertheless can see about as well after surgery as he or she could before the cataract developed. We will learn in later sections, however, that an infant or young child whose vision is occluded for a long period of time by cataracts has a much greater risk of permanent visual impairment, probably as a result of irreversible changes in the visual cortex.

## A Visual Prosthesis

Given that the visual cortex of an adult remains capable of functioning after a long period of nonstimulation, it might be worthwhile to attempt to activate the visual cortex of an inoperably blind person in some way, say by mild electrical stimulation delivered directly to the brain. In this way useful, if crude, visual sensations might be provided to a person whose eyes were no longer functioning. This possibility has been explored by a number of investigators, and the results are exciting from both a theoretical and a practical point of view. It should be noted at this point that subjects in these studies were fully informed of all the procedures that were to be used, and that they gave their consent in advance, knowing that the research was of an exploratory nature and would not be of direct benefit to them.

In the first such study using modern techniques, Brindley and Lewin (1968) surgically implanted an array of small stimulating electrodes under the skull of a 52-year-old blind woman. The electrodes were embedded in a silicone rubber cap designed to fit over the occipital pole of the right hemisphere. When the electrodes were activated by radio control from outside the head, causing mild electric shocks to be delivered to particular points in the primary visual cortex, the woman saw small spots of light, like stars in the sky. Each electrode generally gave rise to only one spot, or *phosphene*, which flickered but remained motionless.

To determine the position of the phosphenes in perceived space, Brindley and Lewin asked their subject to reach into a large perimeter bowl and grasp a handle attached to its inner surface at the center. While directing her eyes toward this spot, she was then to point with her other hand to the position where the phosphone appeared. The spot on the bowl to which she pointed was then noted by the experimenters. They discovered that the perceived locations of the phosphenes were in approximate agreement with the map of the visual cortex discovered by Holmes. That is, stimulation of a particular spot on the cortical surface produced a phosphene in the part of space with which that region of cortex would, in a sighted person, be concerned. For example, she always pointed into the left half of the bowl, consistent with the fact that the electrodes were in contact with the right hemisphere. Electrodes close to the occipital pole produced phosphenes nearly straight ahead, while more anterior electrodes gave rise to phosphenes located farther to the side.

These findings have now been confirmed on other blind persons (Dobelle, 1977; Dobelle, Mladejovsky, & Girvin, 1974) and on sighted people as well (Dobelle & Mladejovsky, 1974). The sighted subjects were hospital patients who agreed in advance to stimulation of the cortex during medically necessary brain surgery on the occipital lobe; as is often the case during brain operations, these patients were conscious throughout and so were able to describe the phosphenes. All these individuals, sighted and blind, reported phosphenes.

How big were the phosphenes? Brindley and Lewin's original subject, who had been losing sight gradually for 5 years, compared most phosphenes to stars, with a few others being blurred or elongated; four subjects studied in Dobelle's laboratory, who had been blind for periods ranging from 7 to 28 years, gave similar reports, saying that the largest phosphenes were the size of a coin at arm's length (Dobelle, 1977). However, a man who had been blind for more than 30 years saw large, elongated phosphenes (Brindley, 1973). Was this subject unique, or does the cortex undergo very slow changes over time, causing the phosphenes produced by electrical stimulation to smear and spread out? This question remains unanswered. In any case, the major conclusion of these studies is that for many years after an adult loses his or her sight, localized phosphenes can be produced by electrical stimulation of the visual cortex.

Furthermore, if groups of electrodes are activated simultaneously, then groups of phosphenes are produced. In the studies described, the subjects were able to perceive not just the location of isolated phosphenes, but the simple patterns formed by multiple phosphenes, like stellar constellations. Dobelle and colleagues (Dobelle, Mladejovsky, Evans, Roberts, & Girvin, 1976) went on to show that even a rapidly presented series of patterns could be appreciated. These were the patterns of spots making up letters, or cells, in braille. Braille is normally presented, of course, in the form of raised dots felt by a fingertip; but in this case the dots were replaced by phosphenes, so that the subject was actually able to see each pattern. He was able to read this visual braille at a rate of about two letters per second.

Scientists in several laboratories are now trying to develop a permanent implant, or *prosthesis*, that will be able to provide useful information to a blind person on an everyday basis, through electrical stimulation of the cortex. Some researchers believe it will eventually be possible to connect the prosthesis to a miniature television camera, mounted perhaps in a glass eye, so that the user's visual cortex can receive information about objects in the environment.

If and when such a prosthesis is developed, its advantages and disadvantages would have to be carefully weighed by any potential user. Among the disadvantages would be the risks that are part of any surgical procedure, the chance that the device would malfunction with the passage of time, and the cost of the device and its implantation. In addition, some users might experience emotional stress in response to this new source of information and its impact on everyday life (Gregory & Wallace, 1963). On the positive side, such a visual prosthesis would actually allow a blind person to see again, although the visual sensations would be cruder than those of normal sight.

## Visual Deprivation in Animals

The work of Novikova, Brindley and others, described in the two previous sections, suggests that the visual cortex undergoes only very slow and modest changes in an adult whose eyesight has been lost. However, other researchers have shown that more severe changes can take place, both in human beings and in animals, if vision is lost early in life. In examining these changes, we will first consider the research on animals, because it tells us more directly what is happening in the brain; then we will use the results from animals to help us understand the vision of congenitally blind people whose eyesight has been surgically restored after a prolonged period without vision.

One of the first researchers to deprive animals of vision was Riesen (1947). He wanted to produce the effects of blindness, and yet be able to test the animals later with visual stimuli, a possibility that would not exist if the animals were actually blinded physiologically at the outset of the experiment. To this end he and his colleagues reared chimpanzees in darkness. A chimp named Snark (Chow, Riesen, & Newell, 1957) was typical of the animals in these studies. Snark was put into a totally dark laboratory soon after birth, and lived there for 33 months. When he was finally brought out into the light, Snark showed almost no response to visual stimuli. He showed neither interest nor fear when objects were suddenly thrust toward him, and he recognized nothing by sight. His visual acuity, tested by determining whether he could learn to discriminate between striped patterns, was about one-tenth that of a normally reared chip.

What was wrong with Snark? Had his visual cortex deteriorated as a result of his lack of visual experience? Perhaps, but a more straightforward reason for his blindness existed: His retinas had degenerated. The ganglion cells, which provide the only route for visual messages to leave the eyes, were almost entirely gone. Snark was blind because little visual information reached his brain.

Scientists are still not sure how to interpret this result. Riesen and his colleagues noted that their chimps often poked their eyes with their thumbs, a behavior that chimps living in a lighted environment do not show. It now seems possible that this harmful pressure on the eyes, rather than visual deprivation itself, caused the retinal damage (Hendrickson & Boothe, 1976), for more recent studies in a variety of other species have found little in the way of retinal damage resulting from dark rearing. The original experiments were very important, however, for they stimulated a great deal of research on the effects, both behavioral and physiological, of visual deprivation.

*Behavioral Effects of Deprivation.* Subsequent work by Wiesel and Hubel (1965a, 1965b) showed that vision is impaired by stimulus deprivation even when the retina is not damaged. They sewed shut the eyelids of kittens, thus depriving them of all patterned retinal stimulation, but allowing some diffuse light to enter the eye. (Since about 90% of blind people have some perception of light, lid suturing actually provides a closer parallel to most human blindness than does dark rearing.) One such kitten had its eyelids sutured on the 10th day of life, shortly before its eyes would normally have opened. When it reached the age of 3 months, the lids of one eye were opened under general anesthesia, so that its vision could be tested. Its eye was in good condition, but its behavior resembled that of Riesen's chimpanzees, for it gave the impression of seeing nothing. In walking around the room, the kitten bumped into large obstacles; and when lowered toward a table, it did not extend its forepaws as a sighted kitten does.

One of Wiesel and Hubel's most important findings was that these perceptual deficiencies occur only if the animal is visually deprived early in life. If the kitten is allowed several months of normal visual experience, subsequent deprivation, even if it lasts for a year or more, will have no substantial effect on the kitten's visual behavior. By the same token, animals that are binocularly deprived for several months after birth will show only modest recovery once their eyelids have been opened, no matter how long they remain in a normally lighted environment. The first few months of life, during which the kitten is susceptible to the harmful effects of visual deprivation, are therefore called the *critical period.*

Even cats deprived throughout the critical period are not totally blind, however. This was demonstrated by Sherman (1973), who raised cats for a year with eyelids sutured, and then tested their visual fields after the lids had been surgically opened. To make these tests, the cat was placed on a table top, and its attention was directed to a piece of meat, held directly in front of it a few feet away. In this way the cat was made to gaze straight ahead, like a human patient staring at the spot in the center of a perimeter. Then an attempt was made to attract the cat's attention to another stimulus, silently presented to the left or right of the fixation object. The animals were tested with one eye at a time, wearing a patch on the other eye. While normally reared cats turn toward a stimulus introduced on either side of the fixation object, the cats that had been raised with sutured eyelids oriented toward a stimulus only if it was presented on the side away from the patch. When the left eye was being tested, only stimuli off to the left were seen; when the right eye was tested, the stimulus had to be off to the right. In technical terms, the cats could see in the temporal half of each eye's visual field, but were unresponsive to stimuli presented in the nasal half of the visual field.

The importance of this result is that it is exactly what would be expected if the deprived cats' remaining vision were mediated primarily by their superior colliculi, rather than their visual cortex. This is the case because each retina sends to the colliculus mainly information about the temporal half of its field of view, but sends to the cortex information about both halves of the field. Later research confirmed the cats' dependence on their colliculi in carrying out this orienting task (Sherman, 1977).

Why do the superior colliculi play such a dominant role in the visual behavior of visually deprived cats? It will be recalled that in cases of human "blindsight," crude vision is apparently mediated by the superior colliculi, but in that situation the visual cortex has been severely damaged in some way. It is hard to avoid the implication that visually deprived cats have also suffered some damage to their visual cortex, damage brought about by the rearing conditions themselves.

*Physiological Effects of Deprivation.* Wiesel and Hubel set out to determine the nature of these pathological changes in the deprived cortex. They themselves had a few years before (Hubel & Wiesel, 1962) made a series of landmark contributions to the study of normal visual cortex, so they had a good basis for evaluating the physiological status of the deprived visual system. The method used in the earlier experiments had been to anesthetize the cat, open the skull over the visual cortex, and lower a fine wire, called a *microelectrode*, into the brain. The animal's eyelids were held open, and it faced a screen on which bars and other patterns of light could be presented. The electrode was advanced slowly, until a series of clicks, issuing from a speaker to which it was connected, signaled that the electrode was near a cortical neuron. Each click represented an action potential, a fundamental unit of neural activity. Many cells "fire" action potentials even in the dark; this spontaneous activity allows the experimenters to know that they are recording from a cell even before they determine the appropriate stimulus for that cell.

Wiesel and Hubel next flashed stimuli on the screen, in order to find patterns that would cause a speedup, or perhaps a pause, in the activity of the cell under study. What they discovered was that cells in the normal visual cortex are very selective in their responses to visual stimuli, with a given cell responding to one stimulus but not to many others. They found, for example, that if a stimulus was to activate a cell, it had to be presented in a particular part of the animal's visual field. The area of the visual field that can influence the activity level of a cell is called the *receptive field* of that cell. Their measurements showed that different cells have receptive fields in different places, depending on where the cell itself is located. For example, cells in the visual cortex of the left hemisphere have receptive fields in the right half of the field of view, and vice versa. These relationships support the principle, discovered in human beings by Holmes and his contemporaries, that particular regions of cortex are concerned with specific parts of the visual field.

Another feature of cortical cells in the normal cat (and in other animals) is that they will respond more vigorously to an edge or line than to other stimuli, such as spots. Moreover, a particular cell can be activated strongly only if the line is oriented in a particular direction: This might be vertical for one cell, horizontal for another, diagonal for a third, and so on. This property of cells is called *orientation specificity*.

From this work on the normally reared animal, Wiesel and Hubel (1965a) now turned their attention to the visual cortex of their lid-sutured kittens. Whereas all neurons in the visual cortex of the normally reared cat respond to some visual stimulus, the investigators found that 3 cells out of every 10 in their formerly lid-sutured cats did not respond to anything. Their spontaneous activity was not altered by any patterns shown on the screen. Of the remaining neurons, which did respond to some visual stimuli, somewhat more than half were normal in their response properties. Their receptive fields were in the expected part of the screen, and they each preferred a bar or edge of some particular orientation. The remaining cells, about 30% of the total, were the most interesting. They responded to visual stimuli, but in an abnormal way, having little preference for one orientation over another. Moreover, these cells fatigued easily: They would fire vigorously when a stimulus was first presented, but required a rest period before another strong response could be elicited.

Subsequent research has confirmed these findings for the most part, although more elaborate testing of receptive fields has revealed that few cells in the deprived cortex are entirely normal (Sherman & Spear, 1982; Singer & Tretter, 1976; Watkins, Wilson, & Sherman, 1978). Despite this agreement in results, however, a controversy has developed over how best to interpret the findings. Do the effects of deprivation represent deterioration of a visual cortex which, at birth, is functioning much as it does in an adult animal, or does deprivation simply prevent the normal development of visual cortex into a maturely functioning structure? In the cat the answer probably lies between these two extreme positions, but in the monkey—visually more mature at birth—the deterioration theory is closer to the mark (Wiesel & Hubel, 1974).

Many investigators have concentrated on following up other observations by Wiesel and Hubel, such as their study (1963) of kittens that have had only one eyelid sutured. This monocular deprivation produces cortical effects that are in a way more dramatic than those of binocular deprivation, with the deprived eye losing out, in competition with the open eye, for the control of cortical cells. In no sense are these animals blind, however, so the subject of monocular deprivation will not be dealt with here.

In summary, cats that are binocularly deprived of visual input early in life lose a considerable amount of their ability to see. This perceptual decline is accompanied by, and probably the result of, a loss by cortical cells of the ability to respond normally to visual stimuli. If the cats are returned to a normal visual environment within the first few months of life, losses can be reversed, but beyond this point they become permanent. In that case the animals are left with crude, limited vision that is apparently mediated by the superior colliculus.

While binocular deprivation is causing the stimulus-specificity of cells in the primary visual cortex to deteriorate, it is having a different, and somewhat surprising, effect on cells located more anteriorly in the occipital lobe, in visual association cortex. Although this brain region normally receives no nonvisual information concerning hand movements, it begins to do so if an animal is deprived of visual stimulation early in life. Juhani Hyvärinen and his colleagues at the University of Helsinki (Hyvärinen, Carlson, & Hyvärinen, 1981) demonstrated this with monkeys who were lid-sutured shortly after birth, and received no patterned visual stimulation until the age of 12 months, at which time the lids were opened and electrical recordings were carried out. While all recordings in nondeprived control monkeys of the same age showed an influence of visual stimulation on cells in visual association cortex, only 39% of the recordings from the deprived animals did so. More surprisingly, however, 18% of the recordings from the deprived animals reflected their motor activity: Cells fired vigorously, for example, when the monkey carried out such tasks as retrieving a raisin from a small box. No such cells were encountered in the normally reared monkeys. These results suggest that, as a result of visual deprivation, new connections may be formed or already existing ones strengthened, between the occipital lobe of the cortex and other brain regions.

*Does a Blind Animal's Visual Cortex Serve Any Function?* What are the implications of Hyvärinen's finding for our understanding of brain function in a blind animal? Does it mean that visual association cortex can play a role in mediating the animal's behavior, even though the normal input to this part of the cortex—visual information—has stopped? Not necessarily. The nonvisual activation of cells in visual association cortex may be simply a neural dead end, without effect on the animal's perceptions or actions. The question is a behavioral one, and only a behavioral experiment could answer it.

Several decades ago, Karl Lashley (1943) attempted to provide such an answer, using rats as experimental subjects. He first trained them to find their way through a maze. When they could hurry through it without errors, he anesthetized them, and blinded them by removal of the eyes. Upon recovery, the rats were at first confused and made errors when put back into the maze, but they soon learned to find their way through it again using nonvisual cues. Finally, Lashley surgically removed the visual cortex (primary visual cortex and part of visual association cortex) of the rats. When they were again returned to the maze, they were totally disoriented, and were all but unable to get through it; moreover, they found relearning the maze to be very difficult, impossible in some cases. This result is surprising because it means that the rats had come to depend on their visual cortex in running the maze, and that they depended on it even when they were blind. If this were not the case, removal of the visual cortex in rats who had already lost their sight should not have disrupted their behavior so drastically.

Orbach (1959) made observations similar to these, in the monkey; his results support Lashley's conclusion that the visual cortex, even in a blind animal, plays a role in mediating certain tasks.

One difficulty with this interpretation, however, is that physical removal of visual cortex in these experimental animals may have indirectly caused subtle damage to neighboring areas of the brain, by interrupting neural pathways important for keeping these other areas in good working condition. One way to address this question would be to replicate Lashley's experiment, using the improved technology available today. For example, temporary cooling of the occipital lobe, to deactivate it for a while, would allow an animal's visual cortex to be put out of commission without being removed. Any behavioral deficits that showed up could be monitored continuously as the temperature of the cortex returned to normal, to see if the animal's behavior also would return to normal. Until such confirmatory studies are done, many scientists will remain skeptical of the idea that the occipital cortex of a totally blind animal—or that of a totally blind person—participates in the processing of information.

Our understanding of how the cerebral cortex responds to sensory stimuli is currently undergoing important changes, however; patterns of neuronal activity in some cortical areas are now known to be more dynamic and malleable than was previously thought to be the case (Merzenich, 1987; Whitsel et al., 1989). In view of the fact that our theories of cortical activity and function are still evolving, it would be premature to rule out the possibility of some functional reorganization of cortex, following the loss of sight. If such reorganization does occur, and does involve the occipital lobe, it seems more likely to engage visual association cortex, than primary visual cortex with its long-maintained map of the visual field.

## Congenital Cataracts and Human Visual Deprivation

We know from the work of Wiesel, Hubel, and others, described earlier, that if an animal is deprived of patterned visual stimulation early in life, its visual cortex undergoes marked changes, which can be demonstrated when the eyelids are unsutured at the end of the critical period. Unlike cells in the normal visual cortex, which fire briskly in response to particular stimuli, many cells in these deprived animals respond sluggishly to a wide variety of stimuli, or else are totally unresponsive. But how about people? Does a baby's vision deteriorate if he or she does not receive normal visual stimulation during the first months of life? The question has important medical implications, because babies are sometimes born with blinding cataracts in both eyes, and the question of when to operate arises.

Modern medical practice is surgically to remove these impediments to vision as soon as possible. In times past, however, with medical care not so advanced as it is today, cataract surgery on an infant was generally not feasible. It thus sometimes happened that a person grew to adulthood without having received any patterned visual stimulation. Some of these adults eventually underwent surgery, however, so that patterned light was finally able to reach their retinas. Had the visual system of these individuals deteriorated as a result of their long period of stimulus deprivation?

A positive answer to this question is suggested by the reports of many cases of this type assembled from the medical literature by von Senden (1932/1960). Although these individuals varied widely in circumstances, such as their age and the degree of blindness before surgery, one result was almost universally encountered: When the bandages were removed following surgery, the person was not able to recognize familiar objects by looking at them. Even after the careful fitting of glasses, so that retinal images were sharp, the form vision of these individuals was very poor. When a conspicuous object was presented, they could tell that something was there, and point approximately to it, but they could not identify it. Objects of the same size, such as a cat and a chicken, were often visually indistinguishable. These patients showed some improvement of their vision with the passage of time, and the gaining of visual experience, but in most cases they never developed anything approaching normal vision. A recent case (Ackroyd, Humphrey, & Warrington, 1974) confirms these early findings. Despite substantial individual differences in the postsurgical visual abilities of such patients (Gregory &

Wallace, 1963; Valvo, 1971), their cases, taken together, provide a striking parallel to the results with animals deprived of form vision, described previously.

How soon after birth should surgery be performed on an infant born with blinding cataracts in both eyes, if the permanent consequences of visual deprivation are to be avoided? A careful study of 24 young patients points to the advisability of early treatment in such cases (Gelbart et al., 1982). These infants had congenital cataracts surgically removed at various ages. In all cases the operations on the two eyes were performed within a day or two of each other, to prevent the eye receiving vision first from capitalizing on its advantage over the other eye, a situation that could result in amblyopia. After surgery, the babies were optically corrected (with contact lenses) to ensure that their retinas received a clear image of objects in the visual field. The patients were carefully monitored over a long period of time, and years later, when they were capable of taking an eyechart test, their visual acuity was tested. Seventeen of the infants had had the cataracts removed before the age of 8 weeks. Later, as children, 15 of these had an acuity of 20/60 or better. Of the 7 patients for whom surgery had not been carried out until after 8 weeks of age, however, only one had an acuity better than 20/60; the other 6 had acuities of 20/200 or worse, meaning that they were legally blind.

This dramatic result, which is consistent with other findings (Parks, 1982), implies that the critical period for the development of visual acuity in people is well under way by the end of the second month. It is by no means over by then, however, for binocular deprivation which does not begin until much later (Ackroyd et al., 1974) can have a deleterious effect on vision. Why should the effect of a few months' deprivation be irreversible, if the critical period has not yet ended? The answer may lie in the abnormal, repetitive eye movements, called nystagmus, which long-deprived infants often develop (Parks, 1982). This nystagmus may interfere with viewing to such an extent that, even after surgery, the pattern of impulses sent to the brain by the eyes is abnormal.

Whatever the correct explanation of these recent results, their practical implication is that surgery for congenital cataracts that are preventing sight ought generally to be performed as early in the child's life as is consistent with his or her overall state of health. It is important to emphasize, however, that not all congenital eye problems can or should be treated by early surgery. In making a decision concerning the best treatment for a particular individual, physicians take into account the nature and severity of the ocular condition as well as a host of other medical considerations.

In the first two chapters of this book we have discussed diseases and other physiological conditions that can damage the visual system, indicating in each case the usual form of treatment and the outlook for recovery of visual function. The remainder of the book, however, deals not with the etiology of blindness, but rather with how blindness, once it has become a reality, affects a person's life. In the next chapter we will begin that undertaking by considering some of the ways in which a blind person's perceptual experiences differ from, and ways in which they resemble, those of a sighted person.

# 3 BLINDNESS AND PERCEPTION

The first two chapters of this book dealt primarily with the physiology of blindness: how diseases of the eye and damage to the brain can result in the loss of sight. The remainder of the book, however, will deal with behavioral and psychological aspects of blindness. The subject of how blind people use their remaining senses to gain an appreciation of the world around them is the subject of the present chapter. In the next chapter, we will consider whether mental imagery and other cognitive activities are influenced by the loss of sight. The last three chapters will take up the social and developmental aspects of blindness, as well as the related topic of how newly blinded individuals adjust to the loss of sight.

## PERCEPTUAL ABILITIES OF BLIND PEOPLE

The question most frequently asked about blindness is whether blind people develop heightened sensitivity of their other senses—especially hearing and touch—as a result of their loss of sight. The answer to this question is, apparently not. It is true, however, that through long practice in deriving information from auditory and somethetic stimuli, many blind people have learned to attend more effectively to nonvisual aspects of their environment than sighted people do. In this section we will first review the evidence that argues against the existence, in blind people, of abnormal sensitivity to sounds or touches, and then discuss the fact that, despite this lack of supersensitivity, many blind people perceive things that go unnoticed by others.

## The Senses Do Not Become More Sensitive

Whether the auditory sensitivities of blind and sighted individuals are comparable is a question that has been asked for hundreds of years, and so it was one of the first issues to be investigated by psychologists when methods for the accurate measurement of sensory ability were developed toward the end of the last century. One of the most careful early investigations was that of Seashore and Ling (1918), who compared 16 blind and 15 sighted high school students on their ability to say which of two successively presented tones was the more intense. They found the two groups to be closely comparable on this test of differential sensitivity, a result that has recently been confirmed using modern equipment and testing methods (Starlinger & Niemeyer, 1981). These latter investigators only used subjects who were found in advance to have normal audiograms, however, so their data may not tell us much about the average auditory abilities of blind and sighted people. Regarding absolute auditory sensitivity—the ability to detect faint sounds—there is no adequately controlled study, but the data that do exist (Benedetti & Loeb, 1972; Hayes, 1941) suggest that blind and sighted subjects are, on the average, equal in this respect. In summary, there is no evidence that hearing ability changes as a result of the loss of sight.

In the case of tactile sensitivity, the study by Axelrod (1959) is definitive. He carefully measured sensitivity to light touch on the fingertip, the stimuli being a series of nylon threads arranged in order of stiffness. On a given experimental trial, one of these threads was pushed end first against the skin, until the hair bowed under the pressure. The stiffer threads were felt easily, but the finest ones went unnoticed by the subject. As a measure of sensitivity, Axelrod determined the degree of hair stiffness that subjects were just barely able to detect. Threshold values of this kind were obtained from 75 children and adolescents who had become blind before the age of 2, and from an equal number of sighted youngsters. The subjects ranged in age from 8 to 20, but for each early-blind subject, a sighted pupil of the same age had been selected, so the two groups were closely comparable on this dimension. Axelrod found that sensitivity varied somewhat, depending on the finger stimulated and the sex of the subjects, but the overall result was that the just detectable amount of force was 48 mg for the blind subjects, 34 mg for the sighted. This difference was not statistically significant, and in any case is in the wrong direction as far as sensory enhancement on the part of the blind subjects is concerned.

Axelrod also tested *two-point discrimination* on the same subjects. In this test, two blunt needles are simultaneously touched gently to a fingertip at a short distance from one another, and the subject is asked whether one or two points of stimulation are perceived. When the points are very close, they are felt as one, but when widely separated the subject can tell there are two. The intermediate separation at which this perception of doubleness is just possible is called the two-point threshold. The experiment requires that an occasional "catch" trial, using just a single needle, be employed so that the subject does not lapse into the habit of saying "two" every time. Axelrod found that the overall two-point threshold, averaged across subjects and fingers, was 1.63 mm for the blind subjects, 1.66 for the sighted. As was the case for light touch thresholds, these two values were not significantly different.

When the three fingers that had been tested were considered separately, however, two-point sensitivity on one of them, the right index finger, was significantly greater in the blind than in the sighted subjects. Axelrod feels that this 0.1-mm difference may indicate a degree of true sensory enhancement. A shortcoming of this piecemeal analysis of the data, however, is that an occasional statistically significant result is to be expected even if there are no true sensitivity differences between the two groups of subjects. Considering all the data, the present author interprets Axelrod's study as showing that there is no appreciable difference in tactile sensitivity between blind and sighted subjects.

More recent research has confirmed the equivalence of cutaneous sensitivity in sighted and blind persons, except for those whose blindness results from diabetic retinopathy. In many of these latter individuals, diabetes impairs touch as well as vision (Heinrichs & Moorhouse, 1969).

The case against supersensitivity does not rest solely on this lack of evidence for it, however. The most persuasive argument against it is in fact a theoretical one: Increased sensitivity would hinder, rather than help, the performance of any person, blind or sighted. The senses are already as acute as they can usefully be. In hearing, for example, the ear is stimulated when sound waves, disturbing the air, beat against the eardrum. But even in a completely silent room, the air molecules are in constant motion, bouncing off one another and colliding with objects in the room. It turns out that the ear of someone with normal hearing is almost sensitive enough to pick up this Brownian motion of the air. If we did hear it, it would sound like the static between stations on a radio. Clearly it would not be desirable to increase the sensitivity of the ear to the point where this hissing white noise was constantly audible, disturbing the listener and muddying important sounds. A similar argument could be made for the sense of touch, in which air currents and the press of clothing would become disruptive if we were more sensitive to them than we are now.

## Some Perceptual Skills Develop with Practice

On the other hand, the information we derive from our senses is often limited by our lack of attention. If we are deep in thought, we may not hear what someone says to us; or we may watch "Lassie" on television without noticing that dogs with different markings play the title role in different scenes. The opposite side of this coin is that, by paying close attention to certain types of sensory information, it is possible to become adept at noticing things that others miss, or seeing subtle differences between stimuli that are confused by others. A professional wine taster is a commonly cited example, but there are innumerable others, from the quality control inspector who checks garments for flaws in stitching, to the zookeeper who can recognize all the individual monkeys in the colony. Not surprisingly, blind people obey this general rule, and are quite capable of learning to make subtle distinctions when such a skill becomes useful to them. Auditory or tactile information that would be superfluous to a sighted person, because it merely confirms or duplicates simultaneously arriving visual information, can often be important to a blind person. Thus a sighted person may see that another person is embarrassed, because that other person blushes or looks away, but in this situation a blind person learns to detect embarrassment by listening for subtle changes in tone of voice.

That many blind persons are skilled in attending to voices has been experimentally demonstrated by playing for them a tape-recorded sentence, and subsequently asking them to choose, from a number of recorded alternatives, the original speaker (Bull, Rathborn, & Clifford, 1983). The spoken sentence was always the same: "I'll meet you outside the National Westminster Bank at six o'clock tonight." Ninety-two blind subjects and 72 sighted ones, ranging in age from 16 to 42, participated in the study. The blind subjects were consistently better at identifying voices than were the sighted. When the voice parade consisted of 9 speakers in a row, for example, blind subjects chose the correct voice on two out of every three trials, while the sighted subjects guessed correctly on only half the trials.

There are several other perceptual skills at which blind people have been shown by experiment to be better, on the average, than the sighted. One such skill will be considered in detail here, because it clearly illustrates the learned nature of those perceptual abilities of blind people that are often regarded as remarkable by the sighted public.

This best known skill of many blind people, sometimes called the "*obstacle sense*," is their ability to detect objects at distances of up to several meters. It often surprises sighted people, and it is perhaps from the existence of this skill that the myth of sensory compensation for the loss of sight arose long ago. Scholars and scientists have been discussing this ability for centuries. Diderot, the 17th-century encylopedist, called it "facial vision," and this rather inappropriate name has stuck. Diderot, and many who came after him, believed that it was air currents or eddies set up by the obstacle, and subsequently brushing against the blind person's face, which gave him or her the necessary clues. This view was based partly on the testimony of blind people themselves, who know that they can detect obstacles but in many cases are unsure how they do it. One adventitiously blinded man described the sensory experience as one "of vague sight or of slight pressure on the face" (Twersky, 1959, p. 19).

In the 1940s, a group of experimental psychologists at Cornell University (Supa, Cotzin, & Dallenbach, 1944) undertook a systematic investigation of the obstacle sense, to quantify it and to determine what sort of sensory information it is based on. They asked four subjects—two blind and two sighted but blindfolded—to walk across a large room, and to stop and raise a hand when they perceived that they were approaching a wall. The two blind subjects did this unhesitatingly, raising their arm while still several meters from the wall. The sighted subjects, however, could not detect the wall until they were nearly upon it, and they often bumped into it. In their first 25 trials, neither blind subject ever ran into the wall, but one sighted subject collided with it 15 times, and the other, 19 times. Clearly the blind subjects were behaving in a different way from the sighted ones. In their second series of 25 trials, however, the sighted subjects made fewer collisions: 6 and 1, respectively. In just a few dozen attempts, then, the sighted subjects were learning the "obstacle sense." They continued to improve with practice, and by the end of the study were about half as skillful at it as their blind fellow-subjects. Clearly, then, the obstacle sense is not something that is unique to blind people; the sighted can also learn this skill with sufficient effort and practice.

But perhaps what the sighted subjects had learned to do, and what the blind subjects did from the start, was to be very cautious: to report the presence of the obstacle after taking only a few steps, in order to avoid a collision. This would not necessarily mean that the subjects were intentionally misleading the experimenter; it could mean simply that they vividly imagined the wall looming in front of them, and mistook such imaginings for perceptions.

To test this possibility, and to make detection of the obstacle more challenging, the experimenters started using a movable board, rather than the wall, as an obstacle. This board, somewhat more than a square meter in size, was mounted on a stand, like a large painting on an easel, and set up in the room in the path of the subject. When subjects were brought into the room and guided by the experimenter into a starting position facing the obstacle, they detected this board as consistently as they had earlier detected the wall, raising their hand when they came within several meters of it. Varying the position of the obstacle failed to disrupt performance, a result which shows that subjects were not simply learning the position of the obstacle with respect to, say, a loose floorboard or the draft from a window. Furthermore, on catch trials when the board was not present, subjects walked the length of the room without raising their hand, proving that their usual responses were based on a genuine perception of the obstacle.

The experimenters now addressed the question of which sensory avenues were being employed in the detection of the obstacle. They first had the subjects wear a veil of felt which covered their head and shoulders, and gauntlets made of leather, in order to eliminate the potential effects of air currents, to which Diderot had originally attributed "facial vision." The coverings were so effective that the subjects could not feel an electric fan directed at them from 10 feet away, but their hearing was only slightly impaired. Wearing this gear, the subjects tried once more to detect the obstacle. They were nearly as skillful at doing so as they had been before, showing that air currents are not necessary for the operation of the obstacle sense.

Suspicion thus focused by default on hearing. To put the role of audition to a direct test, the experimenters fitted the subjects with earplugs made of a mixture of beeswax and cotton wool. These eliminated perception of all but loud sounds. This procedure had the effect of totally eliminating the obstacle sense. Every subject, blind or sighted, now collided with the obstacle on every trial.

In confirmation of this result, additional subjects who were deaf as well as blind showed no obstacle sense, repeatedly colliding with the obstacle. Moreover, they failed to acquire the ability to detect obstacles even after extensive training in the laboratory (Worchel & Dallenbach, 1947).

It is clear, then, that hearing is necessary for the obstacle sense. But is it sufficient? Does the ability perhaps require that auditory information be combined with messages from some other sensory channel? To investigate this possibility, Supa et al. (1944) decided to eliminate all nonauditory cues. They did this by removing the subjects from the large room altogether, seating them in a small room nearby, where they listened through earphones to what was going on in the large room. An experimenter in the large room then walked toward the obstacle holding a microphone, so that the sounds it picked up (which were relayed to the subject's earphones) were similar to what the subject would have heard if traversing the large room in person. Despite this restriction on sources of information, the subjects were still able to detect the obstacle easily, calling out when they perceived that the experimenter was approaching it. This experiment proves that hearing is not only necessary, but is all that is necessary, for the skillful detection of obstacles by blind people, or for that matter by blindfolded sighted people with experience in this task.

This does not, of course, mean that only audition is used by a blind person in everyday life to detect and discriminate out-of-reach objects. There is no doubt that a draft of air from an alley, the interruption of warm sunlight by a shadow, or the smell of a painted surface can serve as a conspicuous clue to the spatial layout of the environment. But these clues are obvious to naîve sighted persons as well as to blind persons, and have never been regarded as mysterious by anyone. What the Cornell studies show is that hearing provides the mainstay of the obstacle sense, the most consistent, reliable, and subtle contributor to this learned ability.

What is it exactly that is heard? Apparently echoes of the person's footsteps are a contributing factor, for subjects in these experiments did worse when walking in socks along a carpet runner, than when wearing shoes and walking on a hardwood floor. Footsteps are not necessary, however; many types of noises will do. A later study showed that the obstacle sense is very acute when seated subjects are allowed to make vocal sounds, talking or clicking their tongues (Kellogg, 1962). The sound does not even need to be made by the perceiver: Clicks and hisses emitted by a loudspeaker toward the obstacle are sufficient (Cotzin & Dallenbach, 1950; Rice, 1967). It is important that the sound contain some components of high frequency (high pitch), for subjects with a hearing loss at frequencies above 8000 Hz do less well at detecting obstacles than those with normal hearing (Rice, 1967); and a tone emitted by a loudspeaker must be of this frequency or higher if it is to make object detection possible (Cotzin & Dallenbach, 1950).

Since the pioneering studies of the Cornell group, it has been shown how precise the obstacle sense is. With it, subjects can turn their head with high accuracy in the direction of an obstacle the size of a saucer 60 cm away from them (Rice, 1967), and such wooden disks can be discriminated if they differ in size by as little as 2.5 cm, or if their distances from the subject differ by as little as 15 cm (Kellogg, 1962). The texture of the object is also discernible to some degree, for a wooden disk can be told apart from a metal one, and cloth can be distinguished from wood (Kellogg, 1962). Even denim and velvet are told apart! It is astonishing that such a powerful perceptual ability lies dormant in most of us, never used unless sight is lost.

## VISUAL AND HAPTIC PERCEPTIONS COMPARED

So far in this chapter we have considered the possibility of differences in perceptual ability between blind and sighted people, when both are limited to the nonvisual senses—that is, when the sighted subjects wear blindfolds or are otherwise prevented from seeing the stimuli. A more intriguing comparison, however, and one with more relevance to everyday life, is between blind people, and sighted people whose vision is not restricted. Do they perceive things similarly? In some ways, of course, their perceptual experiences have got to be different: A blind person cannot experience color, for example. But a lot of information about objects is available to both vision and touch (and, to a lesser extent, hearing). Does this mean that properties of an object such as its shape are perceived in a similar way by a sighted person who looks at it, and a blind person who examines it *haptically* (that is, by actively touching it)?

If not, then how are visual and haptic impressions harmoniously combined when a sighted person both views and touches an object? Questions such as these have long been debated by scholars, and in the following sections we will consider some of the methods used to address them, and some of the answers that have been proposed.

## Approaches to the Study of Haptic Perception

One of the most outspoken early writers on the relation between touch and vision was the philosopher George Berkeley, who maintained that touch is the only sense that provides the mind with spatial information it can understand without prior training, that is, in infancy. Visual input, he argued, is initially uninterpretable, as for instance a story is meaningless if told in a language that the listener has never heard before. As a sighted infant moves about, however, it learns that certain visual sensations go with certain tactile and proprioceptive sensations. It must reach up, for example, to touch an object that appears in a particular part of the visual field, which then comes to be understood to be the "top" of the visual field. Visual space perception, in other words, is a learned ability, which is initially dependent on haptic space perception. In Berkeley's opinion, blind people are relevant to this issue because their understanding of spatial concepts indicates the degree to which the mind is capable, without the aid of visual input, of interpreting haptic information. In line with the rest of his theory, Berkeley believed that congenitally blind people have a reasonably good understanding of space, and perceive the spatial arrangement of objects in the environment accurately, when examining them by touch.

Other scholars, however, took the opposite point of view: that it is vision that has an initial monopoly on the perception of spatial relationships, touch being the poor relation which must learn about space by association—that is, by the complex of sensations that occurs when sighted people touch an object while looking at it.

*Analyzing Multimodal Perception.* It might seem that an easy way to decide between these and other theories would be to ask sighted adults to describe and compare the perceptual experiences that they derive from vision, with those derived from touch. Do visual perceptions have a richer spatial quality than haptic ones? Or the reverse? Unfortunately for this approach, subjects who attempt to answer such questions find that haptic and visual perceptions are complexly intertwined, and so cannot easily be compared. When an object is seen and touched simultaneously, subjects report that a unified perception emerges, in which it is difficult to distinguish haptic from visual elements. Can we really tell by touch that a corner of a book is a right angle, or does it just feel that way because it looks that way? It is hard to be sure.

This fusion of visual and haptic components of a perception can be demonstrated in the laboratory, by presenting a subject with discrepant visual and touch messages. For example, the subject may be asked to reach beneath a cloth, and to examine by touch, through the cloth, an object that lies on top of it. At the same time, the subject views the object, but is not aware that he or she is viewing it through a special lens that distorts its shape. Thus a square object, for example, may produce a rectangular image on the retina. In this situation, subjects typically report that the object not only looks rectangular, but feels rectangular as well (Rock & Victor, 1964). In other words, visual information has distorted the way in which haptic information is interpreted.

A large number of experimental studies have been carried out, using intermodal discrepancies in shape, location, and other stimulus properties. The usual result is that subjects have a unified, multimodal perceptual experience that represents a compromise between the properties of the visual and somesthetic stimuli (Welch & Warren, 1980). In many situations, the visual contribution is weighted more heavily than that from the sense of touch, but this imbalance can be altered by asking subjects to judge haptically salient qualities (Lederman, Thorne, & Jones, 1986), by blurring the visual stimulus (Heller, 1983), and in a number of other ways (Welch & Warren, 1980).

Even when no trickery is used, visual perceptions may influence the way in which tactile information is processed. This is shown by an experiment carried out by Attneave and Benson (1969), who asked sighted subjects to place their hands on a large letter T, made of metal tubing. Embedded in the back of the T, out of view, were six small, vibrating buttons, and subjects were asked to position their hands so that the index, middle, and ring fingers of each hand were in contact with one vibrator apiece. Subjects did this by touching the horizontal bar of the T with one hand and the vertical bar with the other. Next, the subjects were trained to call out particular letters of the alphabet when individual vibrators were activated by the experimenter. Finally, they were asked to reverse their hands, putting the left hand where the right had been and vice versa, and to respond with the first letter that came to mind when a given vibrator was activated. What most subjects did in this situation was to call out the letter appropriate to the vibrator that had been activated, even though a different finger was in contact with it than had been there earlier. When asked specifically to respond either in this way, or in terms of the letters that had been originally associated with each finger, subjects were slower at carrying out this latter task, as if they had to pause and reflect for a moment to remember which finger had been in a specific position earlier.

In this experiment, subjects kept their eyes open, so that they saw the large T, but information about the vibrators was purely tactual, since these were out of view. The results show that this tactile information was being processed in terms of spatial location. Subjects did not simply notice which finger was stimulated on a given trial, but instead, converted this information into a perception of where in space—where on the T—the vibration had occurred. By itself this result says nothing about vision influencing tactile perceptions. This question was addressed, however, in a final phase of the study, in which the experiment was repeated with a new group of subjects, who were instructed to keep their eyes closed. After switching hands, these subjects were equally fast at responding to activation of a vibrator either on the basis of which finger was stimulated, or where in space the stimulation occurred. The earlier preference for spatial responding, which occurred only when the eyes were open, thus indicates that visual information was influencing the rules by which spatial information, presented to the sense of touch, was processed.

To explain results like these, as well as data from his own laboratory showing that closing the eyes reduces the precision of *auditory* spatial judgments, Warren (1970) has proposed that, in sighted people, vision provides a framework into which all spatial sensations can be integrated. Thus, although they are capable of overriding auditory or haptic information when a conflict arises, a person's visual perceptions of the environment normally play a more constructive role, according to Warren: They help one interpret the spatial aspects of nonvisual sensations.

Because of this organizing role played by vision, we cannot learn about purely haptic perception of space by studying people who are viewing as well as touching the stimulus objects. But even if a sighted person closes his or her eyes, visual impressions may not be totally excluded, for he or she may imagine what the touched objects look like, thus bringing visual notions into play. Evidence that visual imagery can affect perceptual performance when the eyes are closed was provided by McKinney (1964), who used an experimental paradigm similar to that of Attneave and Benson (1969). Blind children, and sighted children with their eyes closed, were asked to place their right hand on a table, palm up. The experimenter then briefly touched one of the subject's fingers, and after a short delay asked him or her to point with the other hand to the finger that had been touched. In this baseline condition, blind and sighted children were comparable in accuracy. Group differences in accuracy emerged, however, when the subjects were required to turn their hand over during the delay period. In some trials the subjects were instructed to turn the hand over and leave it in the new position while recalling which finger had been touched, while in a back-and-forth condition, subjects turned the hand over twice, thus returning it to its original palm-up orientation. McKinney found that the blind subjects were less accurate, the greater the amount of motor activity that intervened between the original stimulation and the verbal response: That is, they were less likely to recall which finger had been stimulated if they had turned the hand back and forth, than if they had turned it over only once. This increase in errors with an increasing amount of interpolated activity is a common finding in memory research.

The blindfolded sighted subjects, however, did not show this pattern. Instead, they made the most errors when the hand was palm down; returning it to its original position improved their performance. McKinney interpreted this result to mean that the sighted subjects used visual imagery to aid them in recalling which finger had been stimulated: In other words, that they imagined seeing the hand, and noting on the image which finger was stimulated. For example, if the image were of the front of the hand, and the experimenter touched the index finger, the subject might encode this as "second finger from the right." If now the subject turned his or her hand over but did not modify the image, and continued to think of the stimulated finger as the second from the right, this would lead to the error of pointing to the ring finger. McKinney found that many of the sighted subjects' errors were of this mirror-image type.

We can summarize this group of studies by saying that when sighted people close their eyes, the ability of visual imagery to influence their nonvisual perceptions, by weaving them into a spatial representation of the environment, is reduced (Attneave & Benson, 1969; Warren, 1970), but not completely eliminated (McKinney, 1964).

How, then, can we determine with certainty what purely haptic perception, unaffected by visual factors, is like? An obvious answer suggests itself: by studying the haptic abilities of blind people. Most adventitiously blinded people still have some visual imagery, however, and are therefore subject to the same interaction between haptic and visual factors as are sighted people with their eyes closed. Only when the subjects of an experiment are congenitally blind can it be stated with certainty that visual experience plays no role in their touch perceptions.

*Studying Newly Sighted Individuals.* What is the best way to study a blind person's haptic perception of spatial relationships? One interesting suggestion was put forward by von Senden, a German researcher, half a century ago. He proposed that the nature of a blind person's space perception could be determined by studying people who had been born blind from cataracts or corneal opacities, but who as adults had had sight-giving operations. Von Senden believed that when these individuals first looked at their environment, they would interpret their initial visual sensations in terms of the knowledge and ideas about space that they had gleaned from a lifetime without vision. By finding out how the world looked to these visually naîve people, von Senden reasoned, we could learn how good an understanding of space had been provided by their earlier *haptic* exploration of their environment. To pursue this line of thinking, von Senden assembled from the medical literature many cases of this sort, making note of how the patients responded to visual stimuli.

Although there were differences from one individual to another, von Senden found that most were left, after surgery, with severe visual impairments. Immediately after the surgical bandages were removed, the patients often pointed inaccurately at objects, and even days later tended to make erroneous judgments of depth, thinking that a faraway object was nearby, for example. A more recent case (Ackroyd, Humphrey, & Warrington, 1974) confirms von Senden's report of lingering perceptual impairments. This woman had been blinded by smallpox scarring of her corneas at age 3, but received a corneal graft to her left eye at age 27. Although the surgeon judged the optics of her operated eye to be good enough, following surgery, to permit acuity of at least 20/60, she could see objects only if they moved, or contrasted sharply with their surroundings. She could see the pigeons as they flew about London's Trafalgar Square, for example, but lost sight of them once they had settled onto the gray pavement. It was in *recognizing* shapes that she had the greatest difficulty, however. When she sat at a table on which the experimenter placed either a white paper circle, 9 cm in diameter, or an 8-cm square of the same paper, she was unable to say which was which, even after 1,300 trials.

As was explained in Chapter 2, this deficiency in visual shape perception is probably due, in large part, to changes in the visual cortex that occurred during the early years of life. Von Senden, however, while acknowledging that the visual system in these people was not functioning normally, thought that the main problem was that they did not have a clear understanding of space: to put it bluntly, that they didn't really know what shape and distance were. But why not, if they had been using touch to interact with objects all their lives? Because, von Senden concluded, a genuine understanding of space can only come through vision; congenitally blind people are therefore incapable of any true spatial perception. A blind person, he argued, may learn how many steps there are in a staircase, or that it is necessary to stretch in order to reach an object on a particular shelf, but these memories do not constitute a true appreciation of space.

In the light of what we now know about deprivation-induced changes in the visual cortex of animals, it is clear that von Senden's arguments are not logically valid: His evidence does not warrant the conclusion he drew. Nevertheless his book, *Space and Sight* (1932/1960), became a worldwide scientific classic, and has influenced the thinking of many psychologists and educators.

A view as extreme as von Senden's could not long go unchallenged, and one of the most scholarly challenges to it was offered by Révész (1950), a psychologist in Amsterdam. He argued that haptic perception is just as spatial as vision is. Avoiding the two poles of opinion represented by Berkeley and von Senden, Révész asserted that both vision and touch are independently capable of giving rise to truly spatial perceptions. He argued that the everyday accomplishments of blind people, such as their ability to move about in familiar surroundings with ease, prove that they have a bona fide understanding of space.

The fact that newly sighted people cannot recognize what they see only shows, according to Révész, that the qualitative differences between vision, with its colors and brightnesses, and touch, with its sensations of pressure and temperature, are very great. People who gain their sight after a lifetime of blindness cannot at first relate the visual world to the haptic world, although both are filled with spatial perceptions. This line of reasoning, rather than von Senden's, has been the usual one among scholars, from the time of John Locke onward, who have thought about what the initial visual experiences of a congenitally blind adult would be like. Révész, like von Senden, was of course unaware of the damaging effects that early visual deprivation can have on the visual system.

*Studying the Perceptions of Congenitally Blind Persons.* Interesting as these cases of vision following congenital blindness are, then, they tell us little about the nature of haptic perception. A better strategy for learning about pure haptic perception, uncontaminated by visual influences, is to study congenitally blind people who have *not* acquired sight, as they explore and learn about objects in their environment using the sense of touch.

The nature of their sensory experience can best be understood by contrasting it with the perceptual world of sighted people, in two ways. First, the haptic experiences of congenitally blind people can be compared with the *visual* experiences of the sighted. This type of comparison allows us to learn how blind and sighted people differ when both are using their primary spatial sense. Second, the haptic experiences of the congenitally blind can be compared with the *haptic* experiences of the sighted, which frequently involve visual imagery. This comparison is less relevant than the first to everyday life, because it requires that sighted people be blindfolded or otherwise prevented from using vision, an unfamiliar situation for them; nevertheless, this type of comparison is preferable in some experimental situations, because it allows closely comparable stimulation to be provided to both groups of subjects. In the following sections, we will use both types of comparisons to explore the nature of haptic perception.

In addition, we will discuss some experimental work in which haptic perception in blindfolded, sighted people has been compared with visual or multimodal perception. As we have seen, blindfolding sighted people does not totally prevent visual imagery from influencing haptic perception; nevertheless, some differences between touch and vision are so marked that they are apparent even when the two modalities are not completely independent of one another.

## Differences between Haptic and Visual Perception

*Modality-specific and Modality-selective Stimulus Dimensions.* The most obvious difference between touch and vision is that they produce qualitatively distinctive sensations. Through the sense of touch, both blind and sighted people are able to experience pressure, warmth, cold, and pain, but only those with at least a modicum of sight can experience color, brightness, and darkness.

This is not to say that congenitally blind people cannot talk about color. From their contacts with sighted people, blind people learn that cherries are red, lemons are yellow, and so on, and they are able to use these terms appropriately. They might even be able to make an educated guess about the color of an unfamiliar object, on the basis of its texture or smell. They could not, however, have any first-hand knowledge of redness or greenness.

Similarly, haptics can give no information about faraway objects, such as distant mountains. In many cases the blind person may be able to travel to those objects, and haptically examine them close up, but then they cease to be faraway objects. Thus one cannot perceive great distances haptically, other than by being aware of the travel itself. Some investigators (such as von Senden) have wondered whether this inaccessibility of large-scale distances to immediate haptic apprehension might put congenitally blind people at a disadvantage in thinking about spatial relationships. This is more a cognitive issue than a perceptual one, however, and we will postpone further consideration of it until the next chapter.

In addition to stimulus properties that can be detected by only one modality, there are many other properties that are detectable through both vision and touch, but to which one modality is more sensitive than the other. The sharpness of a knife is more readily assessed by touching it than by looking at it, as is the temperature of a cup of tea, although vision can play a useful secondary role in these perceptual tasks. Shapes, however, can usually be more easily registered visually than haptically (Cashdan, 1968).

The result of these quantitative differences is that the properties that make an object distinctive to a blind person may not be the same ones that make it distinctive to a sighted person. For example, in examining a set of silverware, a blind person might be more cognizant of the heft of the pieces, while a sighted person who was both looking at and handling the same pieces might be struck by the unusual pattern embossed on the handle. Both people would be aware of the heft of the pieces, and of the pattern, but the blind person would find the former property more salient, while the sighted person would take more note of the latter.

Klatzky, Lederman, and Reed (1987) have convincingly demonstrated such differences in the visual and haptic salience of various stimulus properties, although their study did not involve blind people. They presented blindfolded subjects, as well as subjects using vision, with a series of 81 objects, and asked them to sort the objects into a small number of bins. The objects differed from one another along several dimensions, such as shape and hardness, which could be perceived through either modality. (Hardness can be judged visually by how much an object is deformed by the pressure of the hand.) Subjects were not told to sort the objects on a particular dimension, but simply to put "similar" objects in the same bin. The experimenters discovered that subjects sorted in different ways, depending on whether or not they were looking at the stimuli as well as touching them. For example, subjects who used both vision and touch tended to rely heavily on the shapes of the objects in deciding which bins to put them in, while those who were blindfolded attended more to the hardness of the stimuli.

Révész long ago proposed, on the basis of his careful but qualitative studies of the perceptual abilities of blind people, that the shape of an object is more salient to sighted people than to blind people, while the object's composition—what it is made of—is more salient to the blind. In his words, "Form governs the visual, structure the haptic world" (1950, p. 87). Révész would be gratified to learn that these hypotheses are now being experimentally confirmed.

*Simultaneous-vs.-Successive Perception.* Another difference between looking at something and exploring it by touch is that the eye can "take in" a large object all at once, while the hand usually takes a step-by-step approach, examining one part of the object at a time. This difference probably helps to explain the greater salience of shape for vision than for haptics, described in the previous section, because haptically perceiving the shape of a complex object requires the integration of a series of successive impressions, a challenging task that brings memory into play.

However, this simultaneous-versus-successive difference between vision and touch is one of degree rather than of kind. After all, the parts of an object that are haptically examined one at a time—its corners and edges—have shapes just as the overall object does, and these component shapes are perceived. In either modality, then, some shape perception occurs within a single "moment" of perceptual time; the difference between them has to do with how large or complex a shape can be taken in at once. Moreover, the haptic modality has no monopoly on the ability to combine information from a series of sensory impressions, for the eye typically jumps two or more times every second to inspect first one part, then another part, of a complex object. It is therefore not true that only haptics involves the temporal integration of sensory data.

Furthermore, it is now clear that blind people often learn new strategies for exploring objects haptically, strategies that enlarge the hand's perceptual window. One such strategy underlies the fact that blind subjects are generally superior to blindfolded, sighted ones in their ability to judge the straightness or curvature of a long object, such as a plastic ruler held rigidly in a particular conformation by the experimenter (Hunter, 1954). Sighted subjects are likely to say that a ruler which actually curves slightly toward them at the ends feels straight, while blind subjects are less susceptible to this error. Davidson (1972) made videotapes of blind and sighted subjects carrying out this task, and found that the finger movements of the two groups of subjects were different. The blind subjects usually gripped a substantial length of the ruler all at once, using several fingers simultaneously to assess the curvature. Sighted subjects, on the other hand, usually swept one or two fingers along the ruler. Thus it was the sighted subjects who were combining successive sensory impressions! To determine whether this difference in exploratory strategy was the basis of the more accurate judgments of the blind subjects, Davidson gave a new group of blindfolded, sighted subjects the same task, but now carefully instructed them in how to examine the ruler. Half were told to grip it, while the others were instructed to sweep a finger along it. Their resulting judgments of curvature showed that more accuracy was achieved by the gripping than by the sweeping strategy. Gripping, then, like the "obstacle sense," is an example of a perceptual skill that many blind people use to obtain information that sighted people (when not wearing blindfolds) prefer to obtain by looking.

*The Hand Can Change Shape but the Retina Cannot.* Davidson's work on hand position illustrates another fundamental difference between vision and haptics: The hand can assume different shapes in the course of exploring the environment, while the configuration of the retina within the eye never changes. The eye can turn in its socket, and move when the head does, but that is the extent of its flexibility. The hand, however, can reach out in any direction, and can assume shapes that allow the individual to squeeze a cantaloupe, read an embossed label, determine the size of a coin, and otherwise examine objects in the environment.

Most people, whether blind or sighted, make good use of the hand's mobility to extract information from the environment. Lederman and Klatzky (1987) have shown that sighted people, in examining an object with their eyes closed, know how to use particular types of hand movements to learn about specific properties of an object: They rub a finger across the object to determine its surface texture, press on it to assess its hardness, and so on. Many blind people also have these skills; in fact, Davidson's discovery of the "gripping" strategy suggests that some have developed additional haptic exploratory techniques that the average sighted person does not have.

The perceptual advantages afforded by the flexibility of the hand are balanced, however, by the need they impose on the perceiver to keep track of what the hand is doing. The size or shape of an object could easily be misperceived if an individual did not properly take hand shape into account. An extreme example of this sort of perceptual error, on the part of blindfolded, sighted people, was discovered by Aristotle: If the index and middle fingers are crossed, as shown in Fig. 3.1, and a small object such as a pencil eraser is placed between the two fingertips, it feels double (Benedetti, 1985, 1986). A pair of objects is what would be required to stimulate these two skin areas if the person's fingers were not crossed; the illusion, then, implies that the person's perceptual system has not taken into account the fact that the fingers *are* crossed. Errors of this kind are less likely to occur when the perceiver actively explores an object, than when he or she is passively stimulated by it.

In summary, there are at least three aspects of haptic perception—its emphasis on substance properties rather than form, its reliance on the integration of successive impressions, and its ability to capitalize on the mobility of the hand—which distinguish it from visual perception. But these differences should not be regarded as giving an overall advantage to either vision or haptics: Each modality has its strengths and weaknesses. The evidence available to date provides no basis for believing that visual percep-

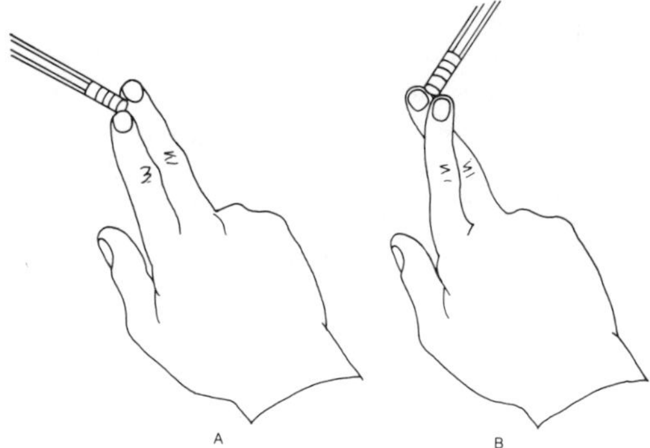


FIGURE 3.1. Aristotle's illusion. If the index and middle fingers are extended normally, as shown on the left, a small object placed between the two fingertips will be correctly perceived; but if the fingers are crossed, as shown on the right, the person will have the illusory sensation that he or she is being touched with two objects. The illusion shows that we perceive tactile stimuli as if our fingers were in their usual relative positions, whether in fact they are or not. (From *Sensation and Perception*, 2nd edition, by S. Coren, C. Porac, and L. M. Ward, 1984.)

tion is either more or less valid than perception derived from touch, or that a sighted person is capable to any greater or lesser degree than a blind person of perceiving the "real" nature of an object.

## Perception of Pictures

While touch may be as useful as vision in allowing someone to identify everyday objects held in the hand (Klatzky, Lederman, & Metzger, 1985), touch is much less useful for identifying objects represented in a picture. The reasons for this difficulty, which we will examine in this final section of the chapter, shed additional light on the relationship between haptic and visual perception.

The most immediate problem for a blind person is that most pictures are executed in a visual medium—pencil or ink, for example—that cannot be perceived by touch. It is easy to overcome this difficulty in the case of outline drawings, however, for there are machines on which embossed drawings can be made. The artist simply "draws" on a special plastic sheet with a blunt-tipped stylus rather than a pencil, and this leaves behind it an elevated ridge that is easily felt. A more serious difficulty is the hand's inferiority to the eye in its ability to resolve fine details: The two differ by an order of magnitude when pictures are examined at arm's length (Phillips, Johnson, & Browne, 1983). While this difference in resolving power can, in principle, be compensated for by enlarging the tangible picture, such outsize displays are often cumbersome and hard to scan quickly (Berlá, 1982). The most fundamental problem, however, is that most pictures are two-dimensional representations of three-dimensional objects, and therefore employ visual conventions, such as an emphasis on outline, and the use of perspective, that the blind person may not be able to interpret without training.

How does the ability of congenitally blind subjects to identify raised-line drawings compare with the ability of sighted but blindfolded subjects to identify the same stimuli? Kennedy and Fox (1977) carried out a study to answer this question. Eight simple outline drawings were prepared, using the plastic sheets described earlier. The drawings were of a hand, a cup, and other common objects. These drawings were then presented to 34 blindfolded, sighted college students. On the average, the subjects identified 2.4 out of the 8 drawings, showing that interpreting haptic pictures is no easy task for sighted people. When the drawings were presented to 7 congenitally blind college students, however, their scores were lower still, with the average subject being barely able to identify a single drawing. Other subjects, who had had some visual experience before becoming blind, and who in some cases had a little remaining sight, generally performed at an intermediate level. The results of the three groups, taken together, suggest that visual experience is helpful in acquiring the ability to perceive tactual drawings accurately. Kennedy and Fox emphasize, however, that some congenitally blind subjects did identify drawings correctly.

Another study, by White, Saunders, Scadden, Bach-y-Rita, and Collins (1970), confirms that two-dimensional representations of solid objects can come to be identified by congenitally blind people, but suggest that some experience with this system of depiction is necessary. In this case the apparatus was an array of vibrators applied to the back. There were 400 vibrators in all, arranged in a 20-by-20 matrix; each vibrator was only a millimeter in diameter at the tip, but they were spaced about 12 mm apart, so that the overall array was about the size of a piece of typing paper. A television camera sent impulses to the array, with different parts of the camera's field of view activating different vibrators. Thus the array reproduced, in tangible form, much of the pictorial information taken in by the camera; it was, in the words of White and his collaborators, a "vision substitution system."

Subjects were at first not able to name the objects at which the camera was aimed, but both sighted and congenitally blind participants learned to do so over the course of several sessions. One congenitally blind subject who wrote about the experience (Guarniero, 1974) said that at first he was always aware that the stimuli were on his back, but that he gradually ceased to notice this, simply perceiving the vibrators as being located in "an ordered two-dimensional space" that was not attached to his body. He learned to appreciate depth cues, such as relative height (the fact that an object high in the picture is usually closer to the horizon, and thus farther from the observer, than an object near the bottom of the picture), but this was more a matter of cognitive interpretation than of actual depth perception. When the camera was repeatedly aimed at the same object, however, he became familiar with the pattern of stimulation, and so could recognize it when the camera was aimed at it again. However, the representation of an object by the vibrators did not seem to him to *resemble* the shape of the object when he examined it by touch in the normal way: "I never discovered any correlation between how something 'looked' [i.e., was depicted by the vibrators] and how it felt" (p. 102).

This investigation shows that blind people can learn to identify objects represented in tactile pictures, and can derive benefits from these representations. But there is an important difference between sighted and blind observers with regard to pictures. Because a drawing typically makes use of outlines and perspective, it resembles in important ways the pattern of visual stimulation obtained when a sighted person turns from the drawing and looks at actual, solid objects. In contrast, tactual drawings are much less similar to the pattern of stimulation which a blind person obtains when haptically examining solid objects. For him or her, the conventions used in drawings represent an arbitrary choice from among many possible systems of depiction; an alternative system, such as a wrap-around format, in which all sides of an object are included in a continuous panoramic representation, might seem equally valid.

Kennedy's (1983) studies of the ability of congenitally blind people to create tangible drawings are consistent with this line of reasoning. He has found that some of these individuals are able to employ perspective, overlap, and other conventions of visual art in their drawings, but that they are equally comfortable in *violating* these conventions to convey a message in some alternative way. For example, some use metaphorical devices, such as drawing a wheel with curving spokes to show that it is rolling, or drawing a man with very long legs to show that he is running. In thus going beyond conventional representation, these individuals demonstrate that for them, drawing is not simply a way of duplicating objects on plastic, but a way of expressing ideas.

It is interesting to note that Kennedy's own interpretation of his data is in some ways different from that offered here. He believes that certain conventions of drawing, such as the use of lines to represent edges in depth, are innate in all people and thus are neither arbitrary nor learned. Indeed, though some of his subjects were able to recognize (Kennedy & Fox, 1977) and to create (Kennedy, 1983) outline drawings, they reported being unfamiliar with pictures. Clearly, further research will be needed to determine with certainty whether the appreciation of outline drawings by congenitally blind people does or does not depend on learning.

## SUMMARY

In summing up this chapter on perception, we can conclude that there are some very real differences in the way blind and sighted people perceive the world, differences that go beyond the obvious fact that blind people do not experience brightness, color, or the shape of faraway objects. The additional differences are of two types. First, although blindness is not accompanied by any increased sensitivity of hearing or touch, blind people have in many cases learned to attend to sources of information about the environment, such as faint echoes, that go unnoticed by most sighted people. Second, the sense of touch, the major spatial modality for blind people, is different from vision in the way it extracts information from the environment, and in the emphasis it gives to different types of information: For example, the limited span of the hand means that local properties of objects, such as their texture, are often more salient than global properties, such as overall shape. The world as perceived by vision and the world as perceived by touch are equally valid, equally rich, but are by no means identical.

In the following chapter, we will turn from the question of how blind and sighted people perceive their environment to the question of how they think about it. Do the perceptual differences between the two groups produce cognitive differences in, for example, their ideas about space? Based on the material presented in this chapter, it seems likely that there will be many similarities, but also some interesting differences.

# 4 BLINDNESS AND COGNITION

As the last chapter made clear, there are important differences between the perceptual world of blind people and the perceptual world of the sighted. Some aspects of the environment can be perceived only through vision; blind people can recall these aspects, if they were once sighted, or can learn about them from sighted people, but cannot experience them directly. On the other hand, properties of the environment that are detectable through touch or hearing are in many cases more salient to a blind person than to a sighted person, whose haptic and auditory impressions are often dominated and obscured by visual ones. In addition, blind people typically learn skills that improve their ability to extract information from the environment through touch and hearing.

An important result of these perceptual differences is that in everyday life, blind and sighted people often accomplish the same goal by using different learned skills—skills that have cognitive, as well as perceptual and motor, components. To take a mundane example, consider the strategies used to recover a small object, such as a paper clip, that one has dropped. Blind people typically begin the search by examining with their hands the region of floor closest to them, without moving their feet; if the item is not turned up here, larger and larger areas of the floor are gradually explored. Sighted people, on the other hand, typically step *away* from the region where they dropped the item, so that they can get an unimpeded view of it. Both strategies work, although the blind person will probably take longer to find the clip if it has bounced far away, while the sighted person will probably take longer if it has fallen into a pants cuff.

It would not be surprising if the learning of different skills by blind and sighted people in many aspects of life favored the development of somewhat different patterns of cognitive strengths and weaknesses. However, everyday interactions with both adventitiously and congenitally blind people indicate that their cognitive abilities closely resemble those of sighted people: In their ability to explain things, to ask penetrating questions, to be creative, to tell jokes and give advice, they are indistinguishable from the sighted. They range from dull to brilliant, just as sighted people do. Nevertheless, it has often been suggested that there are consistent differences between congenitally blind and sighted people in specific areas of cognition, differences that could be measured with carefully designed experimental or psychometric tests. Do such differences actually exist? That is one of the questions that we will address in this chapter. For example, we will review experimental studies that have sought to determine whether blind and sighted people differ in the way they process spatial information, and in their ability to use mental imagery to aid memory.

In contrast to this analytical approach is the more sweeping attempt, undertaken by some investigators, to test for overall differences in mental ability between blind and sighted people. These researchers feel that the cognitive ability of blind people can best be studied by administering multifaceted tests—IQ tests and the like—to large numbers of blind and sighted people, and comparing the group results. We will review this approach early in the chapter, pointing out some of the difficulties inherent in comparing blind and sighted people in this way.

Still other researchers emphasize that the study of cognition in blind people should not be limited to comparing them with the sighted. The information-processing skills blind people use in reading, traveling on foot, and other activities that, in the sighted, depend on vision, are worthy of study in their own right, and in fact are often fascinating. We will consider some of these methods later in the chapter.

## BROAD MEASURES OF COGNITIVE ABILITY

It might seem easy to compare the intelligence of blind and sighted people, simply by giving them an IQ test and comparing their scores. In fact, however, there are substantial problems in the way of such a comparison (Warren, 1984). One is that tests of intelligence developed for use with sighted people often involve the presentation of visual items that cannot be administered to blind people. For example, the person being tested is sometimes given a number of pictures, and asked to put them in order so that they tell a story. Moreover, even test questions that are verbally administered may use visual terminology, such as color names.

There are two general solutions to the problem of the inapplicability of such items to the blind individual. One is to use a test designed for sighted people, but to delete sections or items that require the use of vision, or depend on visual experience. For example, just the verbal part of the Wechsler Adult Intelligence Scale (WAIS) is frequently administered to blind people. When this is done, however, the test does not provide an overall index of a blind person's intelligence, for it leaves his or her nonverbal skills, such as spatial ability, unmeasured.

An alternative solution is to replace inappropriate parts of a test with other components designed specifically for blind people, such as items using tangible shapes and patterns. The Perkins–Binet test (Davis, 1980) is an example of this approach. But since such tests are administered only to blind people, they do not provide a way to compare the intelligence of blind and sighted people. Even if these tests were administered to sighted people, the novel (to them) emphasis on haptic perception might impair their performance, thus nullifying a comparison of the two groups.

Another problem in attempting to compare the intelligence of blind and sighted people is that intelligence is a vague concept, referring to a composite of mental abilities, from the ability to understand a story, to the ability to remember a string of numbers. When Binet developed the first intelligence test, for use with French schoolchildren, he did so for the practical purpose of deciding which students should be put into accelerated classes and which into slow classes; he was interested not in any one mental ability, but in each child's overall capacity. As a result, Binet's test was intentionally a hodgepodge of different types of questions, tapping different cognitive skills. Later tests of intelligence have generally followed his example.

Although some standardized tests of intelligence provide the examiner with separate scores for different types of questions, emphasis is typically given to a combined score, which is said to indicate the person's intelligence, or, if age is taken into account, intelligence quotient (IQ). In evaluating this overall score, however, it is important to realize that the relative emphasis given by the test to particular aspects of cognitive ability is arbitrary. Therefore someone who is especially skilled in the cognitive areas emphasized by the test will have a better overall score than someone whose cognitive strengths lie in other areas. This introduces uncertainty into comparisons of intelligence between blind and sighted people, because the special challenges commonly faced by blind people may tend to foster the development of some cognitive skills more than others.

If one attempts to compare two *populations* of subjects, one blind and one sighted, using standardized tests, then still another problem arises: how to choose from each population a representative group of individuals to be tested. One would like to make the groups as comparable as possible on factors other than intelligence. Thus it would be unwise to compare, say, sighted adults with blind adolescents, for if a difference between the scores of the two groups were found, the investigator would not know whether to attribute it to the age difference, or to the difference in visual status, between the two groups. But age is not the only factor that can influence intelligence test scores. Since intelligence tests do not measure just native ability, but rather, a complex product of hereditary and environmental influences, it is desirable to equate the groups for amount of schooling. For similar reasons the investigator might want to equate for socioeconomic status, level of motivation, and so on. The problem with this approach is that in equating the two groups on one factor, the investigator may unintentionally be introducing differences between the groups on other factors. For example, because of job discrimination, blind people are often employed at a level below that of sighted people of comparable ability. Therefore, if the investigator insists on equating the two groups in terms of income, the blind group is likely to surpass the sighted group in motivation, and perhaps intelligence as well.

The intractability of these three interrelated problems is illustrated by the work of Rubin (1964), who attempted to compare, by means of standardized tests, the cognitive ability of blind and sighted adults. He carefully chose three groups of subjects, with 25 in each group. Those in the first group were all congenitally blind, those in the second group were adventitiously blinded, having been sighted until at least the age of 12, and those in the third group were sighted. To avoid combining totally blind people with legally blind individuals with considerable remaining vision, Rubin limited the two blind groups to people who had, at most, light perception. Because he thought the pattern of results might be different in men and women, he used only male subjects. Only men between 18 and 49 were used, the mean age of each group being about 30, and in addition the groups were equated for amount of schooling (1 or 2 years of college on the average). Finally, Rubin made certain that the three groups were comparable in terms of the professional status of the *father* of each of the subjects, on the premise that this was a large factor in determining the socioeconomic environment in which the subjects were raised. It may fairly be said that the investigator was meticulous in attempting to equate the groups, even at the risk of restricting the generality of his findings.

Rubin administered a series of five tests intended to explore different aspects of mental ability. In the first test, the subject was presented with pairs of words, and asked to say in what respect the two members of a pair were similar. For example, if a subject were presented with the words "island" and "hermit," he might be expected to say that these two are similar in that they are both isolated. In the second test, a series of proverbs was read to the subject, who was asked to explain the meaning of each (Gorham, 1956). Third, the subject was presented with a series of plastic miniatures, representing a heart, an anchor, and other objects, and asked to arrange them in any order he liked, after which he was questioned about his reasons for arranging them in that particular way. The goal of this test was to determine the subjects' willingness and ability to deal with abstract concepts, rather than with mundane ones, such as the relative sizes of the objects (Kahn, 1956). Sighted subjects were blindfolded during this test, a procedure that put them into an unaccustomed perceptual situation; however, any subject who could not identify an object by touch was told what it was. In the fourth test, the subjects were presented with series of numbers, and asked to say what additional numbers ought to come at the end of each series. For example, following the series "1, 2, 4, 8, 16 and 32," the correct answer would be "64 and then 128." Finally, subjects were given a vocabulary test by being asked to define 40 words.

These five tests were not created by Rubin; rather, they were chosen from a wide variety of psychometric tests that have been published and standardized, that is, tried out on large numbers of people. The Similarities Test and the Vocabulary Test, for example, were sections of the Wechsler Adult Intelligence Scale, and the Number Series Completion Test was drawn from the Modified Army Alpha Examination. While the tests represent a variety of mental abilities, they clearly do not cover the range of what is usually meant by the term intelligence, for Rubin wished to concentrate on how blind people deal with abstract concepts and relationships.

After administering a test to two or more groups of subjects, an investigator will almost always find that there are some differences in scores between the groups: It would be a rare coincidence if identical values were obtained. The question is, however, whether the group difference that are found are meaningful, reflecting differences among the populations from which the groups were drawn, or whether they are due simply to unavoidable sampling error in the selection of subjects making up each group. In order to answer this question, Rubin carried out an analysis of variance on the results of each test. This is a statistical procedure to determine whether differences among the groups account for a substantial proportion of the overall variability of the scores. He found that group differences were not significant for any of the five tests. This analysis supports the idea that, when age and background are carefully controlled, there are no appreciable differences in vocabulary, abstract reasoning ability, or concept formation, that can be attributed to visual status.

However, Rubin was not satisfied with this way of examining the data, and he carried out an additional analysis which the present author does not believe was justified. Rubin said that the tests he gave were of two types, the vocabulary test being a measure of "intellectual level," and the other four tests being measures of "intellectual functioning." He was primarily interested in comparing the groups in terms of intellectual functioning, but wanted first to equate them for intellectual level. Now, the congenitally blind subjects had obtained somewhat (but not significantly) higher vocabulary scores than the other groups, so in order to equate the groups statistically for intellectual level, Rubin adjusted the Proverbs, Similarities, and other scores of the congenitally blind subjects *downward* to make up for their large vocabularies. Once these adjustments had been made, a new statistical analysis (called analysis of covariance) showed that the congenitally blind subjects did significantly worse than the other subjects on the Proverbs Test, although not on any of the other tests. He concludes,

> The present study was undertaken to test the hypothesis that the performance of congenitally blind adults on measures of abstract ability would be significantly below that of adventitiously blind and sighted persons . . . On the Proverbs Test the performance of the congenitally blind group was significantly below that of the sighted group, thus providing clear verification of the hypothesis. (Rubin, 1964, pp. 54–55)

The present author believes that Rubin's second statistical analysis is inappropriate, in that the distinction between "intellectual level" and "intellectual functioning" is arbitrary. Presumably intellectual level refers to a basic ability, whereas intellectual functioning refers to how well a person uses that ability. But is a large vocabulary really more fundamental or basic than the ability to understand a proverb? Clearly not. No doubt these two tests measure different things, but to call one a measure of level and the other, a measure of functioning, is not a convincing distinction. Therefore his conclusion about group differences in abstract ability is unwarranted. In fairness to Rubin, his study was carefully planned and meticulously carried out; but the correct conclusion to draw from it is that he found *no* evidence that congenitally blind, adventitiously blinded, and sighted adults differ systematically in the mental abilities that he measured.

This study has been presented in some detail, not because of its results, but because it illustrates the problems and uncertainties encountered in attempting to compare blind and sighted people on arbitrarily chosen cognitive tasks. Can a test involving the manipulation of objects be made fair to both groups by having the sighted subjects wear blindfolds, or does that *introduce* unfairness? Should the groups be equated for educational level? Vocabulary? While there may be no right or wrong answers to these questions, the fact is that the way in which an experimenter answers them will (as we have seen) influence the outcome of the investigation.

Rubin's study is by no means the only one in which standardized tests have been used to make broad comparisons between the cognitive abilities of sighted and blind adults, but other studies along the same lines will not be reviewed here; this one example is sufficient to make the point that if there are cognitive differences between blind and sighted people, we are unlikely to discover them by administering wide-ranging psychometric tests that bear no relation to the special functional demands placed upon blind people in everyday life. It makes more sense to study those areas of life in which blind people must cope with special challenges—areas in which the lack of visual input forces them to do things differently from sighted people. Moreover, the question of "who's ahead" is a pointless and unanswerable one; our approach should instead be to gain insight into the process by which a person's methods of dealing with information are shaped, as are other aspects of behavior, by the unique demands of his or her environment (Warren, 1984). With this goal in mind, let us turn our attention to the way in which blind people address two complex, real-world challenges: how to read, and how to travel, without vision.

## READING

Sighted people read by viewing printed text at an average rate of about 300 words per minute (Gibson & Levin, 1975). Blind people, on the other hand, must read by listening, or by touch, which are much slower methods. (Reading on the part of legally blind individuals with some remaining form vision will be discussed in Chapter 6.) The blind person wishing to read thus faces two problems: how to obtain the material in auditory or tangible form, and how to pick up the information contained in the text at a rapid enough rate to make the reading worthwhile. Let us consider how these problems are addressed, within the context of each reading method.

### Reading by Listening

The oldest, and still one of the most popular methods of reading among blind people, is listening to a friend read aloud. This, however, has a drawback: The friend may try to influence what is read, for example, skipping over some newspaper articles to get to others. If the interests of the two people do not mesh, the reading process is likely to be less than fully satisfying for the blind person. This is not meant to criticize sighted people who read to blind friends, but simply to point out that reading by listening to a friend has its shortcomings. Another popular solution, for those who can afford it, is to hire a reader: someone who reads aloud what he or she is told to. Here the blind person is in control of the situation, and so can independently choose what is read. But further difficulties present themselves. The reader is only hired for certain times, so that reading at other times is not possible. And the blind person may find the sighted person's reading style or voice not to his or her taste: The reading may be careless, have too little or too much inflection, and worst of all, be too slow.

An alternative method of reading by listening is to listen to recordings of books and magazines. Such recordings, in both tape and record format, are made available to state and local libraries through the Talking Books program of the Library of Congress; they are available from other sources as well. While this method does not provide a blind person with unlimited choice of reading matter, it does solve some of the problems of a "live" reader. One can read at leisure, and the voices tend to have clear enunciation, moderate inflection, and a fairly rapid rate, typically about 175 words per minute (Foulke & Berlá, 1978).

A question that is of both practical and theoretical significance is this: In the context of reading, is the brain able to process auditory information as fast as it does visual information? If the auditory system were able to deal with linguistic information only at rates of up to 175 words per minute, then the slow speaking rate of sighted readers would not be a problem for a blind listener, since he or she would not be able to follow the text if it were read faster. On the other hand, it might be that blind people could pick up information at a faster rate, if only it could be presented to them in an accelerated form. To settle this question, a device called a speech compressor (now commercially available) can be used to accelerate tape-recorded speech. Unlike a record player on which a 33-rpm record is played at 45 rpm, the speech compressor does not change the pitch of the voice. Instead, it eliminates small parts of each word, by playing the tape at normal speed for a fraction of a second, then skipping slightly ahead on fast forward, then playing another short segment, and so on. These units that are played and skipped are only a small fraction of a second in duration, so that nothing like a whole syllable is ever left out. The effect is of continuous, normal speech, only speeded up. It turns out that people are entirely capable of following this accelerated speech, not just recognizing the words but understanding the meaning of passages, at rates of up to 275 words per minute (Foulke & Sticht, 1969). This figure is in the neighborhood of the rate at which sighted people read by eye. It seems, then, that the auditory system and the visual system are roughly comparable in the rate at which they can process linguistic information.

Even with the use of a speech compressor, however, reading by listening has some drawbacks. One sometimes wishes to read over a puzzling sentence again and again, or to skip quickly to another part of a book. Such maneuvers are clumsy and time consuming with a tape recorder or phonograph. Fortunately, advances in technology that facilitate searching and indexing will gradually be incorporated into sound-playback devices in the coming years. The ability of present-day compact disk players to play the bands on a disk in any order programmed by the user, gives a hint of what is possible in this regard.

A final problem with reading by listening to a recording, and one that may lie beyond the power of technology to solve, is that blind people who read a lot often come to feel that a recorded voice, however pleasant, is a barrier separating them from the book itself: They wish to read the author's words directly. Individuals who find reading by listening to be unsatisfactory, for this or any of the other reasons described, often choose to read using braille instead.

## Braille

Braille, the reading method of choice for about 8% of blind readers (Josephson, 1964), is a system of representing letters by patterns of raised dots. It was invented in the early 19th century by Louis Braille, a French educator who had lost his sight as a child. Up to that time, tangible reading material for blind people had consisted of embossed letters of the same shape as printed letters. The braille system was radical, not because it consisted of dots, but because the letters differed in shape from print letters. Because of this departure from tradition, braille was initially unpopular with sighted educators of blind pupils, but its ready acceptance by the pupils themselves eventually caused it to prevail over other types of embossed letters. While there are still situations in which tactile stimuli with print-letter shapes are used (see the discussion of the Optacon in Chapter 6), braille has for nearly a century been the most common method of presenting text in a form accessible to touch. Until the 1930s, however, controversy existed among advocates of different styles of braille; fortunately, there is now unanimous acceptance of a single style similar to that originally proposed by Louis Braille.

A braille letter is a pattern of dots within a vertically elongated region called a *cell*. The cell consists of six positions, arranged in two columns of three, each of which may contain a dot. The positions in the left column are numbered 1, 2, and 3; those in the right column, 4, 5, and 6. The meaning of a braille pattern is determined by how many dots are present, and in which positions they are located. For example, a cell containing two dots represents the letter *c* if the dots are in the two top positions (1 and 4), but represents *b* if the dots occupy the top and middle positions of the cell's left column (1 and 2). The 26 patterns making up the braille alphabet are shown in Fig. 4.1; there are also specific patterns to indicate capitalization and punctuation.

On first being introduced to braille, one finds the dots to be very small, and the patterns hard to discern by touch. With practice, however, the letters become recognizable. They are arranged on a page as print letters would be,

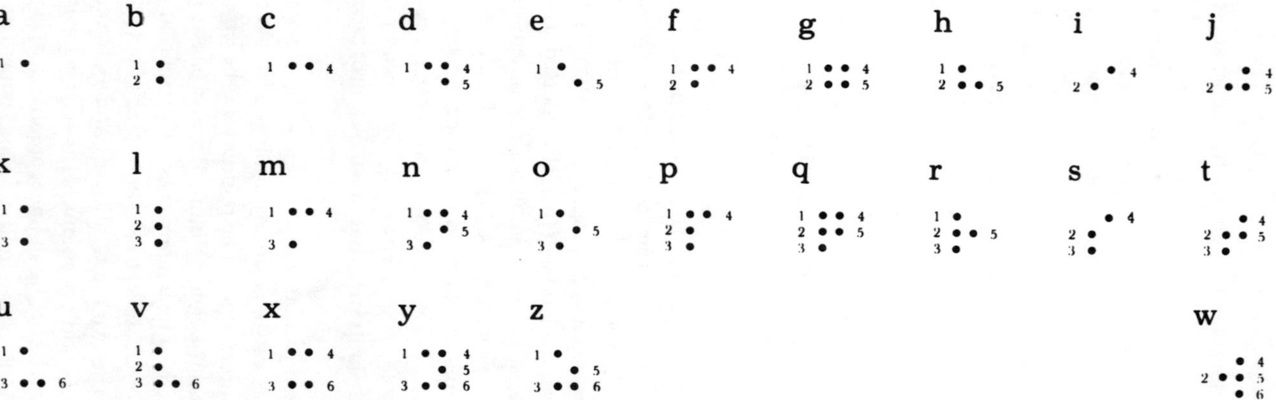


FIGURE 4.1. The braille alphabet. The numeral beside each dot indicates the position that dot occupies within the cell. Louis Braille assigned all the patterns except the one for the letter *w* (shown in the lower right), which in his day was not included in the French alphabet. (From *Programmed Instruction in Braille* by S. C. Ashcroft and F. Henderson, 1963, Pittsburgh: Stanwix House. Reprinted by permission.)

on lines that are to be read from left to right, and an experienced reader of braille is able to read the symbols in rapid succession. In this section, two questions will be considered. First, why is braille easier to read than embossed patterns in the shape of print letters? Second, how fast can braille be read, and what factors determine this rate?

One popular answer to the first question is that braille is more legible than embossing having the print letter shapes, because it consists of dots. Another possibility, however, is that the superiority of braille lies in the *patterns* of the dots, which are simpler than the shapes of the print letters. A careful study by Loomis (1981) has now definitively settled this question in favor of the latter hypothesis. He asked sighted subjects, who had been taught to recognize the braille alphabet visually, to examine by touch a large number of embossed letters. Some were in braille, while others had the shapes of print letters; still others had the shapes of print letters but were made up of dots. The subjects' job in all cases was to identify the represented letter. Loomis found that the accuracy of the subjects' answers was high for the braille letters, but low for the embossed letters with print letter shapes. This was not surprising, since braille was invented to deal with the fact that embossed letters having the print letter shapes are difficult to identify. Loomis also found, however, that the stimuli composed of dots arranged in the shape of the print letters were about as difficult to identify as those embossed with lines; accuracy was much lower for these intermediate characters than for the braille letters. What gives braille its exceptional legibility, therefore, is not the fact that it is composed of dots, but rather, the patterns in which the dots are arranged.

What it is about these patterns that gives braille an advantage is suggested by comparing the number of dots needed to represent a character in braille (3.2 on the average) with the mean number required by Loomis to represent the print-shape letters (8.6). That is, $2\frac{1}{2}$ times as many dots were needed for the print-shape letters. This means that the patterns of braille are simpler than those of the print letters. Readers can easily convince themselves of this difference by trying to represent the print shapes of R, E, or other letters with six or fewer dots: Many of the resulting patterns simply do not contain the necessary information for the letter to be recognized. Braille, in contrast, makes very effective use of the available space to create distinguishable patterns.

Do the virtues of braille exist only when it is presented to the sense of touch, or can braille characters be easily recognized by the visual system as well? To answer this question, Loomis presented visual versions of his stimuli, blurring them slightly to make up for the fact that the eye can resolve smaller details than the skin, and found, again, that accuracy in recognizing braille letters was higher than for the print letter shapes. This fascinating result raises the question of whether reading on the part of sighted people could be made faster or easier by modification of the print-letter shapes. The available evidence offers little support for this possibility, however. In fact, Wallsten and Lambert (1981) have found that even sighted people who know braille well read it by eye much more slowly than they read print. Thus the greater recognizability of the braille characters does not automatically lead to an increase in reading rate.

Let us return, however, to the subject of reading by touch. Experienced braille readers normally achieve reading rates on the order of 100 words per minute, only one-third the rate at which the average sighted person reads print. What accounts for this discrepancy?

An answer to this question is suggested by the fact that a blind person typically uses only the index fingers to read braille (Davidson, Wiles–Kettenmann, Haber, & Appelle, 1980). Many individuals hold the two index fingers close together and move them simultaneously along the line of text, thus examining every character twice; others use the right index finger to do most or all of the actual reading, while the left searches ahead for the beginning of the next line, so that no time will be lost between lines. In either case, only one new character at a time is being examined, since a braille cell is almost as wide as a fingertip. Some highly skilled readers begin reading a new line with the left index finger, slightly before the right index finger has finished with the old line (Bertelson, Mousty, & D'Alimonte, 1985). Except for this brief period of overlap, however, these readers, too, examine the characters one by one.

This letter-by-letter aspect of braille contrasts with visual reading, in which information from 10 or more letter positions is taken in simultaneously (McConkie, 1983). Is the sequential nature of braille responsible for the slow reading rate? It probably is, for when sighted readers, who normally read print at about 300 words per minute, are required to read through a movable "window" that allows them to see only one letter at a time, their rate drops to about 100 words per minute (Wallsten & Lambert, 1981).

Because braille characters are larger than print characters, and because braille must be embossed on heavy paper, a braille copy of a lengthy book takes up several volumes. To cut down on the bulk of brailled material, some words can be represented in an abbreviated way. For example, the two-letter combination "tm" stands for the word "tomorrow." These abbreviated forms are called *contractions*, and text in which they are used is called *Grade II braille*. Grade II braille permits the user to read more than one letter at a time, because multiple letters are represented by a single symbol; it might thus permit an increase in reading rate. Research to test this prediction is inconclusive, however. Some words are apparently recognized more quickly, but others more slowly, when contractions are used (Nolan & Kederis, 1969). In any case, Grade II is much more widely used than Grade I, because of its compactness.

In summary, the main reading methods used by blind people, listening and braille, differ from visual reading (and from each other) in the skills needed to acquire the information in a passage. Each method requires that the user attend carefully to stimuli in a particular sensory modality, and be able to recognize the often complex stimulus patterns in that modality that represent words. The methods used by blind readers may involve a somewhat greater dependence on working memory than visual reading does, in that braille readers usually pick up only one word at a time, and those who read by listening always do so, while visual readers can to some extent see words preceding and following the one at which they are looking directly. This "perceptual window" is not large, however, so that in reading a sentence of average length even a sighted person must rely on memory to a considerable extent.

Reading by any method is, of course, a complex process, involving not just the pickup of information but also the way the person digests this new information and relates it to what he or she already knows. All indications are that these higher-level aspects of reading are the same in blind and sighted individuals. For example, when blind people read braille, the part of the cortex where the greatest increase in metabolic demand occurs (as measured by the amount of blood flowing through blood vessels in the area) is the same as for sighted people reading print: the temporal lobe of the left hemisphere (Jacquy, Piraux, Jocquet, Lhoas, & Noel, 1977), long known to be essential for understanding language.

From a practical point of view, the main difference between visual reading and the reading methods used by blind people is the amount of time involved. Reading braille and reading by listening are both slower than reading print, and in addition, it often takes a long time for a blind person to obtain desired reading material in a form accessible to him or her. In a word, then, the way in which a blind person is able to read extensively, is through perseverance.

## THE COGNITIVE BASIS OF MOBILITY

Mobility is a word with many meanings: the ability to move parts of the body, the ability to change jobs. When used with respect to blind people, however, the term takes on an additional meaning: "the ability to travel safely, comfortably, gracefully, and independently" (Foulke, 1971). Generally speaking, such travel is more difficult for a blind than for a sighted person because information about the environment, especially with regard to buildings or other objects in the distance, is more easily obtained through vision than by any other means. Yet to have mobility skills is important, for a person without such skills must depend on others in many everyday situations, and may feel uncomfortable or embarrassed about this dependence. Being able to get around independently not only reduces such feelings, but also allows the blind person to undertake nonessential activities, such as attending a community meeting, that might be passed up altogether if he or she had to ask a friend to provide transportation.

Mobility depends heavily on mental, as well as perceptual and motor, processes. There are numerous mechanical and electronic aids that can assist the blind person while traveling, but none can replace the cognitive operations that the individual must carry out. Even guide dogs, useful as they are in avoiding obstacles and cars, must not be allowed to participate in choosing the route to follow—if they do, the owner's mobility will suffer! These mobility aids will be discussed in Chapter 6; for the present, however, let us concentrate on the cognitive basis of mobility.

It is generally agreed that there are two major cognitive tasks a blind person must carry out in traveling. The first is to have an understanding of the layout of the area in which he or she is traveling. The second is to know at all times where he or she is within this layout (Rieser, Guth, & Hill, 1982). These two components of mobility will be discussed in turn.

## Knowledge of Layout

An understanding of layout can take many forms, depending on the nature of the terrain and the goals of the traveler. If he or she is in a city, for example, then the fact that the streets are laid out at right angles to the avenues, and numbered consecutively, will no doubt play an important role in his or her conception of the area. If, for example, a blind person is on 57th Street, and wants to shop at a store on 63rd Street, he or she can get there by counting blocks, even if the lengths of the individual blocks along the way are not known in advance. In a more rural setting, unique landmarks, such as the place where a brook flows under the road, or the place where the pavement ends, are likely to be the principal components of the person's knowledge of layout.

But in what form are these facts mentally represented? Does a blind person work mainly with a verbal list of self-instructions: "Turn left at the corner and keep going until you get to the picket fence"? Some of this sort of mental activity does go on, as it does with sighted travelers, but blind people, like the sighted, often have a more flexible understanding of layout. If, for example, they find that a street they had intended to walk along is closed for repairs, many blind travelers, including some who are congenitally blind, can select a different route to reach their destination (Hollyfield & Foulke, 1983). So perhaps a more reasonable hypothesis is that knowledge of layout is stored in propositional form, that is, as a set of factual statements about the environment, such as "The post office is across the street from the restaurant." If someone possesses a large enough number of such facts, and can call them up from memory as needed, then he or she has a good working knowledge of layout. Still another possibility is that blind people have a subjective representation of the environment, analogous to the pictures of a neighborhood that a sighted person can conjure up before his or her "mind's eye." The question of whether blind people, particularly those blind from birth, have such mental images has long been a controversial issue. We will consider it in depth later in this chapter.

From a practical point of view, however, the important issue is not the way in which knowledge of layout is subjectively experienced, but rather, whether the knowledge can be used effectively. A number of studies indicate that congenitally blind people, as a group, resemble sighted people in their ability to register, and later recall and use, isolated facts about layout. When they are asked to *combine* several pieces of layout information, however, congenitally blind people often have more difficulty than sighted people. In one study along these lines, Hartlage (1969) asked sighted and congenitally blind youngsters, age 7 to 18, to complete syllogisms dealing with the relative spatial positions of three people. In one item, for example, subjects were told, "John is in front of Mary. Mary is in front of Bill," and were then asked whether John was in front of Bill, or behind him. The blind subjects answered significantly fewer of these questions correctly than did the sighted ones. On control items dealing with nonspatial information, however, such as whether John was smarter than Bill or not as smart, the two groups of subjects did equally well. The blind participants, then, had special difficulty with the spatial items.

Unfortunately Hartlage's study tells us little about the nature of this difficulty; his results are open to several possible interpretations. One source of this ambiguity is that subjects were allowed to refrain from answering a question if they weren't confident of the answer. Thus a low score for a particular subject might indicate uncertainty, or fear of being wrong, rather than a lack of spatial understanding. If blind youngsters tend to be less confident of their spatial abilities than their sighted peers, this difference could help explain Hartlage's results. Another possible interpretation of the data is that the spatial questions may have been interpreted differently by different subjects. For example, in the spatial question cited earlier, Hartlage assumed that subjects would imagine John, Mary, and Bill all facing in the same direction. An equally valid interpretation, however, might have John and Bill standing side by side, both facing Mary; a subject who interpreted the question in this way would be unable to deduce the "right" answer. If sighted participants in Hartlage's study interpreted the spatial questions in the way they were intended, but blind participants interpreted some of them in a different way, this factor could have contributed to the lower scores of the latter group.

In summary, Hartlage's study indicates that congenitally blind subjects (at least in the age range he studied) have more difficulty with particular types of test items than do age- and grade-matched sighted subjects, but the study doesn't give us a very clear picture of exactly what the two groups are doing differently. While they may in fact be processing or drawing conclusions from spatial information differently, there are other possible interpretations, such as differences between subjects in registering the available information, and in communicating or demonstrating knowledge. This difficulty in interpreting Hartlage's results also characterizes some of the other early studies in which attempts were made to compare spatial cognition in blind and sighted people.

Fortunately, however, a more analytical approach has usually been taken in more recent studies. One example is an investigation by John Rieser and his colleagues (Rieser, Lockman, & Pick, 1980), in which subjects were asked to make two different types of spatial judgments. These investigators asked sighted, adventitiously blinded, and congenitally blind people to recall the spatial arrangement of landmarks, such as doorways, within a particular building. All of the subjects were very familiar with this building, a rehabilitation center for the blind at which some were clients and others were employees. Each subject was asked to consider the landmarks in groups of 3, specified by the experimenter, and to say which 2 of the 3 were the farthest apart, and which 2 were closest together. The same 15 landmarks were used repeatedly in different combinations so that the subjects were asked about more than 100 groups of 3.

Because these landmarks were in a building, rather than in an open space, it was not possible in many cases to walk in a straight line from one to another: Two landmarks might be on opposite sides of the same wall, for example. In that case they would be close to each other in space, though separated by a considerable walking distance. To see how well subjects were able to deal with these two types of separation between landmarks, they were asked to give ratings in terms of walking distances from place to place, and, in a separate experimental session, were asked to rate the landmarks in terms of the straight-line distances among them.

The three groups of subjects responded with about equal accuracy when asked to rate the objects on the basis of the walking distances separating them. When instructed to respond in terms of straight-line distances, however, the congenitally blind subjects were significantly less accurate than the sighted subjects. The adventitiously blinded group performed at an intermediate level.

These results indicate that blind and sighted people are comparable in their ability to recall distances they have walked, whether the paths involved are straight, or include turns. However, when required to combine their knowledge of distance with their knowledge of the turns in the path, in order to evaluate the straight-line distance from start to finish, the blind subjects do less well. The most straightforward way to interpret these findings is in terms of Warren's *frame-of-reference* hypothesis, described in the previous chapter (Warren, 1970; Warren, Anooshian, & Bollinger, 1973). According to this hypothesis, sighted people are able to combine facts about layout into a unified representation that preserves spatial information, and in fact makes manifest spatial relationships that are not explicit in the original list of facts. This frame of reference is not necessarily in the form of an image (although it may give rise to images); its hallmark is, rather, that it helps the person to integrate spatial information in the way that a map would. Warren believes that in sighted people, visual experience plays a dominant role in generating and maintaining the frame of reference, and thereby helps the person to organize and use spatial information obtained through touch or hearing. To some extent, this visual frame of reference probably continues after the loss of sight in adventitiously blinded people. In congenitally blind individuals, however, some other sensory modality must play the organizing role if there is to be a frame of reference. If in many cases congenitally blind people do not develop a strong frame of reference, then as a group they would be expected to do less well than the sighted on tasks such as the distance estimations studied by Rieser et al. (1980).

## Knowledge of One's Own Location

However clear someone's appreciation of layout is, this knowledge is of little benefit if the person is not also aware of his or her location within the environment. That these two types of knowledge are distinct is shown by the fact that a blind person can, on occasion, become lost even in a familiar environment, if snow or some other factor reduces ambient cues to location. Generally speaking, however, blind travelers keep their bearings by picking up information from their immediate surroundings, and integrating this with what they already know about their route.

According to further work from Rieser's laboratory (Rieser, Guth, & Hill, 1982), congenitally blind people are less skillful than either adventitiously blinded, or blindfolded sighted people at taking their own movements into account as they walk about, a skill these investigators call "updating." In this experiment the subjects were brought, one at a time, into a large room containing half a dozen common objects. From a fixed starting place, they were guided in turn to each object, returning to the starting place before going on to the next object. This process was repeated until the subject was able to point accurately, when standing at the starting position, to each of the six objects. Subjects were then guided to one of these objects, and asked to point from this new location to each of the remaining objects (and to the original home base). The three groups of subjects were about equally good at pointing from the original station, but when they attempted to point from the second position, differences in performance occurred among the groups, with the sighted subjects doing the best, the adventitiously blinded subjects pointing somewhat less accurately, and the congenitally blind subjects doing least well. When asked how they went about trying to solve this task, the sighted and adventitiously blinded subjects said that they "saw" the room in their imagination, and that when they walked from the original vantage point to the new one, the image changed to reflect their new position: Objects were now imagined as they would look from this new angle. In contrast, the congenitally blind subjects generally reported that they tried to determine the direction to the objects by mental calculation, using angles and distances. The investigators concluded that congenitally blind people are not as adept as sighted people at the process of updating: Although they can update, they do so in a way which is slower, more laborious, and less accurate. These are features that suggest a less-developed frame of reference (Warren, Anooshian, & Bollinger, 1973).

A result similar to Rieser's was found in another study, in which subjects were asked to walk back to their starting point, rather than simply to point to it (Worchel, 1951). In this study, blind and blindfolded sighted subjects were guided by the experimenter along two arms of a right triangle laid out on a large concrete surface, and were asked to walk from the end of the second arm back to the starting place, along the triangle's hypotenuse. Once again, the blind subjects were significantly less accurate than the sighted. They often ended up in positions several meters away from the actual starting point. Their errors were ones of orientation rather than distance, for they generally walked the correct distance, but in the wrong direction. The difference between the two groups cannot be explained by saying that the blind subjects inadvertently veered as they walked, for the veering tendency is at least as great in blindfolded, sighted people as in blind people (Cratty, 1967). Rather, the blind subjects simply faced in the wrong direction when beginning their attempt to walk along the hyptenuse of the triangle.

Apparently, then, many blind people, especially congenitally blind ones, have difficulty with a particular aspect of mobility, namely, changing direction by the appropriate amount in the middle of a walk, in the absence of auditory or other sensory cues. Whether this finding reflects a difficulty in manipulating spatial information in certain ways, or whether, alternatively, it indicates a lack of skill in turning through a desired angle, is a question that remains to be answered by experiment. The latter possibility is not unreasonable, for it has been shown (Cratty, 1971) that when blind people, wearing earplugs, are asked to turn in place by a particular amount, specified by the experimenter, they often make large errors. For example, when they were asked to turn a full circle, so as to end up facing in the original direction, the average subject turned only about 320 degrees. Errors of this magnitude are sufficient to explain the failure of the subjects in the triangle study to return to the starting point. Moreover, recent work using the pointing technique shows that most subjects' updating errors can be interpreted as indicating misjudgments of the angle through which they have turned and the distance they have walked (Rieser, Guth, & Hill, 1986).

In summary, then, a blind person's ability to keep track of his or her own movements may depend on perceptual and motor factors as well as cognitive ones.

## MENTAL IMAGERY IN BLIND PEOPLE

To understand what mental imagery is, ask yourself whether a frog has lips. When the average sighted person attempts to answer this question, he or she summons from memory a pictorial representation of a frog, and examines it with the "mind's eye" (Kosslyn, 1980). Such an internal representation is called a mental image. The question of where and how such an image is formed is a tangled one from both a philosophical and psychological point of view, but let us avoid controversy by simply defining an image as a mental experience which occurs in the absence of stimulation, but which resembles the experience that occurs when a stimulus is actually present. Thus the image of a frog, conjured up in an attempt to determine whether it has lips, is similar to the experience that would occur if the frog were actually present in front of you.

In this section we will consider the question of whether blind people have mental imagery. For many adventitiously blinded people, the answer is a definite "yes." Years and, in some cases, decades after the loss of sight, they report that they can, at will, form a visual image of a remembered object. To some degree, they can also form visual images of things they have never seen, but that have been described to them or that they have examined by touch. In general, however, such imagery grows weaker with the passage of time, as visual memories fade and as the person becomes more and more adept at picking up auditory and haptic information from the environment. Berger, Olley, and Oswald (1962), for example, were told by three adults who had lost their sight within the previous 15 years, that they continued to experience visual imagery, while two other individuals, blinded 30 and 40 years prior to the interviews, reported having lost this capacity.

Adventitiously blinded people also experience visual imagery in their dreams (Kerr, Foulkes, & Schmidt, 1982); according to some studies (Jastrow, 1888), images may occur in dreams long after they have disappeared from waking life. Such a dichotomy is suggested in the following sonnet by John Milton, the 17th-century English poet, who had lost his sight, probably as a result of glaucoma (Hanford, 1949), some 6 years earlier. Here he describes a dream image of his recently deceased second wife, whom he had never seen.

Methought I saw my late espoused Saint
Brought to me like Alcestis from the grave,
Whom Jove's great Son to her glad Husband gave,
Rescu'd from death by force though pale and faint.
Mine as whom washt from spot of child-bed taint,
Purification in the old Law did save,
And such, as yet once more I trust to have
Full sight of her in Heaven without restraint,
Came vested all in white, pure as her mind:
Her face was vail'd, yet to my fancied sight,
Love, sweetness, goodness, in her person shin'd
So clear, as in no face with more delight.
But O as to embrace me she enclin'd
I wak'd, she fled, and day brought back my night.

For our purposes the last line is particularly relevant, for it implies that visual images were uncommon while Milton was awake, although he still experienced them in dreams. However, the fact that abstract qualities such as sweetness and goodness were apparently substituting for missing details of his wife's veiled face indicates that, even in sleep, Milton's capacity for visual imagery was fading.

In summary, interviews with and first-person accounts by adventitiously blinded people indicate that many of them have considerable visual imagery after the loss of sight, but that it grows gradually weaker over time. The age at which sight is lost is an important factor, as Schlaegel (1953) demonstrated by asking blind adolescents to categorize by sensory modality the first impression that came to mind when the experimenter named each of a series of people, objects, and events. He found that reports of visual images predominated in the case of most individuals who had become blind after the age of 6, but in none of the 13 participants blinded before that age.

Caution should be exercised, however, in interpreting these data, for a teen-ager blinded in childhood may simply not know whether his or her mental representations are visual images. Given this uncertainty, social factors may strongly influence his or her responses. For example, some of Schlaegel's subjects might have previously acquired the habit of describing their mental representations in visual terms, simply because such terms are widely used and readily understood by others.

In the case of congenitally blind people, on the other hand, there is much less uncertainty: We can be sure that they do not have visual imagery. But do they experience some other type of mental image? According to the definition given at the beginning of this section, the ability to recall a familiar tune or smell would qualify as imagery, so in this sense the answer is "Yes." What we really want to know, however, is whether a congenitally blind person has mental images in which the shapes of objects are manifested. Such images would have to be based on information received through the sense of touch, because hearing, though capable of conveying information about the location and approximate size of an object (as discussed in Chapter 3), reveals little about its shape. The question is, then, whether a congenitally blind person has haptic imagery. It will be recalled that in the study of spatial updating (Rieser et al., 1982) discussed in the previous section, the congenitally blind subjects reported that, unlike the adventitiously blind and sighted participants, they did not carry out the task with the aid of a mental image of the room that changed automatically when they walked. On the other hand, when congenitally blind people are asked to recall a familiar object, they typically say that their memory of it is not in the form of verbal statements, but in a more vivid, direct form, as if the recalled object itself were present. Such memories are not explicitly haptic in that the blind person does not usually think about what the object felt like: He or she does not touch it again in memory, but is simply aware of its size, shape, and location. This sounds like imagery, but many scholars, especially von Senden (1932/1960), have argued, largely on philosophical grounds, that congenitally blind people are incapable of spatial images. For decades the question was hotly debated, but only recently has it been put to a direct test.

Such a test was not possible until the 1970s, when the properties of visual images in sighted people were studied quantitatively. As a result of these investigations, psychologists came to recognize that imagery serves not just to help people recall things they saw earlier, but allows them to do everyday thought experiments that help them to plan their actions (Shepard, 1978). Before buying a cabinet for your record collection, for example, you look at the cabinet while trying to imagine your records in it. If it seems that they won't fit, you will probably look for a larger cabinet. An important practical feature of images, then, is their ability to be manipulated.

Roger Shepard and his colleagues at Stanford University have shown that the manipulation of visual images is a very orderly process that can be measured in the laboratory. For example, when subjects were shown drawings of two similar objects, and were asked to say whether the objects were the same, or mirror images of each other, they were able to answer quickly and accurately. If, however, one of the drawings was turned, say, 90 degrees with respect to the other, subjects were able to answer the question only after they had mentally rotated the image of the disoriented drawing into alignment with the other (Metzler & Shepard, 1974). By systematic manipulation of the angular difference between the two pictures, it was shown that subjects rotate the images at a steady rate, which varies somewhat from person to person.

Later investigators realized that this same procedure could also be applied to tangible shapes. When blindfolded, sighted people were asked to examine two similar nonsense shapes, one with each hand, and to say whether they were identical or not, they gave results similar to those obtained using visual stimulation: The greater the difference in orientation between the two stimuli, the greater the time it took subjects to respond (Marmor & Zaback, 1976). Even though they were blindfolded, these subjects were probably using visual imagery, for sighted subjects tend to visualize objects they examine by touch. However, when congenitally blind participants were asked to carry out this task, their results proved to be strikingly similar to those of their sighted fellow subjects, latency once again increasing linearly with stimulus misalignment. This result strongly supports the subjects' own statements that they carried out the task by mentally rotating an image of one of the stimuli, an image that could only have been haptic in nature, since these individuals had never had visual experience.

There was, however, one difference between the two groups of subjects: Those who were congenitally blind seemed (judging from the latency data) to rotate their mental images at only one-fourth the rate of the blindfolded, sighted participants. A third group of subjects, who were adventitiously blinded, had a rate of mental image rotation intermediate between those of the other two groups. These group differences imply that haptic mental images cannot be manipulated at as rapid a rate as visual images can. Other interpretations of the differences are possible, however (Carpenter & Eisenberg, 1978; Hollins, 1986), and more research is needed to settle the issue.

In summary, there is now compelling evidence that haptic mental imagery exists in congenitally blind people. As for adventitiously blinded people, their visual imagery gradually fades after the loss of sight. Does haptic imagery come to substitute for it?

In order to test this possibility, the ability of adventitiously blinded individuals to imagine things in a visual way was compared with their ability to imagine things in a haptic way (Hollins, 1985). Despite important similarities (e.g., Zimler & Keenan, 1983), it is probable that haptic images are not entirely like visual images, but differ from them in the same ways that the haptic *perceptions* of congenitally blind people differ from the perceptions (whether visual or haptic) of sighted people, as discussed in the previous chapter. One of these differences is that sighted people are more adept than blind people at recognizing tangible "pictures"—that is, two-dimensional representations of three-dimensional objects. Congenitally blind people, on the other hand, seem to have a greater ability to perceive vividly both the front and back of a palpated object at the same time.

In order to measure these two "styles" of mental imagery in adventitiously blinded people, where they presumably coexist, it was decided to ask them to form two types of mental images. Some were flat pictorial images, made up of squares in an imaginary checkerboard: An example is shown on the left in Fig. 4.2. It was thought that a capacity for visual imagery would be helpful in generating images like this, and in recognizing them. Other images, however, consisted of filled-in elements in a sort of oversized Rubik's cube, forming an imaginary replica of a solid object, such as the chair represented on the right

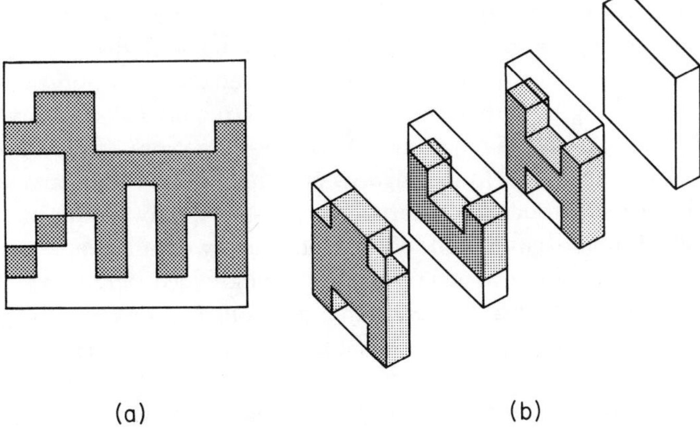


FIGURE 4.2. Patterns representing objects in two different ways, used to test for two different types of mental imagery. The pattern on the left is pictorial in nature, being a two-dimensional representation of a solid object. If a subject could form a mental image based on this pattern, and identify it as a dog, this was taken as evidence of visual imagery. The pattern on the right is more like a statue: The slabs making it up are shown separated in the figure, but subjects were asked to imagine them as pressed together so as to form a single three-dimensional structure. If a subject could form a mental image based on this pattern, and identify it as a chair, this was taken as evidence of haptic imagery. (From "Styles of Mental Imagery in Blind Adults," by M. Hollins, *Neuropsychologia, 23,* p. 563. Copyright 1985 by Pergamon Journals Ltd. Reprinted by permission.)

side of the figure. Haptic imagery was expected to be of benefit in creating and identifying these in-the-round mental representations. For both types of images, a prearranged numbering scheme was used to tell the subjects which squares of the checkerboard, or elements of the cube, were to be filled in. The subject's task was to form the image and then name the represented object.

A number of adventitiously blinded subjects, who had lost their sight at different ages, participated. As predicted, those who had been sighted for most of their lives did as well or better on the test of visual imagery than on the test of haptic imagery, while those who had been blind for most of their lives were more skilled at forming and recognizing the haptic-style images. This study thus shows that the nature of mental imagery gradually changes, following the loss of sight: It remains strong, but becomes qualitatively different from what it was before.

## SUMMARY

In this chapter we set out to learn if there were differences between the cognitive processes of sighted people and blind people, particularly those who were born blind. Similarities, however, were more in evidence than differences. For example, no evidence was found of differences between the two groups in abstract reasoning or in verbal ability. Reading braille and reading by listening are, in general, slower than visual reading, but this reduced speed is apparently due to the nature of the stimulus, and the characteristics of the modality receiving it, rather than to the cognitive mechanisms involved. Similarly, mobility in the environment requires more concentration from a blind person than it does from a sighted person, but this is to a large extent due to the fact that touch and hearing convey spatial information in a more piecemeal fashion than vision does. Congenitally blind people tend to perform less well on some spatial tasks than blindfolded sighted people do; more research is needed to determine the contributions of perceptual, cognitive, and motor factors to this difference. Finally, evidence was reviewed indicating that the spatial imagery of congenitally blind people, which is presumably based on haptic experience, is similar to the visually dominated imagery of sighted people in some ways, but different from it in other respects.

# 5 ATTITUDES AND EMOTIONAL REACTIONS TO BLINDNESS

Early in this century, Helen Keller said, "Not blindness, but the attitude of the seeing to the blind is the hardest burden to bear" (Platt, 1950, p. 57). In those days, many sighted people felt pity, revulsion, and fear when they saw a blind person; it was commonly believed that blind people were in most respects helpless and miserable, but that they were compensated for their blindness by paranormal sensory or mental abilities. Today, attitudes are much more realistic. It is widely understood that, as previous chapters have made clear, blind people are just ordinary folks who can't see: Although life doesn't "compensate" them in any way for being blind, most are capable of achieving happiness and success, in private life and in a career, if given a reasonable chance. This change in public attitudes has not completely run its course, however, for there are still some people with very unrealistic notions of what blindness is like; and even the average sighted person, who expresses sensible opinions about blindness, may feel some anxiety when meeting a blind person for the first time.

In this chapter we will see how attitudes toward blindness have been assessed, in laboratory experiments and in opinion surveys. The way in which blind people are portrayed in fiction will also be examined, for popular stories can tell us, as clearly as any survey, what themes strike a responsive chord in large numbers of people. Against the backdrop of these three lines of evidence, two theories that have been proposed to explain attitudes toward blindness will be considered. We will also review the improvement in attitudes that has taken place over the past several decades, and the reasons for it. Finally, the way in which people who are going blind react to their own loss of sight will be examined.

## ASSESSMENT OF ATTITUDES TOWARD BLINDNESS

The anxiety that many sighted people feel on their first encounter with a blind person is indicated by subtle changes in their behavior. For example, they may speak louder than usual, and their conversation may grow stilted as they make a well-intentioned but unnecessary attempt to avoid words and topics having to do with vision.

In fact, people with any noticeable disability are likely to elicit such reactions from nondisabled people on their first meeting (Davis, 1961; Goffman, 1963). Since the most informative laboratory investigations of this phenomenon have used disabilities involving the legs, such as an amputation or a brace, we will briefly digress from the subject of blindness to consider this related line of evidence.

The common element of these experiments is a comparison of the behavior of nondisabled subjects under two conditions: when they meet a disabled person, and when they meet a nondisabled one. This other person is generally a confederate of the experimenter, who is presented as able-bodied to some subjects, but who pretends to be disabled when meeting other subjects.

In one such study (Kleck, Ono, & Hastorf, 1966), 46 high school juniors served, one at a time, as the subjects. Having been told only that the study was designed to measure physiological activity during a conversation, each subject was ushered into the experimental room, and electrodes were attached to his nonpreferred hand so that skin resistance, generally taken as an inverse measure of emotional arousal, could be recorded. Shortly afterwards the confederate, a student from another school district, entered the room. In fact he had no disability, but for half the subjects he entered in a wheelchair specially designed so that his left leg below the knee could be concealed, giving the impression that it had been amputated. For the remaining subjects, he walked into the room, giving no indication of a disability. At this moment subjects in both conditions showed a drop in electrical skin resistance, but this *galvanic skin response* was significantly greater for the subjects meeting the person who they thought was disabled, than for those meeting the same person without a disability. This suggests that the sight of the disability elicited a strong emotional reaction from subjects. This impression is supported by the fact that participants who had shown especially large skin responses frequently reported, after the session, that they had been flustered and made uncomfortable by the "other subject's" disability.

In a similar study from the same laboratory (Kleck, 1968), a hidden motion picture camera recorded the subject's behavior while he listened to and answered questions posed by the confederate. The film was later examined systematically to determine how much the subject had moved in his chair or gestured during the experiment. It was found that subjects conversing with a supposedly disabled interviewer moved much less during the interaction than did those conversing with the same person when he had no wheelchair. The author suggests that subjects move less in the presence of a disabled person because they are less relaxed.

That feelings of tension and embarrassment may cause subjects to distance themselves from a disabled person was shown by Langer, Fiske, Taylor, and Chanowitz (1976). College students who had volunteered to be subjects in a study on "getting acquainted" were given an information sheet containing a description of the other person they were to meet, including, for some subjects, the statement that she wore a leg brace for a bone condition. After reading this sheet, the subject was asked to enter a room in which the "other subject" (actually a confederate of the experimenter) was already seated, and to pull up a chair for the conversation. The main response measure was the distance from the confederate at which the subject placed his or her chair. Subjects placed their chair at a mean distance of 1.8 meters from the confederate when she wore a leg brace, but at a distance of only 1.2 meters when she wore no brace—a significant difference. Thus they apparently sought to avoid close physical proximity to a disabled person.

More information on this avoidance tendency was uncovered in a later study (Snyder, Kleck, Strenta, & Mentzer, 1979), in which subjects were required to choose a seat next to either a disabled person or a nondisabled one. As each subject arrived at the laboratory, ostensibly to watch and evaluate a silent film, he or she was told that there were two films to choose from, and that these were to be shown simultaneously in adjoining booths. The subject could see that each booth contained two chairs, one of which was already occupied: A confederate wearing a leg brace sat in one booth, while another confederate, without a brace, sat in the other booth. Eighty-three percent of the subjects chose to sit in the booth with the nondisabled person. Since the confederates took turns wearing the leg brace, differences in appearance between them, other than the brace itself, could not account for this result. In explaining their choice, subjects cited a preference for one film over the other, but since each film was paired equally often with the seemingly disabled confederate, the films themselves were probably not the major factor underlying subjects' decisions. Snyder et al. concluded that subjects were motivated by a desire to avoid the disabled person, but were unwilling to admit this motive to the experimenter, and were perhaps not fully aware of it themselves. A control condition, in which the same film was shown in both booths, suggested that when subjects had no way of rationalizing their wish to avoid the disabled person, they were less likely to do so.

Experiments of this type dealing with blindness, rather than with orthopedic disabilities, are less common, but the studies that have been done point to the same conclusion. In one such study (Gowman, 1957), there were three members of the experimental team: a sighted woman, a sighted man, and a blind man. The woman and one of the men—sometimes one, sometimes the other—entered a series of men's clothing stores, and in each store, the male experimenter asked the salesperson to show him a white shirt. When waiting on the sighted man, salespersons invariably directed most of their attention to him, addressing only an occasional remark to the woman. When it was the blind man who asked for the shirt, however, nearly half of the salespersons attempted to interact with the woman instead of with him, saying things like, "Does he want thirty-three sleeves?", and setting the shirt down in front of her rather than in front of him. Two of the clerks apparently tried to avoid the situation altogether, hurrying to busy themselves in other parts of the store.

The idea that interacting with a blind person produces anxiety in many sighted people receives further support from a study carried out at a rehabilitation center, a facility where recently blinded individuals receive counseling and learn new skills, such as mobility (Ward, 1973). The subjects in this study, however, were not the clients at the center, but rather, a group of sighted students who had come there as part of their training to become rehabilitation workers. The study consisted simply of interviewing these trainees regarding their feelings and attitudes during their stay at the center. It was found that trainees who had had little or no contact with blind people before they came to the center began to feel bad shortly after arriving there. They reported feelings of uneasiness, fear, revulsion, and depression. Some realized their feelings were caused by the fact that, for the first time, they were coming into prolonged contact with blind people. Other trainees, however, while reporting the same negative emotions, didn't know what was causing them: They blamed the weather, or an impending illness. Fortunately, these feelings declined in intensity after a day or two, and in most cases disappeared altogether.

Was it really their encounters with blind people that had made these trainees feel anxious and upset? Yes, for other trainees, who had known blind people in the past, experienced no such reactions on their arrival at the center. Apparently, then, some sighted individuals experience a wave of negative emotion when they first interact with blind people, but these feelings subside after a time.

Blindness is, of course, a serious physical impairment, which cuts off an important channel of sensory experience, and makes many everyday activities more difficult to carry out. No one wants to be blind. It is therefore not altogether surprising that sighted people, on meeting a blind person, might think, "It's too bad that person is blind . . . I hope I never become blind," and that this train of thought should produce some anxiety. Whether this anxiety can fully explain the reactions of sighted people such as the sales people and rehabilitation students just mentioned is a question that laboratory experiments have so far not been able to answer.

Descriptions by many blind individuals of their encounters with the sighted in everyday life, however, suggest that the answer is "no" (Chevigny, 1946; Kirtley, 1975). They report remarks and actions by sighted people that reveal, in addition to emotional tension, a number of misconceptions about blindness. In particular, many sighted people seem to feel that blind people are unable to lead satisfying lives—that they are completely dependent on others and are chronically unhappy. For example, blind people with guide dogs are sometimes approached by strangers who say something like, "I'll bet your dog cheers you up a lot." Although phrased in a positive way, such a remark implies that the blind person's life is basically an unhappy one. But are such notions the exception or the rule among sighted people? Unfortunately we cannot tell on the basis of these valuable, but anecdotal, accounts.

In order to put the study of attitudes toward blindness on a more rigorous footing, Cowen, Underberg, & Verrillo (1958) developed a questionnaire dealing with this subject. It consists of statements such as "A blind person can never really be happy," with which respondents indicate strong agreement, mild agreement, mild disagreement, or strong disagreement. In designing the questionnaire, the experimenters asked a panel of judges who worked with blind people (a rehabilitation worker, a nursery-school teacher, and so on) to look over a large number of statements and to pick out those which they thought indicated a negative attitude toward blind people, as well as those indicating a positive attitude. Only statements that were declared positive or negative by all five judges were included in the final questionnaire. The positive statements were all to the effect that blind people are normal, apart from their lack of vision, while most of the negative statements alleged that blind people are helpless and unhappy.

In scoring a subject's responses, strong agreement with a negative statement received four points, mild agreement three points, mild disagreement two, and strong disagreement, one. This order was reversed for the positive statements. Thus a high score on the test indicates a strong negative attitude toward blind people.

The main purpose for which Cowen and his colleagues wanted to use this *Attitude to Blindness* questionnaire was to determine whether the opinions of sighted people regarding blindness are related to their views on other topics. To answer this question, they asked respondents—101 students in adult education psychology classes—to fill out three additional questionnaires. One of these measured prejudice against Blacks, a second was designed to assess negative feelings toward members of minority groups in general, and the third measured a dimension of personality called authoritarianism, which may be defined as an extreme respect for authority combined with a tendency to categorize people and things as good or bad (Adorno, Frenkel-Brunswik, Levinson, & Sanford, 1950). Comparing the scores obtained on the different tests, it was found that those people who scored high on one test were likely to have scored high on the others as well; that is, scores on the four tests were significantly correlated. This suggests that attitudes toward blindness are related to other aspects of one's personality. Negative attitudes toward blind people are apparently just one manifestation of a tendency to rely on stereotypes.

Later investigators have used the Attitude to Blindness scale as a way of determining the effect of some experimental manipulation, such as a series of conversations with a blind person, on the attitudes of sighted respondents. We will discuss one of these studies in the section on changing attitudes, later in the chapter.

More extensive attitude surveys have subsequently been conducted by other researchers (e.g., Lukoff & Whiteman, 1961; Siller, 1970). An important finding of these later studies is that attitudes toward blindness are complex, and cannot be adequately described with a single dimension such as "positive versus negative." For example, an individual might express the belief that blind people are generally not capable of doing very much for themselves, and yet might state a willingness to have a blind person as a close friend; another individual, however, might express just the opposite views. Siller (1970) also showed that a person's pattern of attitudes toward one disability is usually similar to his or her pattern of attitudes toward other disabilities.

An interesting difference of opinion regarding attitudes toward blindness was discovered by Lukoff and Whiteman (1961). They questioned large numbers of sighted people about their attitudes toward blindness, and also asked blind people what they believed the attitudes of the sighted to be. The investigators found an appreciable disparity between these two sets of data. Although most sighted people were not well informed about blindness (as determined by "information questions" included in the survey), and said that they felt sorry for blind people, they expressed few negative opinions regarding their capacities or personality. Blind participants in the study, on the other hand, reported that they found stereotyping of blind people to be very common among the sighted. In attempting to explain this discrepancy, Lukoff (1972) points to the fact, uncovered in his research with Whiteman, that those sighted people who frequently approach blind strangers with offers of help tend to have a more patronizing attitude than the average sighted person. From such encounters, Lukoff theorizes, blind people would gain the false impression that patronizing attitudes are very widespread. The investigators conclude that stereotyping of blind people does occur, but is not as pervasive as is sometimes thought.

Kirtley (1975), however, has offered a different interpretation of the

Lukoff–Whiteman data. He points out that people are often unwilling to admit to holding opinions, such as prejudices, that they know are frowned on by society: No one wants to give the interviewer a bad impression. Moreover, people are sometimes not entirely aware of their own feelings: They may harbor beliefs that can subtly affect their behavior, without realizing that this is happening. Kirtley argues, in other words, that unrealistic attitudes toward blind people are more common than Lukoff and Whiteman's data suggest.

Kirtley's argument may be illustrated by considering the responses to individual items in a survey administered to 104 high school students in New York City (Gowman, 1957). Explicitly negative statements about blind people were overwhelmingly repudiated: For example, 95 of the respondents disagreed with the statement, "I think some blind people are blind because they are being punished for something they have done." However, equally unrealistic statements with a positive connotation, such as "The blind, in general, seem to have a special spiritual quality," received widespread endorsement. As regards the everyday competence of blind people, a majority of subjects agreed with any positively phrased statement, whether it implied that blind people are generally capable ("The blind, in general, can do just about everything with very little help") or incapable ("I think somebody who knows something about the blind, and can see, should be with them most of the time"). According to Kirtley, it is difficult to determine sighted people's true feelings about blindness from surveys of this kind.

Reserving judgment on this controversy, let us conclude simply that surveys confirm the existence of misconceptions about blind people, but do not tell us with precision how widespread such attitudes are.

It is worth pausing at this point to consider why attitudes toward blindness and other disabilities have been the object of so much inquiry and concern to social scientists, educators, and rehabilitation workers, and to disabled people themselves. One reason for the importance of these attitudes is that they affect the quality of human relationships. A sighted person who feels nervous and depressed when talking to a blind person, and who is preoccupied during the conversation with how devastating it would be to become blind, is unlikely to get much out of the conversation—or put much into it. Any interests that he or she shares with the blind person will probably remain undiscovered.

Evidence that personal interactions between a disabled and a nondisabled person are often stifled in this way was provided by one of the wheelchair studies mentioned earlier (Kleck et al., 1966). As part of the interview that took place during that study, the subjects were asked to rate, on a 10-point scale, the importance that they assigned to academic achievement, sports, and appearance. The ratings they assigned to academic achievement were found to be consistently higher, and those assigned to sports and appearance consistently lower, when the interviewer was pretending to be disabled, than when he was not. The authors interpreted this result, which has been confirmed and extended by later studies (Hastorf, Northcraft, & Picciotto, 1979; Strenta & Kleck, 1982), to mean that the subjects shaded their true opinions so as to spare the feelings of the disabled interviewer. Moreover, subjects in the disabled-interviewer condition showed less individuality in their ratings than those in the control condition, and spent less time elaborating their answers. Clearly, the effect of such tendencies in everyday life would be to inhibit frank communication and so reduce the value of the conversation to either participant.

Another very practical way in which unrealistic attitudes toward blindness can harm blind people is by making it hard for them to find a job suited to their interests and abilities. Employers who are made anxious by interacting with a blind person, or who believe that blind people are not up to the stresses of a challenging job, are more likely to hire a sighted applicant than an equally qualified blind one, even when the work does not actually require vision.

Finally, repeated encounters with pitying sighted people can affect a blind person's feelings of self-worth, and attitude toward society. Some become increasingly dependent on family, friends, and institutional supports, as if conforming with the views of those around them; others become hostile and defensive, reacting angrily if unnecessary help is offered (Cutsforth, 1933/1980; Gowman, 1957). A great many, however, maintain a balanced view of the situation, speaking out against misconceptions on the part of the sighted, but attributing them to ignorance rather than to thoughtlessness.

In short, unrealistic attitudes toward blind people can have a wide range of social and psychological effects. But recognizing the existence of such attitudes, and understanding their impact, still does not explain them. Where would someone get the idea, occasionally expressed, that the average blind person cannot get dressed or eat a meal, unassisted? Do these notions occur spontaneously to sighted people, or are they part of a culturally-transmitted stereotype? To answer this question, we will examine the way in which blind people are portrayed in folklore and other popular stories of the past and present. This should allow us to determine whether unrealistic attitudes toward blindness are part of our cultural heritage.

## BLINDNESS IN LITERATURE

Blind fictional characters have been common from antiquity to the present, and extensive studies of this subject have been made (Kirtley, 1975; Monbeck, 1973; Twersky, 1955). Our purpose, however, is only to consider a handful of the best known of such characters, to determine whether they are portrayed as ordinary men and women who just can't see, or as profoundly abnormal individuals.

We will begin with Oedipus, the best-known blind person in Greek mythology. In order to placate the sun god Apollo, this proud king of Thebes—while still sighted—relentlessly pursues an investigation into the murder of his predecessor. Oedipus, an adventurer who was acclaimed king when he came to the city years earlier, has until now had little interest in its history. But the investigation reveals that he himself is the assassin, for a stranger whom he fought and killed on approaching Thebes was the previous king. Moreover, the murdered ruler was Oedipus's own father, and the king's widow, whom Oedipus married when he assumed the throne, is his mother. He did not recognize his parents because they had sent him away as an infant. When he learns these horrible facts, Oedipus gouges out his eyes and goes into exile. But blindness transforms him, turning the hard-driving man of power into a benign, saintly figure with the gift of prophecy. In Sophocles's play *Oedipus at Colonus* he goes to Athens to die, in order that his earthly remains may protect that city from harm.

To our question of whether Oedipus is portrayed in an unrealistic way once he is blind, the answer is a clear "yes." He combines clairvoyance with a profound unawareness of his surroundings: For example, he cannot tell, by listening, whether he is in a town or in the countryside. Another important aspect of this story, however, is that it uses light and blindness as symbols of abstract concepts. Light represents knowledge and inquiry, while blindness represents a withdrawal from reality; thus Oedipus blinds himself to cut himself off from the world, as well as to atone for his violent and incestuous misdeeds. As we shall see, the use of blindness as a symbol for psychological or metaphysical concepts has been common in literature, and probably accounts for the leading roles that blind characters often play.

In another part of the ancient world, the writers of the Bible were also using light and blindness as symbols, but this symbolism is somewhat different from that in Sophocles's tragedy: In many passages in both the Old and New Testaments, light represents divine revelation, and those who are not receptive to religious values are said to be "blind." These metaphors have remained an important feature of religious literature up to the present day. Perhaps one reason for the pervasiveness of this traditional symbolism is the fact that some people who undergo sudden religious conversions experience at that moment a sensation of dazzling light (James, 1902/1961, p. 205–206).

The most intense and sustained use of light and blindness as symbols of religious concepts occurs in Dante's *Divine Comedy*, one of the greatest literary achievements of the Middle Ages. In this allegorical journey through hell, purgatory, and heaven, angels and saints give off dazzling light, and God is manifested as pure light. The inferno is dark, but as Dante climbs the Mount of Purgatory and makes the celestial journey through paradise, the light grows brighter and brighter. On several occasions, Dante himself is temporarily blinded by the dazzling lights, thus demonstrating his initial inability to comprehend divine truths. But Beatrice, the soul who is guiding him through heaven, is able to restore his sight with her "eyebeams" (Dante, 1321/1970).

In one region of purgatory, he encounters souls who are being punished with blindness: "to those shades . . . God's rays refuse to offer their delight; for each soul has its eyelids pierced and sewn with iron wires" (Dante, 1321/1961, pp. 141–142). In a revealing aside to this scene, Dante tells the reader that he is uncomfortable in the presence of blind people: "Somehow it seemed to me a shameful act to stare at others and remain unseen." Perhaps his discomfort arose in part from a conviction that blindness was a spiritual disability as well as a sensory one.

On a more mundane level, a number of European folk tales involve blind characters whose loss of sight has a symbolic value, usually representing a punishment for sin. Rapunzel, a fairy tale of uncertain age which was transcribed by the Grimm Brothers in the last century, is such a story. Rapunzel is a girl imprisoned in a tower by a cruel witch. A prince, traveling near the tower, hears her voice but can find no door through which to reach her chamber. But Rapunzel has very long hair, which she lets down from her window. The prince climbs up her hair, and the two become lovers. When the witch learns what has happened, she is determined to punish the young people for their indiscretion. She cuts off Rapunzel's hair and abandons the pregnant girl in a desert; then she uses the hair to trick the prince into climbing the tower. When he reaches the window the witch pushes him off, so that he falls into some briars, which pierce his eyes and make him blind. Helpless and remorseful, the prince wanders aimlessly for years until he meets Rapunzel, now accompanied by their twin children. Rapunzel weeps, and her tears, falling on the prince's eyes, magically restore his sight. After being legally married, they live happily ever after.

The 19th century was the period in which blind characters appeared most frequently in English literature, usually to convey some moral to the reader. In *Jane Eyre* (Brontë, 1847/1945), for example, blindness again serves as a punishment for sin. Jane, the novel's heroine, is a young woman who takes a job as governess in the home of Edward Rochester, an enigmatic man who mocks her at first but later proposes marriage. Just before the wedding, however, Jane learns that the first Mrs. Rochester is still alive—insane and confined to an upstairs room. Angered over her employer's duplicity, and determined not to become his mistress, Jane flees. But one night she "hears" Edward's voice, and returns to find that an accidental fire has killed his wife and left him blind. Now a helpless and dependent figure, sorry for his earlier treatment of Jane and his wife, he explains his condition by saying: "Divine justice pursued its course . . . Of late, Jane—only—only of late—I began to see and acknowledge the hand of God in my doom." They marry, and in an ending reminiscent of the Rapunzel story, his vision improves!

A common feature of the stories reviewed so far is that characters go blind as a result of their misdeeds, but are purified and transformed once their sight is gone. It is worth asking why authors have traditionally considered blindness such an appropriate punishment for wrongdoing, and why it works such a remarkable transformation on the personalities of these fictional characters. A plausible answer is that, for the author and his or her readers, vision is not just a sensory channel, but a symbol of power and (to judge from the misdeeds that are being punished in most of these stories) sexuality.

The theme of blindness as weakness is paramount in Rudyard Kipling's *The Light that Failed* (Kipling, 1899), a novel about a war correspondent named Dick who achieves fame for his battlefront sketches. Returning to England, he settles into sedentary, urban life, and devotes his attentions to Maisie, his childhood sweetheart. She is a cold and self-centered artist who keeps him on a string, rejecting his love while repeatedly summoning him to her studio so he can give her artistic advice. Unable to resolve the situation, Dick becomes more and more listless and unhappy, a decline that is accelerated when he suddenly loses his sight as a result of an old war wound. Feeling that his life is now worthless, he returns to the Sudanese battlefield, and stands in the line of fire, so that he can die in the environment where he had earlier achieved something meaningful.

For a modern reader, the most striking aspect of this novel is the idea, accepted without hesitation by all the characters, that blind people can't work for a living, enjoy themselves, or do much of anything except wait for death. Kipling explains that Dick "was dead in the death of the blind, who, at the best, are only burdens upon their associates" (p. 176). The author goes out of his way to emphasize Dick's helplessness, for example, by making him crawl on his hands and knees rather than walk. But blindness is not really the main subject of this book, for it is two-thirds over before Dick loses his sight. Instead, the overall theme of the novel is the way Dick falls apart after abandoning the active life; Kipling apparently made Dick go blind because he thought of that as the ultimate downward step short of death.

In recent decades there has been a trend, which will be discussed in a later section, toward depicting blind people in a more commonsense way. However, the literary tradition of portraying them as very strange, and using blindness as a symbol of punishment, ignorance, or weakness, continues to be represented. For example, in *The Name of the Rose* (Eco, 1980/1984), a best-selling mystery novel set in a 14th-century monastery, the villain turns out to be Jorge, a blind monk. When sighted, he had brought to the monastery the world's only copy of a treatise by Aristotle, praising laughter. But now the demented Jorge considers laughter incompatible with his grim view of religion, so he smears poisonous ointment on the manuscript in order to kill anyone who tries to read it. In the end he eats, and thus destroys, the poisoned manuscript. "You are the Devil," the novel's hero tells him, "and like the Devil you live in darkness" (p. 581). Thus Jorge's blindness is explicitly used as a symbol of the ignorance that he wishes to preserve.

In this short overview, we have seen that unrealistic attitudes toward blindness are definitely a part of our cultural heritage: Although blind fictional characters have sometimes been portrayed as having normal values, feelings, and living skills (in the novels of Sir Walter Scott, for example), it has until recently been more common for an author to use blindness as a metaphorical way of telling readers that there is something unusual about a character's personality. Authors who use this literary device are drawing on feelings about blindness which already exist in their readers—feelings to which they, in turn, contribute. The fact is, however, that no one is certain how these feelings developed, or what their psychological basis is. In the following section we will examine two theories that attempt to answer these questions.

## EXPLANATIONS OF ATTITUDES TOWARD BLINDNESS

### The Lack-of-knowledge Theory

One possible explanation of unrealistic attitudes toward blindness is that most sighted people simply don't know much about it (Lukoff, 1972). When they see a blind person and wonder what his or her life is like, they fall back on imagination and guesswork. What they most vividly, and correctly, realize is that they would be profoundly depressed if they lost their sight. That this depression would lift with the passage of time, and that it would not occur at all in congenitally blind people, are facts that do not occur to them; and so they conjecture that the average blind person has an unhappy life. Further, sighted people have a hard time understanding how they themselves could cook or carry out other daily activities if they were blind, and so they imagine that these activities are beyond the competence of the average blind person. And if they see a blind person with a cane walking along a busy street without bumping into anyone, they may attribute this skilled performance to some extraordinary sensory capacity, because they are unaware of the months of training that he or she has received.

Unfortunately, once such misconceptions about other people develop, they can be hard to change: The person holding them sometimes becomes committed to them, and has difficulty in giving them up. For some individuals this is because the beliefs have come to serve a psychological purpose. For example, thinking of blind people as very different from oneself may help a sighted person to dismiss the fear of someday becoming blind (Monbeck,

1973). If an attitude such as this becomes deeply entrenched, it fulfills the definition of a *prejudice*: a strongly-held opinion that is not based on evidence.

In summary, the lack-of-knowledge theory asserts that unrealistic attitudes toward blind people arise when sighted people who don't know much about blindness rely on their own intuition, mixed perhaps with misinformation passed along by others or derived from popular culture, in forming their opinions on this subject. The strong points of this theory are that it is clear and simple, and that it is consistent with the repeatedly demonstrated fact that the general public is not at all knowledgeable about the causes and nature of visual impairment (Lukoff & Whiteman, 1961; Clark, Martire, & Bartolomeo, Inc., 1984). Attempts to test the theory, by measuring attitudes before and after subjects are presented with information about blindness, have had mixed results (Lukoff, 1972; Skrtic, Clark, & White, 1982); but this is not surprising, given the fact that attitudes, regardless of how they were first formed, are often resistant to change.

A more serious difficulty for the lack-of-knowledge theory is that it fails to explain why blindness is more dreaded than are other, equally handicapping conditions. Deafness, for example, imposes about the same amount of difficulty on everyday life, yet is contemplated with much less foreboding by the average person (Gallup, 1976; Gowman, 1957). It is the disparity between the real but manageable hardship imposed by the loss of sight, and the enormous fear, like the fear of death, that the thought of blindness evokes in many sighted people (Carroll, 1961), that has prompted some investigators to suggest that factors other than ignorance may be at work in producing unrealistic attitudes toward blind people. We will call this alternative viewpoint the *symbolism theory* of attitudes toward blindness.

## The Symbolism Theory

According to this hypothesis (Chevigny & Braverman, 1950; Greenacre, 1926; Hart, 1949; Kirtley, 1975; Monbeck, 1973; Schauer, 1951), most people unconsciously harbor some strange ideas about the eyes, and these ideas influence the stories we make up, our dreams, and our emotional reactions to blindness. The most important of these ideas is that the eyes are instruments not just for seeing, but for influencing others, especially in a sexual or aggressive way. Expressions such as "She melted under his gaze" and "Their eyes shot daggers" hint at such an attitude.

Where does this belief about the eyes come from? According to some theorists, its roots lie in the early development of the individual (Chevigny & Braverman, 1950), when the act of looking, interwoven with fantasy, is an important means by which children vicariously interact with their environment. Whatever causes this belief nowadays, a form of it already existed in antiquity, as a respected scientific theory: Classical scholars such as Pythagoras, Plato, and Euclid thought that the eyes shot out a beam of rays that struck the viewed object, where the rays interacted with ordinary light to produce visual experience (Riggs, 1985). Seeing, in other words, was thought to be something that your eyes did to light and objects, rather than a process by which light, bouncing off objects, stimulated your eyes.

If people still believe, unconsciously, that looking is one way of influencing the environment, it follows that blindness ought to be regarded not just as a sensory loss, but as a loss of power, a loss of one important method of carrying out one's desires. This, according to the symbolism theory, is the basis for the widespread belief that blind people are incompetent or ineffectual, compared with the sighted.

A second unconscious idea is that seeing and understanding are the same thing. This notion gives rise to expressions like "I see what you mean," and words like "clarify" and "enlighten." It also contributes to our attitudes toward blindness, according to the symbolism theory, because it implies that blind people are cognitively, and perhaps spiritually, deficient.

The eyes thus have a double symbolism: To the unconscious, they are a channel through which sexual or violent impulses are expressed, and also a window through which knowledge, especially spiritual knowledge, enters. It is a short step from this paradoxical conception to the idea that blindness is a punishment for sin. Few people would acknowledge such a belief nowadays, but it was widely accepted as an obvious truth in earlier times, declining in acceptance only in the present century. According to the symbolism theory, however, it lingers on at an unconscious level in many people.

A variation on this theme is that blindness prevents, rather than punishes, sinfulness, and that blind persons are therefore more absorbed in spiritual matters than are their worldly, sighted contemporaries: that they have an "inner light" which compensates them for their presumed insensitivity to physical light (it not being widely realized that most blind people have light perception), and makes them uncannily sensitive to the feelings and thoughts of others.

The symbolism theory of attitudes toward blindness asserts that this network of irrational and somewhat frightening beliefs is present to a degree in everyone, but that people differ widely in the psychodynamic role played by these beliefs—that is, in the extent to which they influence our conscious thoughts and our behavior in everyday life. According to the psychiatrists and clinical psychologists who propounded the theory, these beliefs remain dormant in the average person most of the time, but may come to play a more active role in people whose psychological equilibrium or overall view of reality has become distorted. Some mentally ill persons, in other words, seem to be very much in the grip of these ideas about the eyes and blindness. The annals of psychiatry and clinical psychology contain many cases in which irrational thoughts about blindness are part of the emotional problems of the individual.

One example is the case of a 36-year-old man who reported a sudden loss of vision while shopping with his wife and mother-in-law (Brady & Lind, 1961). Medical examination showed that there was no physiological basis for the loss of sight: that is, his blindness was "hysterical." It became clear to his doctor that he was a very dependent individual, who was constantly harassed at home by his wife and mother-in-law. As is common in hysteria, his feelings of anger and powerlessness had been converted into a seemingly physical symptom.

After a long period of psychotherapy, this patient was treated with behavior modification techniques. He was asked to press a lever at 15-second intervals, and rewarded with praise for successfully carrying out this task. Then a light was introduced into the situation; it came on when he was supposed to press the lever. Although he denied seeing the light, it caused shaking and other signs of emotional upset, and his performance at the task actually grew worse. Over the course of many sessions, however, his performance gradually improved, and during this improvement he began using visual metaphors to describe his relationship with his wife, saying that they didn't "see eye to eye," and that he was so angry he "couldn't see straight." Suddenly the excited patient reported that he could see again, thus bringing his period of hysterical blindness to an end. The behavior modification procedures were eventually terminated, and he was given counseling to help him cope with everyday problems.

What is interesting about this case from our perspective is that the man's feelings of frustration found expression in the form of a visual loss, vision apparently being for him a symbol of the hostility he dared not express. When at last he did express it, using visual metaphors to do so, the hysterical symptom was no longer necessary, and so it ceased to exist.

There are many other ways in which symptoms of emotional illness may involve the eyes, from excessive blinking in the presence of a hated person, to mutilation of the eyes as self-inflicted punishment for some thought or deed (Favazza & Favazza, 1987; Hart, 1949). What is common to such behaviors is that the person uses vision as an unconscious metaphor for actions of an emotional nature.

There is little reason to challenge the symbolism theory of attitudes toward blindness as an explanation for symptoms of mental illness, in cases such as these. It is debatable, however, whether unconscious symbolism plays a major role in shaping the average person's feelings about blindness. In maintaining that it does so, some advocates of the theory point out that (as we learned earlier) folklore and literature contain many examples of blindness serving as a symbol of incompetence, wickedness, or saintliness. In their opinion, the popularity of these stories shows that the symbols they contain are understood and appreciated, at an unconscious level, by the general public. But does unconscious eye-symbolism actually influence the interactions of sighted and blind people in everyday life? At the present time there is no proof that it does so. Experimental research addressing this question would be an interesting addition to the scientific literature.

The lack-of-knowledge theory and the symbolism theory are not, of course, incompatible, nor do they rule out the possibility of additional, equally valid, explanatory principles. Most researchers in the area believe that a full understanding of attitudes toward blindness will require a combination of theoretical perspectives. For example, the lack-of-knowledge theory may be especially useful in explaining the mild embarrassment felt by many sighted people when they first meet a blind person, while the symbolism theory may be needed to understand the feeling of those who have a stronger emotional reaction.

## RECENT CHANGES IN ATTITUDES TOWARD BLINDNESS

Whatever the cause of traditional attitudes toward blind people, the happy fact is that these maudlin, destructive feelings are on the wane. In comparing the views of society in previous decades with those prevailing today, people who have been blind for many years generally feel that public attitudes are slowly changing for the better. This change is clearly reflected in the balanced, realistic way that blind people are now frequently depicted in popular culture, as in the play *Butterflies are Free* (Gershe, 1969) and the film *Places in the Heart* (Donovan & Benton, 1984). No one is completely sure what is causing the improvement, however.

The work of educational agencies, such as the American Foundation for the Blind, which publishes a scholarly journal as well as books and pamphlets intended for a variety of audiences, has no doubt played a role. Similarly, the autobiographical works of blind authors have had an educational impact on the reading public. The writings of Helen Keller (1905, 1929) opened up this genre: She was the first to bring to national public attention the problem of misconceptions about blindness. The idea that societal attitudes are the main obstacle confronting blind people was more vigorously espoused by Jacob Twersky in his hard-hitting novel *The Face of the Deep* (1953), which contains much autobiographical material. And the recent, widely acclaimed memoir, *Ordinary Daylight* (Potok, 1980), while not concerned primarily with public attitudes, presents a sophisticated picture of a recently blinded individual. It is important to note that in these and other examples, blind people themselves have undertaken the responsibility of informing the public about blindness.

Another important impetus for change has been the civil rights movement. Originating in the struggle of Blacks for equality, it sensitized the public to the evils of discrimination generally, and inspired other groups, including blind people, to challenge the status quo. Through organizations such as the National Federation of the Blind, they have fought for equal access to educational and employment opportunities.

Still another factor has been the presence in society of large numbers of blinded veterans following each of this century's wars (Gowman, 1957). The strong public conviction that veterans, having served the country, deserve a job, has helped to dispel the opposing notion that blind people must be sheltered from the rough-and-tumble of competitive employment. Moreover, the rehabilitation movement, which developed partly in response to the needs of blinded veterans, has grown much more effective over the years in preparing recently blinded individuals to meet the new challenges they face in the workplace and in other aspects of everyday life. Educational strategies designed to meet the special needs of blind children, while mainstreaming them whenever possible, have also become increasingly successful. The resulting integration of large numbers of competent, independent blind people into general society has had a very beneficial effect on public attitudes. These legal, institutional, and societal changes will be discussed more fully in Chapters 6 and 7.

Organizations that receive donations of time and money from the public, in order to provide services to some members of the blind population, have had a mixed effect on societal attitudes. On the negative side, some of these organizations appeal to the public's fear of blindness in their fund-raising activities, portraying "the blind" as despairing people who are in need of charity and sympathy because they "live in darkness." Although such an approach may increase donations, it has the unintended side-effects of fostering harmful stereotypes.

Fortunately, such methods are nowadays the exception rather than the rule: Most service organizations help to increase the sighted public's understanding of blindness, by spelling out to potential donors the needs that the organization addresses, and by bringing volunteers into frequent contact with blind people. There are many thousands of such volunteers nationwide, whose activities include reading to blind people, helping them with shopping, and transcribing requested items into braille (Pogorelc, 1972). Those volunteers who have a patronizing view of blind people when they begin to work for an organization (Carroll, 1961), often develop more realistic attitudes as they gain more experience.

That attitudes can be changed by such everyday interactions has been experimentally demonstrated by Cole (1970/1971). The subjects in his study, college students enrolled in a child psychology class, were divided into small discussion groups which met regularly during the semester. Shortly after the start of the term, each group was joined by an additional student, who was actually a confederate of the experimenter, posing as a member of the class. For most of the groups, the newcomer was blind, but for two control groups a sighted confederate was used. At the beginning and again at the end of the semester, each student filled out a number of questionnaires, including the Attitude to Blindness scale. A variety of questionnaires, dealing with different subjects, were completed in order to reduce the chance that any student would suspect that an experiment on attitudes toward blindness was being conducted. As an additional way of monitoring attitudes, the group discussions were videotaped, and the videotapes were later studied to determine the manner in which the sighted students addressed the blind member of the group, as well as to make a record of any attitudes toward blindness that were expressed. As for the confederates, they simply tried to make a constructive contribution to the group discussions, which generally had nothing to do with blindness. At the end of the study, each student was asked to describe the extent of his or her previous contact with blind people.

The main result of the study was that those subjects who had had no previous contact with blind people underwent a substantial improvement in their opinion of blind people over the course of the semester: Their Attitude to Blindness scores dropped dramatically. Students who *had* had previous contact with blind individuals showed little or no attitude shift as a result of their discussion-group interaction with the blind student, suggesting that previously formed opinions, whether positive or negative, can be hard to change. Not surprisingly, students in the two control groups, which had been joined by sighted confederates, showed no change in Attitude to Blindness scores. In summary, Cole's study shows that the attitudes of many people can be changed, for the better, by extended interaction with a friendly and capable blind person. It is presumably changes of this type that are now occurring more and more in settings outside the laboratory, and that are the major cause of the gradual improvement in societal attitudes toward blindness.

## REACTIONS TO THE LOSS OF SIGHT

In this final section, we will turn from a consideration of how sighted people feel about blindness, to how blind people feel about it. The answer to this question depends very much on whether they became blind early in life, or at an age that allows them to remember what it was like to be sighted. Those in the former group do not "miss" sight; they know that the faculty exists, that life in a world where most people can see would be more convenient if they could too, but they do not long to see the sunset. It is more difficult to summarize the feelings of adventitiously blind people, because the extent of their visual memories, and the ways in which the loss of sight changed their lives, span a wide range. Those who have been blind for only a few years do sometimes regret that their sight is gone; they can remember the pleasures and opportunities that vision afforded. For the most part, however, they are concerned with the present and future more than with the past, and think about vision only to the extent that everyone thinks, sometimes, about earlier periods in their lives. Moreover, the visual world is recalled less and less vividly with the passage of time (Berger, Olley, & Oswald, 1962), so that visual memories necessarily play a small role in one's thinking if decades have passed since the loss of sight.

This acceptance of blindness on the part of those who have been without sight for a substantial period of time contrasts sharply, however, to the emotional upheaval that most adventitiously blinded people suffer at the time their sight is lost. This traumatic experience is very difficult to go through, in part because a person who loses sight as an adult still has, for a time, the attitudes toward blindness that he or she held as a sighted person. If these were negative, as we have seen is often the case, then the newly blinded person will have a residue of feelings of pity, and perhaps even of loathing, now directed toward himself or herself. In addition, the loss of sight is a heavy blow, apart from any preconceptions the person has about it; to be cut off from what was previously a major source of contact with the world necessarily produces a profound emotional reaction.

While the feelings and behavior of a newly blinded person in the period immediately following the loss of sight of course differ from one individual to another, a consistent overall pattern is usually discernible: He or she acts and feels like a person in mourning (Blank, 1957; Carroll, 1961; Cholden, 1958; Schulz, 1980). There is debate as to why the reaction takes this form. Some say that the loss of anything important, whether a loved one, a part of the body, or even a treasured object, brings on this same reaction, which is called one of "mourning" only because the death of another person is the most widely recognized of these precipitating events (Blank, 1957). Carroll (1961), on the other hand, argues that the reaction resembles mourning because in fact many newly blinded people think of blindness as akin to death. Moreover, he maintains, the person's life is so different after blinding from what it was before, the adjustments that need to be made are so far-reaching, that the blind person is a different individual from the sighted person he or she once was; in a way, the sighted person has "died," to be reborn as a blind person. Lowenfeld (1981) has criticized this point of view as unduly metaphorical, and—more importantly—as unhelpful to the blind person, whose successful adjustment to blindness often involes maintaining a strong sense of continuity with the period of his or her life preceding the loss of sight.

Although the reaction is interpreted differently by different workers in the field, their descriptions of it are in close agreement. It usually occurs in stages, the first being one of shock, the second, one of depression. This in turn is usually followed by a recovery of the person's normal mood, and an interest in learning to cope with the practical problems which blindness presents.

The stage of shock is one in which the person does not come to grips emotionally with the fact of blindness. In psychodynamic terms, the person's ego is not prepared to assimilate this major loss, and insulates itself from reality. This insulation may take several forms. The person may have a feeling of unreality, as if the events he or she is experiencing are happening to someone else, or are only a dream; he or she may sit motionless for long periods of time, giving little if any response to questions. Particularly if some sight is left, the person may deny that any visual impairment exists, attributing the absence of useful vision to some external factor, such as dimness of the light. Alternatively, the person may believe the loss of sight to be temporary, insisting that another doctor will be able to do what his or her present ophthalmologist has been unable to accomplish.

This period of shock may last only a few days, or stretch on for weeks, depending on such factors as the suddenness and completeness of the visual loss, how definite the physician is in explaining the nature and future course of the impairment, and the individual's emotional makeup (Cholden, 1958).

The shock is followed by a period of deep depression, during which the reality of blindness and its implications get through to the person. He or she feels that the joy has gone out of life, that it is not worth living. The practical problems imposed by the blindness seem insuperable, and the person feels that he or she is a worthless burden to the family. The professional consensus is that this phase of the reaction to blindness is a necessary one, which ought not to be postponed by encouraging unrealistic hopes for a return of sight. The depression may last for weeks, but should eventually lift, so that the person gradually comes to show again a normal interest in everyday life.

Because the blind person's ability to progress through these emotional phases depends to a large extent on the reactions of family members to the situation, it is important to ask what their thoughts and feelings are likely to be during this period of crisis. As in the case of the blind person, individual differences account for the details of their reactions, but there is an overall pattern which is common to most people (Schulz, 1980). This is the same pattern of shock and depression, although usually in milder form, that the blind person himself or herself shows. In the shock phase, family members may refuse to accept that the blindness is a permanent condition; and in the depression stage they may have feelings of guilt for unkind things said or done years earlier to the now-blind person. It sometimes happens that a spouse or other family member seeks to escape from his or her own depression by rejecting the blind person—either by leaving, or by withdrawing emotional support and interacting only on a superficial level (Bauman, 1972; Schulz, 1980). Many families, however, are drawn closer together by the crisis, and even if family members don't always say and do the most appropriate things, the blind person benefits from evidence of their caring.

But when the blind person's depression is lifting, and he or she begins to take an interest in life once again, the protective behavior of family members, which was so comforting during the early period of blindness, can gradually come to be *over*protective. Family members may urge the blind person to "be careful" when moving about; may hurry to do for the blind person things that he or she is trying to accomplish independently; and may avoid burdening him or her with everyday family problems and decision making. Although this solicitous behavior is well intentioned, it has the effect of hindering the blind person's recovery of self-confidence. Another common source of tension within the family is that the blind person may be unable to continue in his or her previous job. Emotional stresses ensue as belt tightening becomes necessary, or as another member of the family becomes the breadwinner.

The best way to reduce these interpersonal strains, as well as the blind person's lingering feelings of depression and inadequacy, is for him or her to receive counseling and acquire new skills, in order to become as active a contributor to the family and to society as before. Those who accomplished this in previous eras had to do so largely on their own, improvising new ways of doing things without sight. Nowadays, however, there is an organized, systematic way of once again becoming competent and independent, both at home and in the workplace, through the process known as *rehabilitation*. It is the subject of the next chapter.

# 6 THE REHABILITATION PROCESS

In this chapter we will consider the way in which people who have become blind as adults adjust to this new situation, a gradual process known as rehabilitation. One of its most important elements is for these individuals to deal with, and begin to put behind them, their emotional reactions to the loss of sight, discussed in the previous chapter; they need to accept the reality and permanence of their blindness, but also to realize that it is not an insuperable obstacle to self-fulfillment. Another major component of rehabilitation is for the adventitiously blinded individual to learn methods, developed by past and present generations of blind people and rehabilitation workers, for efficiently carrying out a wide range of activities without vision. Mastery of these techniques and problem-solving strategies helps the person to accomplish his or her goals with respect to personal management, household tasks, returning to the workplace, recreational activities, and other aspects of life.

An adventitiously blinded person's rehabilitation can be greatly facilitated if he or she makes use of the many counseling and training services that are available today, from workers in the professional field of blindness rehabilitation. In the following sections we will first discuss the historical development of the rehabilitation movement, and then turn to a consideration of the nature of present-day rehabilitation services. The second half of the chapter deals with the variety of reading and mobility aids that currently exist: Some of these play an important role in the rehabilitation process.

Although the discussion is couched in terms of adventitiously blinded people, most of the material presented in this chapter—except for the section on psychological counseling following the loss of sight—is relevant to congenitally blind adults as well. The special challenges facing the blind child, and his or her parents, will be taken up in the next chapter.

## HISTORY OF REHABILITATION TRAINING

In antiquity, no organized assistance, let alone training, was available to blind people in helping them adjust to their disability. A lucky few were respected as bards or soothsayers, but most probably found themselves at the bottom of the economic ladder, dependent on others or working at a subsistence level. In the Middle Ages, asylums or refuges for blind people started to come into existence; these charitable enterprises provided food, shelter, and other necessities for some blind people, but made no attempt to train them for re-entry into the outside world.

The first systematic attempt to provide specialized training to blind people occurred in Europe in the 18th century, with the founding of schools for blind children. These became more numerous in the 19th century, and spread to America. Teaching was largely oral until Louis Braille invented the embossed-dot alphabet in the 1820s, making it possible for reading to be included in the curriculum. Music was heavily emphasized in these schools, the hope being that graduates could be employed in that field.

Samuel Gridley Howe (1801–1876), founder of the Perkins School for the Blind in Massachusetts, was among the first to champion the idea that blind pupils should be prepared for entrance into a wider range of occupations. It was his goal that they should be able to live normal, independent lives as adults. A solid academic curriculum qualified Howe's brightest pupils as teachers or civil servants; crafts were introduced to allow those who were manually inclined to become artisans; and a number of other career possibilities were explored for those with other aptitudes. Although he was mainly concerned with the long-term education of blind children, rather than the intensive retraining of blinded adults, Howe's widely publicized conviction that blind people are as diverse in their interests and capabilities as sighted people helped to set the stage for modern rehabilitation training.

Sheltered workshops were another forerunner of the rehabilitation movement. These were institutions, some established in the last century, in which blind people labored to make mops, brooms, and other craft items which were sold on consignment. A financial floor for many blind people, sheltered workshops were given a boost by the Wagner–O'Day Act of 1938, which encouraged the purchase of their products by the federal government. While a step toward rehabilitation in that they provided gainful employment, sheltered workshops fostered segregation of blind people in the workplace, and often lacked the resources to provide good vocational training. Many sheltered workshops are still in operation, but with the opening up of a wide range of career opportunities for blind people in recent decades, the workshops have become a less prominent part of the overall employment picture. The changing role of workshops, and the upgraded rehabilitation services many now offer, are described by Koestler (1976).

Rehabilitation, in the modern sense of the term, began in the wake of World War I, as hundreds of servicemen, disabled by combat injuries, presented a need for retraining that would allow them to return to active civilian life. But federally sponsored rehabilitation in this early period was intended mainly to help people with motor disabilities, such as paralysis or loss of an arm or leg. By and large, blind people were expected to get help from the pre-existing state commissions for the blind (Rives, 1972), which provided counseling and cooperated closely with the sheltered workshop system. Europe was ahead of the United States in this regard, with the founding of special rehabilitation centers for blind people, such as St. Dunstan's Hostel in England, and the development of new techniques, such as the use of guide dogs in Germany.

A major step in the development of rehabilitation services for blind people in this country was taken in 1929, when The Seeing Eye, Inc., was founded by philanthropist Dorothy Eustice. This nonprofit organization, supported largely by private donations, brought to America the European idea of guide dogs, and championed the goal of *full mobility:* that blind people ought to be capable of going wherever they want, without a sighted human guide. Clients came to the Seeing Eye headquarters, in Morristown, N.J., where they were matched with a dog and given a month of intensive training (of which more is said later in the chapter). Very modern in outlook, Eustice eschewed sentimentality and insisted that the dogs were workers rather than pets; she argued persuasively that they ought to be allowed to accompany their owners into restaurants and other public facilities, as they now are by law in every state. Seeing Eye continues to operate today, very much along the original lines; other guide dog schools have also come into existence.

However, not every blind person is a good candidate for a guide dog. Many people don't have the temperament needed to care for a dog and keep it in training, while others have only modest travel requirements that would not give the dog sufficient exercise. Additional mobility aids were clearly necessary.

The most important of these, the *long cane,* was invented during the 1940s by Richard Hoover, a rehabilitation instructor working with blinded World War II soldiers at Valley Forge General Hospital, in Phoenixville, Pa. Hoover realized that traditional, or *orthopedic* canes—stout sticks that people can lean on—are of little assistance to an able-bodied blind person: While they can be used to explore the ground for 30 cm or so in front of the person, a user walking at a normal pace would be unable to adjust his or her steps in time to take advantage of information gained from such exploration. What was needed instead was a cane that could be extended to a distance of a meter or so in front of the person, so that if, say, a hole in the sidewalk were encountered, he or she would be alerted in time to navigate around it. To meet this need Hoover developed a long, slender, lightweight cane, and began teaching blind soldiers how to use it.

As word of the Valley Forge innovation spread, representatives of state agencies and of other nations visited the hospital, to learn about this new type of mobility training (Williams, 1972). At about the same time, Congress passed the Vocational Rehabilitation Act Amendments of 1943, providing substantial funding to the states for the expansion of rehabilitation services, and explicitly making them available to blind people. The additional staff and resources provided by the Act made it possible for mobility programs using the Valley Forge methods to be set up in various parts of the country, and so allowed the long cane to become the most widely used mobility aid, which it remains to the present day. Another outgrowth of the Valley Forge techniques was the establishment, in 1960 and later, of graduate programs to train mobility specialists.

During this same period a new concept, that of the *rehabilitation center*, was gradually emerging (Koestler, 1976). An important figure in this movement was Father Thomas Carroll, who argued that rehabilitation should be an intensive, carefully integrated effort on the part of a number of professionals, rather than merely an assortment of unrelated training activities (Muldoon, 1986). He demonstrated the feasibility of this idea at a rehabilitation center, now called the Carroll Center, which he founded in Newton, Mass., in 1954; his approach has since been widely adopted. In an influential book, *Blindness: What it is, What it Does, and How to Live with it* (Carroll, 1961), he argued that psychological services are a major part of rehabilitation.

The development of a network of rehabilitation centers was greatly aided when Congress, in its 1965 revision of the Vocational Rehabilitation Act, provided funds for their construction (Rives, 1972). Centers are now firmly established as an efficient way for an organized program of rehabilitation services to be provided to adventitiously blind people.

Against this background of stability, however, dramatic changes are occurring in the technology of mobility aids and other types of rehabilitation aids. An emerging question for the next decade is whether these innovations, some of which are still at the research and development stage, will bring about a qualitative change in the level of rehabilitation services available to the average blind person. The question is in part a financial one, since many of the most helpful new devices are expensive, and beyond the means of someone who has lost his or her job because of blindness.

These recent developments will be discussed later in the chapter, in the section dealing with sensory aids. First, however, let us consider the overall nature of rehabilitation training as it exists today.

## PRESENT-DAY REHABILITATION SERVICES

When an adult becomes blind, he or she is well advised to contact the state agency that provides specialized services to blind people. In some states this is an administratively distinct unit, such as a Commission for the Blind, while in other states services are provided through a Department of Vocational Rehabilitation or other multifaceted government agency. In some areas, accredited private agencies offer comparable services (American Foundation for the Blind, 1988).

### Informing Clients of Available Services

Whether public or private, these agencies are a valuable resource, for they provide their client—that is, the blind person—with information about the range of services available to him or her. Different people may be interested in different types of services: A lawyer might ask about training in braille and other reading methods; a homemaker would want to learn how to cook and carry out other household activities without sight; a cab driver, having lost his or her job, might need career counseling, and information about financial support during the transitional period of unemployment. In addition, all would probably want to learn personal-management skills and mobility techniques, and might request psychological counseling, to find out if the strong emotions they were feeling were normal, and to learn how to minimize the stress of their changed situation on family relationships.

The agency representative would explain that there are two ways of obtaining rehabilitation services. One is for the client to continue to live at home, availing oneself of services that are available locally. Some people have compelling reasons for staying near home: The blind person might be an invalid who requires a lot of care from family members, or might have family responsibilities that make long-term absence from home a severe hardship. In such a situation, the client can meet with service providers in their offices, or, if that is not feasible, they can visit the client's home for a series of sessions.

For many adventitiously blinded people, however, rehabilitation skills can best be learned by going to a rehabilitation center. As explained earlier, this is a facility, either publicly or privately owned, in which instructors of various rehabilitation skills are located together, along with rehabilitation counselors and other specialists. Clients who live near a center may commute to it, but more often, the client lives at the center during the period of training, which normally lasts from 1 to 6 months. Rehabilitation centers have the advantage, over home instruction, of "total immersion" in the subjects to be learned. The client is able to concentrate without interruption on the skills he or she is acquiring, making learning more efficient than that derived from occasional lessons. Moreover, the client's exposure to other blind people at the center, including some who are at a more advanced stage of retraining, increases his or her understanding of the potential benefits of the rehabilitation process, and facilitates acceptance of blindness.

Another difference between home lessons and rehabilitation at a center is that the latter approach normally involves periods of separation from family members. Although emotionally stressful for both the client and his or her family, this temporary separation can benefit clients with overly protective families, by taking them out of an environment in which their attempts at independence are discouraged. On the other hand, it may be difficult in this situation for family members to learn new attitudes and behaviors that will facilitate the blind person's continued adjustment once he or she returns from the center. To minimize this problem, many rehabilitation centers schedule "family weekends" and other opportunities for family members to visit and learn more about the training the client is receiving, and the progress he or she is making.

The agency representative will normally make a recommendation to the client as to which instructional setting seems more appropriate for him or her, based on a consideration of all of these factors. Since the skills to be learned are very much the same whether taught at home or at a center, we will confine our description of rehabilitation training to that which takes place in the latter type of setting.

Soon after arriving at a center, the client is introduced to his or her *rehabilitation counselor*. This person's job is to get to know the client, so as to recommend the optimal mix of types of training. This involves a series of discussions with the client, as well as the administration of a number of tests. For example, the client's remaining vision is carefully measured, to determine whether low vision aids—discussed later in the chapter—would be of benefit. Also generally included are tests of mood and personality, designed to guide psychological counseling by a clinical psychologist or psychiatrist.

## Psychological Counseling

The job of the psychologist or psychiatrist is a demanding one: to help the client accept blindness while overcoming the gloomy view of it that he or she probably held before the loss of sight. The situation is often complicated by family members who have urged the blind person to keep hoping for a return of sight, thus postponing the adjustment process and increasing his or her fear of blindness (Cholden, 1958).

One of the main functions of psychological counseling is to make clear to the client the distinction, discussed in Chapter 5, betwen *becoming* blind, which is always an emotionally devastating event, and *being* blind, which is usually not accompanied by depression or any other particular emotional state. It is primarily the change in visual status that is disturbing, rather than blindness itself. Once the adventitiously blinded person appreciates this distinction, he or she will understand that feelings of deep depression are entirely normal, even justified, when sight is lost; but that, with the passage of time, it is possible to adjust to blindness so that life becomes as full and rewarding after the transition as it was before.

Blindness does not, of course, eliminate pre-existing emotional problems, which may in fact be brought to a head by the stressful period through which the newly blind individual is passing. Psychological counseling for many clients thus cannot be limited to the reaction to vision loss, but must address the whole person.

There is no one agreed-upon method of psychological counseling. Strategies vary, depending on the personality of the client, and the stage in the reaction to the loss of sight that the client has reached when he or she arrives at the center: Someone who, several months after the loss of sight, still speaks of an imminent return of vision, might require a different sort of counseling from someone who had already experienced, and recovered from, a deep depression. The professional background of the psychologist is also a factor. Some are inclined by training to break through the client's defenses and get him or her to confront problem areas directly; others, preferring to let clients work through problems at their own pace, will suggest broad outlines for a counseling session, but let the client do most of the talking. Group sessions, in which several clients are brought together, are often helpful in allowing each person to see that his or her problems are not unique (Cholden, 1958). If possible, the client's family should also receive psychological counseling, for they, too, are undergoing a stressful transition.

## Training in Independent Living Skills

Even while these sessions with the psychologist continue, the client is receiving rehabilitation training in several areas. The first things to be learned are personal management skills, such as how to use a braille watch, and how to keep track of money (bills of different denominations are folded in different ways).

Methods of carrying out household chores, such as cooking and home repair, are also taught. Many of these techniques have been widely used by blind people for decades: For example, in pouring a cup of coffee, one hooks a fingertip over the rim in order to know when it is full. New techniques are steadily being invented, however, as the home environment changes and different needs arise. Commercially available specialty items, such as modified kitchen implements and carpentry tools, make many tasks easier and safer.

One of the most useful skills clients learn is that of labeling. Braille labels can be made by the client and used to identify clothing, cans of food, household chemicals, and other objects. In addition, many prelabeled items, such as embossed telephone dials, appliances, playing cards and game boards, are commercially available.

Given the importance of labeling, most clients learn at least the rudiments of braille; a minority choose to study it more intensively. Other reading aids, from "Talking Book" records and tapes to electronic devices and specialized computers (described on pp. 124–128), are also introduced.

Throughout their stay at the center, most clients take regular lessons in mobility. The nature of mobility training, the travel aids that are currently available, and others that are in the testing stage, make a complex and exciting story that is taken up in detail toward the end of the chapter.

## Vocational Preparation

One of the main goals of rehabilitation centers is to prepare the client for re-entry into the workforce, and services that are job-related are therefore usually given heavy emphasis. For example, many of the discussions between the client and his or her rehabilitation counselor deal with choosing a career. Some people can return to their old line of work, perhaps with some carefully worked-out changes in the way they do their job, but many cannot.

To help these latter individuals in weighing their options, a test of interests such as the Kuder Occupational Interest Survey (Kuder, 1966) is typically given. In this test the client is asked to consider triads of everyday activities, such as carpentry, reading, and gardening, and to say which of the three he or she would enjoy most. Through a large number of such questions, the test-giver seeks to determine the types of work that would be most satisfying to the client.

Additional tests of a more "hands-on" nature are often given, by specialists called vocational evaluators, to assess the client's aptitude for a particular career, such as secretarial or factory work. Unfortunately, few tests have been devised to measure potential for highly skilled or professional employment (Vander Kolk, 1981). Not every test is necessary or appropriate for every client; a particular test ought to be given only when the counselor and client are in agreement as to its potential usefulness.

Toward the end of a client's period of rehabilitation, much of his or her time may be spent in preparing for the specific career chosen. Most rehabilitation centers offer training in a number of occupations. For example, in training people to become medical transcribers—whose job it is to type hospital documents on the basis of tape-recorded dictation by physicians—the blind person is taught how to operate the dictation equipment, how to type, and how to use a multivolume braille medical dictionary.

Because a series of laws, beginning with the Randolph–Sheppard Act of 1936, provided funds for training blind vending-stand operators, and gave them priority in federal buildings, the operation of stands and related facilities is another widely taught vocation. Though periodically modified by Congress and challenged in court, the Randolph–Sheppard program still involves more than 3,000 vendors and vending facilities, fewer than half of which are on federal property (Partos & Kirchner, 1986).

Many clients, however, will not want to pursue any of the career options for which specific training is offered in the center, and for them, vocational development ought to make use of resources outside the center, in the community. Cooperation with groups and businesses beyond the confines of the center is therefore one hallmark of a successful vocational rehabilitation program.

Perhaps the most important part of vocational counseling is to make clients aware of their own capabilities, and to help them develop a flexible problem-solving approach to the obstacles presented by the lack of sight. Recent technology, combined with old-fashioned ingenuity, can often provide a way for blind people to carry out jobs from which they have traditionally been excluded. For example, many jobs in which money handling is required have traditionally been off limits to blind people, because of their inability to see the difference among bills of different denominations. However, a recently developed electronic aid called the Talking Paper Money Identifier (American Foundation for the Blind) solves this difficulty: It uses a light pen to recognize bills, and synthetic speech to tell the user what they are. Blind people who are familiar with a variety of such resources probably have better career prospects than those who have concentrated exclusively on learning a specific vocational skill during the rehabilitation period.

## Evaluating Rehabilitation Services

In concluding this survey of rehabilitation services, it is appropriate to ask how well the system works. Once clients leave a rehabilitation center, do they continue to use the skills they learned there, and can they find suitable employment?

There is evidence that many people do make subsequent use of their rehabilitation training. A 1980–1981 interview survey of 60 people whose cases had been closed by the Michigan Commission for the Blind between

1977 and 1979 found that more than a third used braille, and roughly half traveled out-of-doors independently (Ponchillia & Kaarlela, 1986). Some of the people interviewed had declined to receive braille or mobility instruction, and some probably did not master these skills during training; the figures therefore underestimate the degree to which rehabilitation skills, once learned, are maintained.

How helpful is the training received in a rehabilitation program, as far as employment is concerned? It is difficult to answer this question conclusively, but we can begin by asking what proportion of clients have found employment by the time they "graduate" from a rehabilitation program. Kirchner and Peterson (1982) have addressed this question by examining data supplied by the Rehabilitation Services Administration on all visually impaired clients whose cases were closed during 1980 by the programs it oversees. Of the roughly 31,000 such individuals, 47% were gainfully employed at the time of case closing. This is nearly a threefold increase over the 17% who were employed at the time they *entered* the rehabilitation program. It falls short, however, of the roughly 60% of the general population, aged 16 and older, who were employed during that year (U.S. Bureau of the Census, 1984).

Gainful employment is not the only indicator of successful vocational rehabilitation: The proportion of clients who were working (exclusively) as homemakers was also greater at the time their cases were closed (32%) than when they were referred to the agency (16%). Almost four-fifths of departing clients, then, worked as homemakers or were gainfully employed, or both.

There are, however, complicating factors that must be kept in mind when attempting to draw conclusions from these statistics. First, there is no "control group" of recently blinded individuals who were monitored during 1980 but who did not receive rehabilitation services. (Agencies of course encourage all eligible persons with whom they are able to establish contact, to avail themselves of appropriate rehabilitation services.) Thus we cannot be sure that the increase in employment seemingly brought about by rehabilitation programs might not actually be due, in some degree, to the passage of time: While most adventitiously blinded people are temporarily distraught by the loss of sight, some might be able to return to work after several months, even without formal rehabilitation training. One way for future researchers to address this issue would be to compare the employment records of people who have been in different types of rehabilitation programs—say, programs that use different methods of counseling. Clear differences in employment outcomes between the two programs might indicate the relative usefulness of the two types of counseling.

Another difficulty in interpreting the existing employment data is that they do not tell us what happened to the clients *after* their cases were closed. Perhaps some who were employed lost their jobs, while others found jobs. Finally, the figures give no indication of job satisfaction: We do not know what proportion of rehabilitation clients were in work appropriate to their talents and interests.

Despite all of these reservations, the Kirchner–Peterson data still suggest a cautiously optimistic interpretation: that rehabilitation programs do much good, although they do not completely achieve their goals.

This same conclusion is drawn by many rehabilitation counselors themselves, in evaluating their own programs. In a recent survey of 167 counselors in 97 public and private rehabilitation agencies, most rated themselves as being partly successful in helping their clients with career development (Bagley, 1985). Asked to rate the extent to which they were able to meet various career-related needs, on a scale from 1 (never) through 2 (occasionally) and 3 (often) to 4 (always), the average rating was a moderate 2.78. Interestingly, the counselors felt that they were most successful in helping clients to "learn about low vision aids and other special equipment which might help them in training or on the job." Many identified an absence of information about local career opportunities for their clients, and the lack of an organized plan for capitalizing on such opportunities, as factors hindering the rehabilitation process.

Anecdotal reports by former clients suggest that they, too, give rehabilitation programs mixed reviews. The system is widely acknowledged to provide valuable training in a variety of practical skills. Many former clients believe, however, that vocational counseling tended to steer them toward "safe," well-established careers, rather than into more challenging fields. No doubt what is needed by the average rehabilitation counselor is more detailed information on the many careers, including professional, managerial, and technical ones, in which blind people have been successful, and the special methods, if any, that they use in performing their jobs without vision (Peterson, 1985). Such information would provide general guidance even if a client decided on an innovative, untried career.

Vocational preparation, with follow-up monitoring, is generally the last step in the rehabilitation process, and with it, our overview of rehabilitation services ends. One factor in rehabilitation, however, will now be discussed in greater detail: the use of sensory aids, especially recently developed ones, that give promise of substantially benefitting blind people.

## TECHNOLOGY AND REHABILITATION

Most sensory aids for the visually impaired fall into one of three categories. First are optical or electronic devices that help people with low vision to make the most of their remaining sight; second are aids that help people who do *not* have useful remaining vision to read and carry out related tasks; and third are mobility aids. These three types of aids are discussed in the following sections.

## Low Vision Aids

It will be recalled from Chapter 1 that only about 10% of legally blind people are totally blind, the remainder having at least the ability to distinguish light from darkness. In fact, roughly half of those who are legally blind have a visual acuity of 5/200 (the ability to see at 5 feet what someone with normal vision can see at 200 feet) or better, and more than one in five are on the borderline of legal blindness, with a visual acuity of about 20/200 (National Society to Prevent Blindness, 1980).

Any remaining vision is of some value, and a visual acuity of 20/200 is very useful indeed, in many cases allowing the person to read newspaper headlines and other large print. Special optical and electronic devices can often be of benefit by enlarging print or other visual stimuli so that they are within the range of the person's acuity (Faye, 1976; Jose, 1983).

*Optical Aids.* The simplest low vision aids are positive *spectacle lenses* worn like ordinary eyeglasses. Normally, glasses compensate for a person's near- or farsightedness: For example, a farsighted person whose eyes are actually focused at a distance of 6 meters, when he or she is trying to read a book held in the lap, can wear positive lenses to allow the book to be sharply imaged on the retina. But the same principle can be applied to a person with low vision, even if no refractive error is present. Say that a person with diabetic retinopathy is trying to read a book held in the lap, but is prevented from doing so by reduced acuity, despite the fact that the book is sharply imaged on the retina. A positive lens worn in the spectacle plane will now cause the book to be *out* of focus when held in the lap; the person's eyes will instead be focused at a nearer distance, say, 10 cm from the face. When the book is moved to this nearer distance, it will be imaged sharply on the retina, and, because of its nearness, the letters will loom large enough in the field of view for the person to read them. In other words, a positive lens worn in the spectacle plane allows targets to be seen as larger, not because it magnifies them, but because it allows them to be held closer to the face than would otherwise be possible. For example, a lens which allows an object to be examined from a distance of only 2–3 cm permits the retinal image to be about 10 times larger than it would be if the object were held at a normal reading distance (Faye, 1976, p. 89). A limitation on this type of aid is that it is difficult to hold an object very close to the face without blocking the illumination on it.

Another approach is to use a positive lens as a *hand magnifier*, holding it a short distance above the book or other object to be examined. Doing so increases the size of the retinal image without requiring the book to be held at any particular distance from the eye; the only requirement is that the lens be kept at a distance of approximately one focal length from the book—a distance ranging from 30 cm or so for the weakest lenses down to about 3 cm for the strongest. The effect of these lenses ranges from less than a doubling of the image size, up to about a twelvefold magnification, for people with very low acuity (Faye, 1976, p. 79). With these strongest lenses, however, only a small amount of print can be seen through the lens at any given time, simply because it is so greatly magnified.

The aids mentioned so far are designed to help with near vision. They are not of benefit when one wishes to read a street sign, or identify a person half a block away. For this type of situation, a different and more elaborate magnifying device, such as an *afocal telescope*, made up of multiple lenses, may be of benefit.

*Electronic Aids.* Other types of visual aids are electronic in nature, such as *closed-circuit television*. With this device, a television camera faces downward onto the printed material, and an image of the text appears on an adjacent television screen. Its major advantage over positive spectacles is that the paper is at a comfortable distance for page turning, letter writing, and (with a special attachment) typing; and, in contrast to the hand magnifier, it leaves both hands free for these activities. An additional positive feature of a closed-circuit television is that it can be made to display either black letters on a white field, as in normal reading, or white letters on a black field. Many people with cataracts and other visual impairments find troublesome glare to be reduced by this reversed-contrast arrangement. Moreover, the system is usually equipped with a zoom lens that can provide as much as fortyfold magnification (Faye, 1976, p. 76), an enlargement that is beyond the reach of either the spectacle lens or the hand-held magnifier. On the negative side, however, is the fact that a closed-circuit television is not easily portable: Someone who uses it for home or office reading will need another type of aid to read labels in the grocery store.

Similar in appearance to a closed-circuit television display, but based on different technology, are large-print computer displays. A variety of hardware and software configurations are available to make computers accessible to individuals with low vision.

Still other devices, using other optical and electronic principles, are available. Considerable expertise and judgment are required to determine the optimal aid, or combination of aids, for a particular person. The low-vision specialist who advises the client on this subject—an optometrist or ophthalmologist with supplementary training—must take into account the client's visual acuity and field defects, visual requirements, and other factors, such as motor ability in holding or operating an aid. Moreover, the client must be thoroughly trained in the use of an aid if he or she is to derive maximum benefit from it (Jose, 1983).

## Nonvisual Reading and Computer Aids

People who cannot benefit from low vision aids, because their visual impairment is too severe, must use nonvisual methods of reading. The two most common of these, as discussed in Chapter 4, are listening to another person read aloud, whether in person or by means of a sound recording, and reading braille. However, electronic devices now make it possible for a blind person to read print without the mediation of a reader or transcriber. Instead, a machine is used to convert the print into tangible or audible form.

*The Optacon.* One such instrument, the Optacon (Telesensory Systems, Inc.), allows the user to feel the shape of print letters. This device consists of a miniature camera, which is held against the printed page, and a rectangular array of vibrating metal rods which convey tactile information to the user. The camera contains a 5 × 20 grid of tiny phototransistors, onto which the print is imaged; these receptive units communicate with the Optacon's electronics, which in turn activate the rods in the tactile array. Light falling on a particular phototransistor affects the vibration of a particular rod, with the result that the pattern of vibrating rods mimics the shape of the letters lying within the field of the camera.

The user holds the camera with one hand, moving it along a line of print, while the index finger of the other hand remains motionless on the vibrating tactile array (see Fig. 6.1). The field of the camera is only slightly larger than a letter of average print, so that the user receives information on a letter-by-letter basis, as is the case when Grade I braille is read. It will be recalled from Chapter 4, however, that embossed patterns having the shapes of the print letters are harder to identify than braille letters, and this raises the possibility that Optacon patterns, though vibrating rather than stationary, might likewise be more difficult to read than braille. This seems to be the case. Although individual reading rates vary widely (Craig, 1977), 35 words per minute may be considered typical for experienced Optacon users. This is less than half the rate at which braille is normally read. Moreover, many hours of training and practice are usually required for even this moderate level of speed to be achieved.

What, then, is the advantage of the Optacon? The answer is that it makes accessible to the user the vast array of printed materials that are not available in braille. Major magazines and best-selling books are regularly "brailled" by the Library of Congress, but less popular material is not. The many short documents that fill everyday life, such as doctor bills, office memos, and club newsletters, are likewise not in braille. Blind people have traditionally bridged this gap by asking or hiring a sighted person to read such items. The Optacon frees its user from this requirement, by allowing the blind person to read directly from the printed document. Because reading with the Optacon

FIGURE 6.1. How the Optacon is used. This man is reading a printed document by scanning it, one line at a time, with the miniature camera. The camera is operated by the dominant hand, the left in this case. With his right index finger he receives information about the scanned text through a tactile array of vibrating rods. The control unit housing the tactile array contains circuitry that activates the rods in response to signals arriving through a cable from the camera. A zoom control on the camera allows the user to adjust it for different sizes of print. Also shown in this picture are a folding cane, and a braille slate and stylus for making notes. (Photograph by Telesensory Systems, Inc. Photography Dept. Reproduced by permission.)

is relatively slow, however, it is seldom used to read books or other extended material.

*The Kurzweil Reading Machine.* There is another reading aid which is more suitable for long items: the Kurzweil Reading Machine (Kurzweil Computer Products, Inc.). Because of the cost of this device, the number of individuals who own one is limited, but it is available for use in a number of libraries, schools, and other public facilities. It is a desktop machine consisting of three parts: a computer, a keyboard, and a box called the *scanner*, which has a glass window like that of a photocopy machine in its upper surface. The user places the printed material face down on the window, and operates keyboard controls that activate a camera lying beneath the glass, causing it to locate and sweep across the print: It scans one line after another, automatically adjusting its movements to take the distance between lines into account. The computer recognizes letters by comparing patterns sent to it by the camera with codes stored in memory. The computer then uses this information to trigger synthetic speech, with the result that the printed material is read aloud by the machine. The loudness and pitch of the machine's "voice," as well as its speaking rate (up to 250 words per minute), can be adjusted by the user.

Because letters and numbers differ somewhat in appearance from one printed or typed document to another, the computer may initially have difficulty in reading a particular book or magazine, mistaking some characters for others. After reading a page or so of text, however, it learns how to identify the characters in that particular typeface without error.

The synthetic speech in the Kurzweil Reading Machine is based on standard rules of English phonetics (for example, that *c* is given a hard pronunciation when followed by *a*, *o*, or *u*, but a soft pronunciation when followed by *e* or *i*) rather than on recognition of particular words. Thus words that violate the rules will be consistently mispronounced by the machine. The user can, however, instruct the machine to spell out words that he or she cannot understand. An additional aid to understanding is that the machine takes punctuation into account in order to give sentences the proper inflection.

In a way, the Optacon and the Kurzweil Machine are analogous: One converts print into tactile patterns, the other converts it into sound. There is, however, a fundamental difference between them. The Kurzweil actually recognizes letters, while the Optacon merely puts them into tangible form, leaving the job of recognition up to the user.

*Computer Systems.* The principle of a computer controlling synthetic speech, which is embodied in the Kurzweil Reading Machine, can be applied to other computers as well. A number of companies now make synthetic-speech devices, and the software necessary to allow output from a computer to activate them. A blind user can thus type commands into a computer using a keyboard, and listen to the machine's responses. Programming is possible using this method, as is the use of pre-existing programs to read out files of information that are stored on tape, disks, or in the computer's memory.

Even braille itself can now be used in new ways. Analogous to the synthetic speech output devices are others that produce a brailled version of the computer's messages to the user. These may take the form either of hard-copy braille, produced by an embosser, or paperless braille, in which rods, similar to those in the Optacon but arranged into discrete braille cells, can be elevated through holes in a sieve-like surface to mimic the dots of braille.

A person may have different computer needs in different situations: Businesspeople, researchers, and students may find that no one reading aid can do everything they want. It is possible, however, to combine or interface these devices so as to produce a more versatile information-processing system. For example, a system in operation at the University of North Carolina at Chapel Hill (Kessler, 1984) includes a Kurzweil Reading Machine, an Information Through Speech computer and a Facit printer (Maryland Computer Services, Inc.), and an LED–120 braille printer (Triformation Systems, Inc.). A visually impaired student using this system to work on a term paper might begin by making the Kurzweil machine "read" a number of scholarly articles. Selected passages could be sent directly from the Kurzweil to the IFS Computer, in digital form, for storage. Later, the student could enter his or her essay at the computer, which repeats in synthetic speech the material typed in at the keyboard, and check on the accuracy of statements by referring again to the scholarly articles stored earlier. Once composed, the term paper could be printed out using the Facit printer (in either regular or large print), while the student would keep a braille copy produced by the LED–120 printer.

It is possible to assemble existing machines into a variety of such computer systems, accessible to blind people, with the optimal configuration being determined by the needs and degree of residual vision of the users. Moreover, as synthetic speech, computer vision, and other fast-moving technical fields continue to advance, we can expect that existing devices will be steadily improved, and new ones designed. With so many types of hardware and software available, blind people and organizations serving them have a problem that did not exist a few years ago: choosing among competing computer products. Careful planning and investigation are necessary before any computer purchase is made, whether the purchaser is an individual desiring speech output for a home computer, or a corporation or university planning an elaborate system for use by more than one person. To help in this decision-making process, the American Foundation for the Blind established in 1986 a National Technology Center at its New York headquarters. The Center will test existing equipment, develop new instruments when feasible, and gather and disseminate information about the cost, reliability, and customer satisfaction ratings of various devices. Rehabilitation centers can also play an important role in this process by giving interested clients some hands-on experience with computer equipment.

A problem for potential users, however, is the high cost of many reading and computer aids. Some rehabilitation programs will supply a particular aid to a client at no charge, if it will help him or her to be employed at a higher level than would otherwise be possible; some companies will purchase an aid to allow a visually impaired employee to perform a particular job; some aids are available for use in libraries and other public settings; and some blind people can afford to buy a reading or computer aid out of their own pocket. Often, however, none of these alternatives is available. Creative solutions to this funding problem will be increasingly needed in the future, to ensure that the expanding array of electronic sensory aids is accessible to all who can significantly benefit from them.

## Mobility Aids and Their Use

Present-day mobility training teaches skills that were virtually unknown at the turn of the century. In this section we will discuss these skills, and the mobility aids that they require.

The most important aids at the present time are the long cane and the guide dog: Their value has been repeatedly demonstrated since their introduction decades ago. Starting in the 1960s, however, another approach to the problems of mobility has been gathering momentum. This is the attempt to build electronic travel aids that will sense environmental objects and inform the blind person of their presence. In the following sections, the two traditional travel aids, and a number of more recently developed electronic devices, will be considered in turn.

Before we begin, it is worth noting that the information provided by the "obstacle sense," discussed in Chapter 2, is *not* sufficient for mobility. Even those individuals who are very adept at this echo-detecting skill find that it is unsatisfactory for locating dropoffs and obstacles close to the ground (Bledsoe, 1980), and is severely disrupted by environmental noices such as those caused by rain and traffic; thus it does not afford safe travel, although it can provide much useful information.

*The Long Cane.* The most widely used mobility aids are the long cane, a metal tube with a curved handle, and its cousin, the folding cane. Both have a tip of solid nylon or a similar hard material. With the one-piece construction of its shaft, the long cane is the more rigid and lighter of the two; but many users are willing to forgo these advantages for the convenience of the folding cane, which can be stashed in a briefcase or coat pocket when not in use. Aside from these differences, the two devices are very similar, and statements about the long cane in the following discussion apply to the folding version as well.

While the use of the long cane is a complex skill, the basic idea is to extend the cane forward and down, so that its tip is just off the ground, and to swing it from left to right repeatedly while walking. The arc traced by the cane should be wide enough to alert the blind person to any obstacles that he or she is approaching, and to provide additional information, such as the location of the edge of the sidewalk. The user should swing the cane to the left while stepping forward with the right leg, and vice versa, so that advance warning of an obstacle on one side is obtained before the leg on that side moves forward (Hoover, 1950). The cane is tapped against the ground at each end of its arc, in order for the user to detect dropoffs, to obtain information about the texture of the ground, and to provide a sound that facilitates echo location.

Once they become skilled in its use, many blind people find that the cane satisfies their mobility needs. Others, however, find that it does not give them information about the terrain early enough. Since the average user's cane is only 1.2 to 1.4 meters in length (Farmer, 1980), the user must stop quickly once an obstacle is detected if collision is to be avoided. An additional shortcoming of the cane is that it does not help the person to detect overhanging obstacles, such as store awnings or tree limbs.

*The Guide Dog.* Based on his or her professional experience, the mobility instructor may recommend another mobility aid to some clients. The most time-tested of these is the guide dog, but it is only suitable for certain individuals (Whitstock, 1980): those with the temperament needed to care for a dog and maintain a good working relationship with it, and with the physical strength to handle it. A guide dog is especially appropriate for those individuals who want to travel on foot a lot, through new environments, since this activity will exercise the dog and allow its skills to be challenged constantly. A substantial amount of residual vision in a legally blind person can be an argument against using a guide dog, since the person tends to rely on his or her own vision, causing the dog's unused skills to deteriorate.

Should the mobility instructor and the client decide that a guide dog would be desirable, the client then applies to one of the guide dog schools located in various parts of the country (American Foundation for the Blind, 1988). The client's application is carefully reviewed to determine suitability, and, if the school decides that the applicant could benefit from a dog, he or she goes to the school to receive a dog and be trained to work with it.

The majority of guide dogs are German shepards and retrievers, obtained by the schools as donations, or from their own breeding programs. Most schools follow the lead of The Seeing Eye in asking families living near the school to raise the animals for the first year, in order to socialize them and give them a wide range of experiences similar to what they may later encounter in a client's home. This is typically done in collaboration with an organization such as the 4–H Clubs.

After this initial year, dogs return to the school and are trained for several months before the arrival of their future masters. During this period they learn to obey simple commands, to stop at curbs and other dropoffs, to avoid obstacles (including overhanging ones), and to wear a harness with a rigid U-shaped handle that their master will hold. Perhaps the most difficult skill to teach the dogs, but one of the most valuable, is intelligent disobedience (Whitstock, 1980). Dogs must learn to refuse a command that would lead their owner into danger, such as into the path of an oncoming car.

Once trained, a dog is assigned to a client who has recently arrived at the school. After 4 weeks of working with and learning to take care of the dog, the client takes it home, where it can be expected to work for about 10 years. After this, the dog is typically too old to work hard, and becomes a pet—either its owner's or someone else's—while the blind person returns to the school for a new dog.

Either a long cane or a guide dog is sufficient for mobility, and under normal circumstances they are not used simultaneously. Even someone who uses a guide dog, however, can benefit from cane skills. The cane becomes important when the dog is sick and cannot work, or on occasions when the person does not want to be accompanied by the dog.

Despite the great value of the long cane and guide dog, many blind travelers wish they could obtain more information about the environment than either of these traditional aids is able to provide. It is the goal of many scientists and engineers to design electronic devices that will fill this need, by obtaining information about the environment and communicating it directly to the blind person. A variety of such devices have been built and tested, with mixed results: Some proved unsatisfactory, while others were found to be of value and are now commercially available. New instruments, now on the drawing board, will capitalize on the lessons learned from earlier models. Rather than attempting to survey all the electronic travel aids that have been built, we will concentrate on three that are representative of this rapidly changing field: the Laser Cane (Nurion Industries, Inc.), the Sonicguide (HumanWare, Inc.), and the computer-based aid of Collins (1985) and Deering (1985), which is still in the research and development stage.

*The Laser Cane.* This device is a modified long cane that uses laser beams (too weak to be harmful) to probe the environment (Farmer, 1980). The beams are of an infrared wavelength, and so are not visible. There are three beams, all of them narrow, which emanate from lasers located close together on the front of the cane, a few centimeters below the crook (see Fig. 6.2). One beam travels upward, and so encounters overhanging obstacles, such as tree limbs; another travels slightly downward, striking posts, vehicles, and other objects in front of the person; the third beam is aimed more steeply downward, and is designed to detect dropoffs such as the edge of a curb. These are called the up, forward, and down channels, respectively. When the beams encounter objects, they are reflected diffusely. Light is scattered in all directions, but a small fraction of it returns in the direction of the cane, where sensors located about 30 cm below the lasers detect it. There are three sensors, facing in different directions so that each is able to receive light from one channel only.

To warn the user, each channel activates a tone. These are distinguishable, being high, medium, and low in pitch for the three channels, respec-

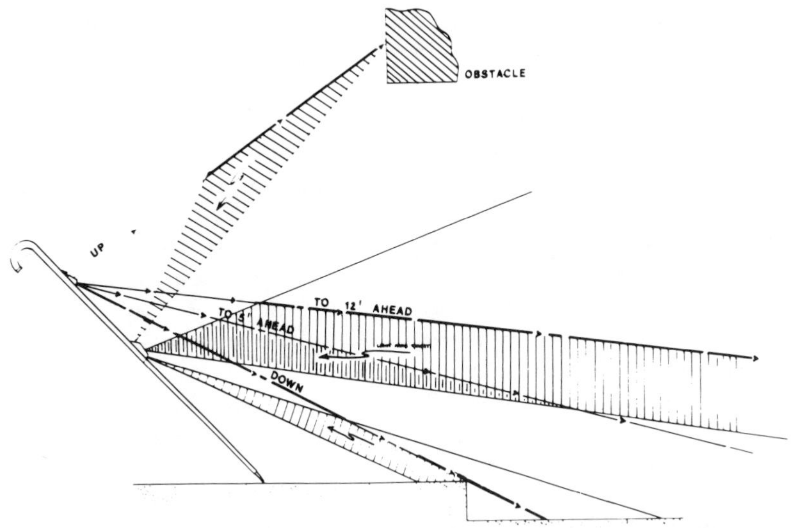


FIGURE 6.2. The Laser Cane. The lines with arrows pointing away from the cane represent the three beams of infrared light that originate near the crook. The beams labeled "up" and "down" are fixed, while the intermediate beam can be made to travel in either of two directions, depending on whether the user is in a cluttered environment (for which the beam labeled "to 5′ ahead" is appropriate), or in a more spacious one ("to 12′ ahead"). The hatched angles extending from the center of the cane indicate the zones of acceptance of the three sensors, which are oriented in such a way that each picks up reflections from a different one of the three laser beams. A traveler using the Laser Cane in this situation would be alerted to the overhanging obstacle by a high-pitched tone, and informed of the downward step by a low-pitched tone. (From "Mobility Devices," by L. W. Farmer, in *Foundations of Orientation and Mobility*, R. L. Welsh & B. B. Blasch (Eds.), 1980, New York: American Foundation for the Blind. Copyright 1980 by the American Foundation for the Blind. Reprinted by permission.)

tively. The up and forward channels sound their tones when an obstacle is detected, while the down channel emits a tone to indicate a dropoff. The forward channel activates a vibrating pin in contact with the user's index finger, as well as the medium tone; some users prefer to switch this tone off and rely on the vibration alone. An additional control can change the range of the forward channel from 3.6 to 1.5 meters (i.e., from 12 to 5 feet), the shorter range being more appropriate in a cluttered environment.

The principle used by the down channel to detect dropoffs is a clever one. There will be a moment, as the user approaches a curb, when the downgoing beam just skims over the curb and reflects off the street. Since the detector is lower on the cane than the emitter, reflected light will be temporarily unable to reach it because the curb is in the way. It is this interruption of the down beam that triggers the Laser Cane's low-pitched tone.

The Laser Cane has a clear advantage over an ordinary long cane, in that it gives warnings of obstacles and dropoffs sooner, and is capable of signaling overhanging objects. These capabilities give some users a greater feeling of confidence than they have with an ordinary long cane (Goldie, 1977). The device has some limitations, however: It can fail to alert the user to the presence of a glass door, through which the beams may pass unreflected, while a shiny opaque surface may reflect beams away from the cane and thus prevent a warning. Proficiency in the use of the Laser Cane requires considerable training, even for those who already know how to use a long cane. The Veterans Administration training course, for example, involves some 80 hours of lessons (Farmer, 1980). This and the cost of the device are presumably the main factors that keep the Laser Cane from being more widely selected as a travel aid by long-cane users.

*The Sonicguide.* This device, also called the Binaural Sensory Aid, presents an even richer array of information to the user. Like the Laser Cane, it depends on the reflection of emitted signals, but these are pulses of ultrasound, rather than of infrared light. A more important difference, however, is that while each channel of the Laser Cane can, by design, indicate the presence of only one obstacle at any given moment, the Sonicguide presents the user with simultaneous information about any and all objects that are currently reflecting signals. Just as the narrow beams of the Laser Cane make its selectivity possible, the Sonicguide's broad emission of ultrasound, filling an area that is 30 degrees of arc from top to bottom and 40 degrees from side to side, allows its signal to reflect from numerous objects (Warren & Strelow, 1985).

The transmitter and receivers of the Sonicguide are located in eyeglass frames worn by the user. Ultrasound is emitted from the center of the frame, just above the nose, and on reflection is picked up by two receivers flanking the transmitter and somewhat above it. Returning ultrasound is converted to audible sound and presented to the user through small plastic tubes that fit into the ear canal, without blocking out ordinary sounds from the environment.

Unlike the Laser Cane, which emits three tones of unvarying pitch, the pitch of the sounds presented to the user by the Sonicguide varies systematically with the distance of the obstacle being detected: the greater the distance, the higher the pitch. This is made possible by the fact that early parts of an ultrasound pulse reflect back from objects in time to be mixed with later parts of the same pulse that are just leaving the transmitter. Each pulse steadily drops in frequency while it is occurring, like a sliding musical note, so that the reflected waves are always higher in frequency than those outgoing waves they meet on their return to the instrument. The closer an object is in the environment, the briefer will be the round trip made by the ultrasound, and the smaller the difference in frequency between the transmitted and reflected waves present at the receiver. It is this frequency difference that determines the pitch heard by the user (Warren & Strelow, 1985).

Another feature of the Sonicguide is that its two receivers, one on the left and one on the right, give the sounds presented to the subject a stereophonic quality. Reflections from an object off to the right will strike the right receiver broadside, but the left receiver at a glancing angle, resulting in a difference in the intensity of ultrasound picked up. Since the left channel is connected to the left ear, and the right channel to the right ear, the result of these reflections will be a louder sound presented to the right ear than to the left. When such differences occur in everyday life, they are effortlessly perceived as coming from a source that is off to the side. With training, the same is true of sounds from the Sonicguide.

Because the pitch of the sound indicates the distance to a reflective surface, a smooth object, such as a wall, will produce a purer tone than an object consisting of multiple surfaces at different distances, such as a bush. The latter will produce a scratchy, rough sound (Farmer, 1980). Skilled users come to recognize the sounds of particular types of objects.

In summary, then, the Sonicguide is a rich source of information as to the location and nature of objects within a broad arc in front of the user; it does not, however, provide much warning of dropoffs or objects close to the ground, and should therefore be used in conjunction with a guide dog or long cane. Not surprisingly, it takes many hours of training to become skilled in the use of this device, but those who have worked through this initiation phase typically find it to have been worth their while in terms of the additional information that they can now extract from the environment (Thornton, 1975). As with the Laser Cane, cost and the effort involved in learning to use the device explain why it is not more widely used.

Although the makers of most electronic travel aids recognize that training is required before users can benefit from an aid, not enough research has been done to determine the best possible methods of training. Should trainees be allowed to learn by trial and error, under the watchful supervision of a mobility instructor, or should the instructor give step-by-step instructions? Do artificially simple training exercises facilitate or hinder later training in a complex environment? For most of the electronic mobility aids, these questions have not been answered by careful laboratory research.

Yet Warren and Strelow (1985) have shown that laboratory experiments can sometimes suggest training strategies that are not intuitively obvious. They asked blindfolded, sighted subjects to sit at a table and to use a

Sonicguide to locate vertically oriented pieces of pipe that were suspended in air above various positions on the table. On a given trial, a single object was presented, and the subject was asked to point to a spot on the table directly below the pipe, based on auditory signals presented by the Sonicguide. To measure the effectiveness of training, subjects were first given a series of training trials, then a series of test trials. In each training trial, the subject reached up and examined the pipe by touch after pointing to a spot on the table. Since these pointing responses were often in error, the subject would frequently need to explore the space in front of him or her in order to find the pipe. After 72 training trials, the test phase of the experiment began. Subjects were still asked to point as before, but were no longer allowed to reach up afterwards to determine if they had pointed accurately.

Some subjects in these experiments simply wore the Sonicguide in the normal way, in that they were free to turn their head from side to side while listening to the auditory signals. In this situation it is relatively easy to position the head so that the sound is equally loud in the two ears, which in turn means that the person is facing the object. Subjects became skilled in doing this, with the result that in the testing phase, their directional errors were a modest 6 degrees, on the average. In the case of other subjects, however, Warren and Strelow rigidly attached the Sonicguide to the table, so that subjects had to hold their head still in order to use it. No longer able to solve the task by turning their head until the sound was balanced in the two ears, subjects had to learn the particular amounts of loudness inequality at the two ears that corresponded to particular object directions. Yet they also did reasonably well at this more challenging task, making errors during the test phase (in which head movements were still prevented) that averaged 12.5 degrees. A third condition, in which the head was motionless during training but allowed to move during testing, produced errors that averaged 9.5 degrees.

The surprising result of the experiment, however, came from a fourth group of subjects who were free to move their head during training, but had to hold the head still during testing. These subjects had directional errors averaging 19 degrees, a large figure approaching that which would be produced if subjects were only guessing as to the objects' locations. The implication is that with the head free to move during training, subjects turned to face objects, on a trial-and-error basis, and never bothered to learn that a sound that was, say, 7 decibels louder in the left ear indicated an object 10 degrees left of the midline. When deprived during testing of their ability to turn the head, they were not able to interpret these interaural differences well enough to point toward the objects.

This finding is of practical importance, for it shows that if potential users are free to move their head at all stages of training, they may not learn to make optimal use of the Sonicguide's directional information. Yet it is important that the interaural-difference cue be learned, for in everyday life a blind person often needs to identify the direction to an object—such as an approaching bicycle—immediately, without hunting for it by turning the head from side to side. It follows, then, that training with the Sonicguide ought to include considerable practice with the head held motionless. Other improvements on existing methods of training, with various aids, probably await discovery through systematic laboratory investigations of this kind.

*Computer-based Aids.* More recently conceived electronic travel aids rely on a computer to process incoming information before it is passed on to the user. One such device, currently being developed at the Smith–Kettlewell Institute of Visual Sciences in San Francisco, uses optical information in a way that mimics, in a simplified way, some of the neural processing strategies that occur in a normal visual system (Collins, 1985; Deering, 1985).

This mobility aid obtains its information from a small television camera that is mounted above the user's shoulder. The video signal from the camera is sent to the computer, where it is broken up into a grid or matrix that is 64 units on a side. The computer takes note of the intensity of light falling within each of these 4,096 tiny areas of the picture. This digitizing process converts the television picture into a form that can be more easily processed by the computer. Adjacent areas of the picture are then compared with one another to locate abrupt changes in light intensity, which may indicate borders or edges. Once all elongated edges have been identified, the computer examines groups of them, searching for meaningful combinations of edges that will indicate the presence of particular types of objects. This is done by comparing the patterns picked up by the camera with others that are stored in the computer's memory. For example, the computer might recognize two long vertical lines, close to each other, as a pole. Synthetic speech is then used to inform the user of the identity of the object. At the same time, one of 16 mechanical stimulators worn under a headband is activated, gently tapping the user's forehead in a position that indicates the direction to the object; distance is indicated by the number of taps.

This computerized travel aid is not yet ready for everyday use. The main difficulty is that only objects with simple shapes can be recognized. But the field of computer vision is advancing rapidly, and before the end of the century there will probably be computers that can recognize a large number of common objects. The important thing about this aid is the conceptual advance that it represents: It uses a computer to free the user from much of the mental work required by earlier electronic travel aids. Other researchers are working along similar lines (Tou & Adjouadi, 1985).

In summary, there are already a number of useful electronic travel aids, and the long-term outlook is good for the development of new devices, incorporating small but powerful computers, that will make mobility a less taxing activity for blind pedestrians than it is now.

## REHABILITATION OF DEAF-BLIND PEOPLE

So far our discussion of rehabilitation of blind people has not taken account of the fact that many of them have additional disabilities. For example, a large number have severe impairments of both vision and hearing. Since each of these sensory impairments affects roughly half a million Americans, that is, one in every 500, it might be expected that there would be about 1,000 people in the country—one out of $500^2$—who are at least partially deaf and blind. In fact, however, the figure is above 10,000, according to data compiled by the Helen Keller National Center for the Deaf-Blind (Kirchner & Peterson, 1980). The reason for this large number is that blindness and deafness are statistically correlated: Some risk factors associated with blindness are also associated with deafness. For example, prenatal conditions such as rubella, and childhood diseases such as scarlet fever, can affect both vision and hearing, as do certain inherited conditions such as Usher's syndrome, a combination of retinitis pigmentosa and degeneration of the auditory receptors. Automobile accidents, wartime injuries, and other traumas severe enough to damage one sensory system often damage others as well. Finally, both vision and hearing tend to deteriorate with age, so that many elderly people have severe losses in both systems.

Rehabilitation of deaf-blind people is a profoundly challenging and complex topic, which space does not permit us to deal with in depth here. Just as there are degrees and types of vision loss, which suggest different rehabilitation techniques and aids to the blindness rehabilitation worker, so are there many patterns and degrees of hearing impairment. When these two impairments are combined, rehabilitation efforts must begin with careful assessment of the person's remaining sensory capacities. Those who are totally deaf and blind (a small minority) necessarily depend on the sense of touch to receive most of their information about the world.

Linguistic communication, which is accomplished verbally by blind people, and through sign language or other vision-dependent methods by deaf people, presents a major problem in the case of people who are both deaf and blind. The method normally used to solve it is the manual alphabet, in which the hand of the "speaker," cupped in the hand of the recipient, assumes configurations that represent letters. An alternative method, that of drawing letters on the palm, has the virtue that it requires no training on the part of the speaker, but is sometimes difficult for the recipient to follow in that the drawing of one letter apparently produces after-sensations that interfere with the perception of succeeding ones (Heller, 1986).

A related problem for many deaf-blind people is social isolation (Yoken, 1979). Acquaintances without sensory impairments, and even those with a single impairment, may avoid them, or at least not take the trouble to communicate with them effectively.

Despite these communication difficulties, however, successful rehabilitation is possible. Many deaf-blind people can learn to read braille, or have enough residual sight to make use of low vision reading aids, so that their educational horizons need not be limited, and a range of vocational options is available to those who receive appropriate training. Some electronic aids on the market today, such as the Optacon, the Laser Cane (the central channel of which has a tactile output), and computer and telephone accessories that use braille, are of value to them; and likely future aids will further expand their opportunities. Additional information on deaf-blindness is available in McInnes and Treffry (1982), Meshcheryakov (1974/1979), and Walsh and Holzberg (1981).

Deaf-blindness is not the only multiple sensory loss: With advanced diabetes, for example, some people experience both a deterioration of vision and an impairment of the sense of touch. Furthermore, a substantial number of visually impaired people also have a motor disability, such as paralysis or spasticity. In still other individuals, sensory losses may occur in combination with mental handicap, a subject that is treated in depth by Ellis (1986). Data from government surveys indicate that such multiple impairments are common. Nearly three-fifths of the visually impaired population have an additional sensory loss, or a motor or cognitive disability (Kirchner & Peterson, 1980).

As the number of impairments increases, so does the complexity of the rehabilitation process. If rehabilitation workers are to help multiply handicapped individuals reach their full potential, they need to understand clearly the nature of a given person's impairments, but even more important, to get a clear idea of the person's underlying—and sometimes hidden—potential. Sometimes a client's disabilities may require individualized rehabilitation services that go beyond the competence, or the resources, of a local rehabilitation center; in that case the individual may be referred to a regional or national center that specializes in multiple disabilities (Koestler, 1976). Even the best present-day rehabilitation methods, however, are inadequate to the needs of some clients. What is required above all is systematic research, to develop and evaluate new rehabilitation strategies, sensory and performance aids, and training methods.

# 7 THE BLIND CHILD

Eleanor H. L. Leung
Mark Hollins

According to the National Society to Prevent Blindness (1980), there were in 1978 some 6,500 legally blind children under the age of 5 in the United States. It is widely believed, however, that their number is increasing, and will continue to do so in the future (Ferrell, 1984).

Demographic factors, particularly the age of the mother, are expected to play a role in this increase. Although women can bear children from their early teens until their middle forties, the uncomplicated birth of a robust, full-term baby is most likely when the mother is in her twenties. Mothers in their early teens, in contrast, with their still-developing reproductive systems, are more likely to give birth prematurely, which greatly increases the chance of visual impairment. Another problem in the case of pregnant teen-agers is that, because of social factors and because their education is incomplete, many do not seek or obtain adequate prenatal care. The result is that their babies often have low birth weight or other health problems that may include visual impairment. Women who become pregnant in their late thirties and beyond face other but equally serious hazards, particularly the gradually increasing risk of birth defects. Despite these problems, however, the proportion of babies born to mothers at the extremes of the child-bearing years is increasing, as larger numbers of teen-agers become sexually active soon after reaching adolescence, and as many women in their twenties decide to postpone children until their careers have been well established or other goals have been met (Clarke–Stewart & Koch, 1983).

Another important factor in the expected increase in the number of blind children is that medical advances have made it possible for many premature infants, who in the past would have died, to survive. This improvement in health care helps to explain the "second epidemic" of retinopathy of prematurity, which has been widely reported in recent years (Kolata, 1986), although not yet fully documented.

In view of the anticipated increase in the number of blind children, it is very fortunate that major, qualitative improvements have recently been made—and continue to be made—in our understanding of how a blind child develops, and how that development can be facilitated. Authoritative reviews of this rapidly expanding field of knowledge reflect both its scientific (Warren, 1984) and educational (Scholl, 1986) aspects.

Perhaps the most crucial insight has been the realization that the parents of blind children must become active participants in their development (Ferrell, 1986b; Stotland, 1984). Before the 1970s, many parents were led to believe that decisions about their blind child's education and social development were best left to professionals and institutions. Infancy and the preschool years were widely regarded as periods of passive coping until it was time for primary responsibility for the child's training to be taken over by experts. Most parents of a young blind child knew they were supposed to provide a supportive environment in which the child would feel loved, and to minimize the child's feelings of differentness—both admirable goals—but many didn't have a clear idea of how to do these things, or of what else to do. When the child reached school age, he or she was typically sent to a full-time residential school, or a special education day program that did not solicit parental input.

New approaches to the education of blind children were gathering momentum, however. Attitudes toward blindness were gradually changing, partly as a result of the dramatic increase in the number of blind children that occurred during the 1950s and 1960s. Thousands of infants developed retinopathy of prematurity in the decade before 1954, when oxygen was shown to be a factor in the etiology of this disease, and thousands more were born blind as a result of prenatal rubella, contracted during the epidemics of 1964 and 1966. These large cohorts of blind children could barely be accommodated by residential schools and other segregated, special education programs. As educators began to seek alternative educational strategies, and as the parents of blind children began to demand a larger role in their education, the need for mainstreaming became increasingly obvious.

The Education of the Handicapped Act, passed by Congress in 1975, formalized and increased the pace of the mainstreaming process. This law (P.L. 94-142) states that all school-age children, regardless of their disabilities, are entitled to a free public education in the least restrictive setting, even if local programs specially designed to serve their needs have to be created. The impact of this law, and of the changes in public opinion of which it is a manifestation, has been enormous: 80% of all legally blind children in the United States now reside at home and attend regular schools, compared with 19% in 1948, when the residential school movement was at its peak (Roberts, 1986). In 1986, the provisions of this law were extended to handicapped children under 5 years of age (P.L. 99-457).

Moreover, research in the last 20 years has led to a greatly improved understanding of how blind children develop (Warren, 1984), and special educators have started to put into practice many of the lessons learned from this research (Scholl, 1986). Since some of these practical implications have to do with ways to facilitate social and cognitive development during the preschool years, educators now increasingly encourage the parents of a blind child to take an active role in the child's education virtually from the moment of birth. Several handbooks offering suggestions along these lines have recently been written for the parents of visually impaired children (Ferrell, 1985; Kastein, Spaulding, & Scharf, 1980; Scott, Jan, & Freeman, 1977).

Blind children, compared with sighted children, often show lags in one or more areas of development. Not all blind children experience these delays, however, and those who do, show considerable individual variation in their rate of development. Moreover, a child may show rapid development in one area, such as language, but progress more slowly in another area, such as mobility. These individual differences depend in complex ways on a number of factors, such as the degree of residual vision and the presence of other impairments, but particularly on the amount of early training, whether formal or informal, that the child receives. The age norms presented in this chapter for the attainment by blind children of specific developmental milestones are therefore merely estimates, because they were determined at a time when active parental involvement and early educational intervention were less common than they are today. These recent trends may be expected to lead to the earlier emergence of many skills, requiring a revision of developmental norms for blind children in the near future.

The aim of the present chapter is to describe the unique problems these children encounter in a visually oriented world. Special emphasis will be given to the infancy period, and therefore to children who are blind from birth or shortly thereafter, because it is in infancy that the blind child's needs and behavior have traditionally been least understood, but about which most has been learned in recent years. Although all aspects of development are intertwined, we will for the sake of exposition divide the subject into two broad areas: the development of a child's ability to relate to other people, and the development of his or her ability to interact with and understand the physical environment.

For simplicity we will usually refer to a child either as "he" or "she" in the remainder of the chapter: An arbitrary decision was made to use "he" in the section on social development, and "she" in the section on interaction with the physical environment. Every statement in the chapter, however, is intended to apply equally to girls and boys.

## SOCIAL DEVELOPMENT

### Parent–Infant Interaction

When a parent or other caregiver approaches a sighted infant, the infant will often gaze at the adult's face, smile, and vocalize. Initially, these behaviors may not be truly social in nature: The infant emits them almost reflexively, without expecting a response in return. Nevertheless a response from the parent is typically elicited. In addition to feeding the infant, changing his diaper or otherwise providing physical care, the parent typically smiles back at the infant, looks into his eyes, touches him affectionately, and talks to him. Parent and infant soon become engaged in a repetitive, sometimes rhythmic sequence of smiles, vocalizations, and touches, accompanied by mutual visual regard (Brazelton, Koslowski, & Main, 1974; Stern, 1974). This sequence of reciprocal behaviors is periodically interrupted for a brief rest period whenever a member of the pair, usually the infant, looks away. Looking at the other person, or not doing so, thus becomes a form of communication or signaling between parent and child. Other examples of "body language" develop as time passes: By 6 months of age, the child's facial expression conveys a variety of emotions, from coyness to indignation; by 9 months, he reaches toward an out-of-reach object to demand it; and by 12 months, his points elicit parental naming of objects.

A blind infant will also smile and vocalize, but cannot establish eye contact with others. Selma Fraiberg, a child psychiatrist who carried out a detailed longitudinal study of the social and cognitive development of blind infants (1977), found that the parents typically feel discouraged when their visual regard is not reciprocated and their smiles are not returned. Unable to infer the child's interests and feelings from the direction in which his eyes are pointing, the parents may feel they are powerless to establish a close bond with him. The blind infant's facial expression is similarly uninformative: It conveys happiness or unhappiness, but, typically, little else. As a result of this lack of visual feedback from the infant, the normal turn-taking aspect of parent–infant interactions may not develop fully in the case of a blind infant and his parents.

Fraiberg (1979) found, however, that there are ways for parents to establish a close relationship with a blind infant, and to read his signals accurately. Although it is true that the infant's smile can only briefly and occasionally be elicited by the parent's voice, tactile stimulation, such as "bouncing, jiggling, tickling, and nuzzling," is very effective in making the infant smile or laugh.

Instead of looking exclusively at the infant's face, Fraiberg suggests, parents should attend to the movements of his body—particularly his hands. By the end of the second month, the infant is using them to seek out the mother's hands and face during feeding. In the next few months a pattern is set up in which periods of active fingering alternate with periods of immobility or withdrawal of the hand. This behavioral sequence is reminiscent of, and may be analogous to, the bouts of looking and smiling by which the sighted infant interacts with his caregiver. Paying close attention to the "body language" signals of the child, and reciprocating them tactually while speaking to him, are an important way for parents to facilitate his social development.

Fraiberg's (1977) careful observations revealed another important fact: The stages of attachment of the infant to his parents are comparable with those manifested by a sighted infant, although certain aspects of this developmental process were delayed in most of her subjects. One aspect that was not delayed was their growing tendency to respond in different ways to their parents and to a stranger. By 3 months of age, the babies often smiled in response to their mother or father's voice, but not to the voice of a stranger; and between 7 and 15 months, the infants struggled and cried when held by a stranger. These are normal behaviors, and appropriate for these ages.

The blind infants' changing responsiveness to separation from their mother often did not follow the schedule characteristic of sighted infants, however. At about the age of 8 months, the average sighted child will become upset if his mother leaves the room. Blind children show the same reaction, Fraiberg found, but not until the end of the first year; and when separation distress does occur, it is very intense. In cases of prolonged separation, as when the mother went to work or to the hospital, the blind children showed abnormally severe distress, with extended screaming, and regression to more infantile forms of behavior. Upon the mother's return, the children clung to her, in some cases clawing at her face and arms, behavior that Fraiberg interprets not as hostility, but as a desperate attempt to hold onto her.

Why do some measures of attachment, such as fear of a stranger, indicate a normal rate of social development, while another measure—separation distress—indicates a developmental lag? One answer, according to Fraiberg, is that a blind infant is often slow to realize that people (and objects) continue to exist once they are out of reach and not making any noise. As awareness of this fundamental truth gradually develops, the young child passes through a period of stressful uncertainty as to whether a departing parent will ever return. Only as the child grows confident of his parents' permanent existence and affection is he able to accept temporary separation from them. (The subject of "object permanence" is an important one, to which we will return several times in this chapter.)

Another factor that can have a much more serious effect on social development is that, in some cases, parents attempt to keep some "emotional distance" between themselves and their blind infant, either because they seek to avoid the distress his blindness causes them, or because they are unable to read the infant's social signals, and so wrongly conclude that he is not anxious for their affection. One clinical case that illustrates the harmful effects of withdrawal by the parents is that reported by Omwake and Solnit (1961). Their patient, referred to as "Ann," was blind nearly from birth as a result of retrolental fibroplasia. Ann and her twin sister were born 2 months prematurely, and Ann was very small. Because of respiratory problems, she was given oxygen at high concentration; at the time no one knew that this treatment was itself a cause of the blinding retinal disease being found in so many premature infants. Ann's mother, already upset at the unexpected arrival of twins, sank into a profound depression on learning that Ann was blind. As time passed, the mother dealt with her depression by withdrawing her emotional commitment to Ann. The day-to-day care of the blind infant was delegated to a maid, and when contact with Ann was unavoidable, the mother interacted with her in a tense and wooden manner. The father and other members of the family likewise showed little interest in the child.

At the age of 3½, Ann was brought to a psychiatric clinic because she was emotionally disturbed. She clung to her mother, would not permit the therapist to touch her, and did not respond to the therapist's attempts at communication. When in the 14th session, her mother left the room, Ann reacted violently, writhing and screaming. After this episode she was somewhat more at ease, and gradually came to accept the friendship of the therapist, who related to Ann by playing songs for her on a piano. Eventually the child began to engage in doll play with the therapist, acting out her feelings toward family members. Ann gradually improved, and as she did so, her family began to accept her. When the therapist ended her account of Ann, after 5 years of therapy, the child still had problems, but seemed to have a good chance for normal emotional development.

It is to be hoped that problems as severe as Ann's will become increasingly rare as the needs and capabilities of blind infants come to be better understood by their parents, and by the general public.

## Development of Language Skills

By the end of a child's second year of life, words are expected largely to replace gestures and other types of "body language" as the predominant form of communication, whether the child is sighted or blind. A blind child's family eagerly awaits his first words in the hope that the child's language development will proceed normally. But a large potential impediment exists which threatens to hinder such development: The rate at which information about the size, shape, and position of objects can be picked up is slower for a blind child than for a sighted one. Thus a sighted child can scan a shelf of toys in a few seconds, while an equivalent haptic inspection would take a blind child minutes, at least. He may therefore have difficulty following the normal flow of a conversation between two adults and/or older children that deals with their surroundings. Imagine, for example, a conversation between two sighted children in a garden: "There's a caterpillar on your cucumber plant." "That's not mine–mine is the one next to the flowers." A blind child will understand this conversation if he already knows what the words mean, but if he has not yet learned to recognize caterpillars or cucumber plants, he may not be able to locate and examine them in time to profit from hearing the conversation. A sighted toddler would be able to see immediately what plants were in question and what a caterpillar was.

In view of this difficulty in surveying the environment quickly, it is remarkable that most blind children have an essentially normal language development. The linguistic stages through which they pass are closely comparable to those of sighted children (Landau & Gleitman, 1985), although typically somewhat delayed. By school age, the delays have been largely overcome so that the average verbal abilities of the two groups are similar (Burlingham, 1961; Matsuda, 1984; Simeonsson, 1986). In this section we will examine the similarities and differences between the language development of blind and sighted children, and how they and their families are able to overcome the potential difficulties mentioned earlier.

The age at which sighted children can say two words ranges from about 10 to 23 months; half can do so at 14 months (Bayley, 1969). The median age for blind children, on the other hand, is about 18 months, with one in five achieving this milestone only after reaching age 2 (Fraiberg, 1977; Norris, Spaulding & Brodie, 1957). These first words are typically the names of important people or objects in the child's life, such as "mama," "dada," "cookie," or "juice."

Why are many blind children delayed in speaking their first words? The potential difficulty mentioned at the beginning of this section seems an unlikely explanation, for the child has no doubt heard these simple words many times while being encouraged to touch their referents. One possibility is that the concept of object permanence mentioned earlier–the realization that objects continue to exist even when they are out of reach–is acquired later by blind infants (Fraiberg, 1977); if they are not in contact with an object, and it is not making noise, they have no evidence of its existence. Sighted infants, on the other hand, can see a myriad of out-of-reach objects and thus may more easily develop the idea that objects are independent entities, deserving of a name. A related possibility is that sighted children are more easily *reminded* of out-of-reach objects: The sight of cookies in a cookie jar may trigger cognitive processes that culminate in verbal activity.

Whatever the explanation for the sometimes-encountered lag in the average blind child's utterance of his first word, moderate delays in the enlargement of his vocabulary are easier to understand. A toddler normally increases his vocabulary by using the words he already knows in new, and sometimes inappropriate ways, thereby eliciting a new, more appropriate word from a parent or sibling. For example, a sighted child who already can name his juice cup, may call an open baby food jar "cup," to which the parent will respond, "No, that's a jar." The parent understands the child's train of thought. A blind child, on the other hand, may go through the same generalization process, but with a different result (Landau & Gleitman, 1985; Millar, 1978). He may find the similarity between the cup and the jar unremarkable, but be impressed by the similarity of texture between the plastic cup and, say, plastic keys, so that when playing with the keys, he will call them "cup." If he does not hold the keys up for the parent to see, the parent does not know he is referring to them. Even if the keys are held up, the parent, more cognizant of shape than texture, does not immediately perceive the similarity between the keys and the cup, and so does not understand that the child is trying to name the keys. The parent's response, instead, might be to bring the child something to drink! Thus even a highly intelligent blind child with devoted parents may meet with some difficulty in enlarging his vocabulary.

Another problem is that haptic exploratory skills are difficult to master, and so a blind child may have difficulty in making subtle discriminations between objects (Landau & Gleitman, 1985; Warren, 1982). For example, if two toy vehicles look very different, yet feel similar on cursory haptic inspection, a blind child may have difficulty in learning to give them different names, even after an adult has labeled them separately.

Later linguistic development can be measured along a number of dimensions. On some of these dimensions, blind children are, on the average, equal in performance to sighted children, while in other ways they lag behind them. Fraiberg (1977) found, for example, that blind children respond to verbal requests, imitate words, and express their "wants" on the same age schedule as sighted children. However, their ability to combine two words denoting different ideas into a sentence lagged 6 months behind sighted children. Furthermore, adverbs, prepositions, auxiliary verbs, and other words that help to turn the telegraphic speech of young children into the smoothly flowing sentences of older children, are often slow to enter the blind child's vocabulary (Laudau & Gleitman, 1985). What causes these lags in language development?

One possible explanation is that parents talk to blind children in a way different from the way they address sighted children. Striking evidence for this interpretation has recently come from studies in which videotapes were made of blind children, in their second and third years, as they interacted with their parents. Rowland (1984) found, for example, that verbal turn taking, characteristic of conversations between a sighted child and parent, was often absent in the verbal interactions of a blind child and his parent. The parent tended to talk a lot, almost constantly in some cases, but the child showed little tendency to respond, either verbally or gesturally, to parental speech. Although the children vocalized a normal amount, they typically did so when the parent was *not* trying to hold a conversation with them. Rowland speculates that the children were unresponsive because the pauses in one person's verbal output that normally serve as a cue for the other to respond, were absent in their parent's speech.

It is worth recalling at this point that the turn-taking social behavior of parent and child normally starts in infancy, long before the baby is able to talk in words. The failure of turn taking that Rowland has uncovered in the behavior of 1- and 2-year-olds may well have had its start in the early months of life. Thus the slow development of language skills that many blind children experience may stem from difficulties they have had in communicating nonverbally with parents or other family members. Research by Urwin (1983, 1984) supports this hypothesis: She examined the development of speech in blind children whose parents were adept at acknowledging, interpreting, and reciprocating, the child's behavioral signals, to such an extent that turn-taking social interactions frequently occurred. *These* children, she found, showed little or no delay in the development of language.

This same theme is reinforced by the results of another study in which the interactions of blind children between the ages of 1 and 3, and their parents, were taped and later studied in detail (Kekelis & Andersen, 1984). For comparison with the data of the four blind children, two sighted children and their families were also included in the study. Kekelis and Andersen found that, with some exceptions, parents talked to their blind child in a way that was abnormal, and somewhat lacking in content. For example, in attempting to consolidate his language skills, they devoted a great deal of time to naming objects, and asking the child to name them, but they provided little additional information about the objects. Similarly, the parents' conversation with the child dealt mainly with the child's own activities, seldom venturing into a description of other things going on in the environment. Presumably, parents limit the subject matter of the conversation in this way because they realize that the child, at least before he can walk, has a much vaguer understanding of the out-of-reach environment than he does of his own body and actions; but in restricting their talk to these child-centered topics, parents fail to provide raw material for further language growth on the child's part. Finally, a large proportion of their speech to the child was in the form of commands, intended to encourage him to interact with his environment. When these imperatives were not obeyed, they were typically repeated again and again so that the parent's speech became, in the opinion of the investigators, intrusive.

In contrast, parental speech to sighted children contains more statements than commands (Newport, Gleitman, & Gleitman, 1977), and provides the child with a detailed, rich, and no doubt stimulating, account of his environment.

Kekelis and Andersen noted that abnormalities in the speech of the blind children reflected those in their parents' speech. Repetitive naming of objects was common, and the children talked largely about their own activities. The researchers suggest that more normal, creative conversational ventures on the part of a blind child's parents might help to broaden the child's interests, activities, and verbal behavior, even if he does not always completely understand what the parent is saying.

Factors other than what his parents say to him are probably at work in shaping the blind child's speech, however. For example, much of his verbal behavior may be motivated by a desire to get and hold the attention of the parent, rather than to communicate a semantic message (Urwin, 1983, 1984). A sighted child can hold the parent's attention with gestures and facial expression, while using speech primarily to convey meaning; but a blind child must use speech for both of these purposes. The substantive content of the child's speech will suffer if he uses verbal behavior primarily to achieve the first goal. One way in which he can easily hold the parent's attention is by imitation, parroting what has just been said to him or something he heard earlier, such as a line from a song. Perhaps this explains why *echolalic* speech is often present in the verbal behavior of blind children. Unhappily, parents who repeatedly test their child's vocabulary by asking him to name familiar objects, may inadvertently be encouraging echolalia.

In summary, a blind child and his family are often caught in a "feedback loop": The child's lagging verbal development causes the parents to concentrate on teaching basic vocabulary and concepts, with the result that the child is not exposed to the more advanced verbal stimulation that he needs.

As was stated at the outset, however, most blind children eventually do develop normal language skills, and are able to use them for effective communication—a subject to which we will return in the next section. But the way in which language competence is achieved, and how it can best be facilitated in language-delayed children of various ages, are questions that remain very much in need of scientific investigation.

This description of language development in the blind child has so far not touched on one controversial topic: the use by blind children (and adults as well) of words that refer to something visual. Many blind people say things like "I'll see you tomorrow," or "I'm going to watch the parade," as a way of conveying that they will meet you tomorrow, or listen to the parade. The use of visual terms in this way has traditionally caused concern on the part of some psychologists and educators, who feel that blind people who use these terms are saying something different from what they mean, or using words that they literally (in the case of congenitally blind people) cannot understand (Cutsforth, 1933/1980).

In the opinion of the present authors, this concern is, for the most part, misplaced. Many vision words have acquired a rich, multifaceted meaning, which can be partly understood, even by a person who has been totally blind from birth. Thus "see" really means "meet" and "understand," as well as "have a visual sensation of," and it is entirely valid and appropriate for a blind person to use it in this way. It is of course true that a blind person could use visual terms inappropriately, for example, by using color words to refer to the texture of objects, but such errors are rare, and are usually no more problematical than the occasional misuse of words by a sighted person.

An in-depth study of one blind child's language (Landau & Gleitman, 1985) makes clear that the use of visual terms need not be a source of confusion to the child; their meaning can be, to a large extent, understood, and they can be used appropriately to add to the richness of the child's language. The child in this study was Kelli, a congenitally blind girl whose language development, like her cognitive development in other areas (Landau, Spelke, & Gleitman, 1984), was comparable with that of a sighted child. The researchers found that as Kelli grew, her use of visual terms became increasingly appropriate. For example, she at first used color names indiscriminately (as many sighted children do in their first years), but by age 4 she understood that she had no way of perceiving the color of an object, and she requested help from a sighted person when asked what color an object was. A year later she knew that objects can be colored, but that events and abstractions cannot.

Far from merely parroting visual words, Kelli made a genuine, and to a large extent successful, attempt to understand their meanings on the basis of the context in which they were used. For example, when asked at age 3 to look up, down, behind or in front, she moved her exploring hands in the appropriate directions. "Look" was not synonymous with "touch" for her, because when asked to touch an object, she would simply hit or stroke it, while when asked to look at it, she manually examined the object. When asked to let the experimenter look at the back of her pants, Kelli at age 3½ would turn around if she had originally been facing the experimenter, but would remain in her original orientation if the experimenter were behind her. Kelli understood that sighted people could "look" with their hand or with their eye, but that only the first type of looking was possible for blind people. She had a comparable understanding of other visual terms.

What Kelli's example shows is that visual terms can make a valuable and enriching contribution to a blind child's vocabulary, if she has been able to obtain a reasonable, if incomplete, idea of their meaning from context. There thus seems no reason for sighted people to discourage a blind child from the use of visual terms, or for them to avoid the use of such terms in the child's presence, as has often been done in the past.

## Later Social Development

As the blind child grows, and comes into contact with more and more people outside the home, social development takes on new meaning. The challenge for the child is not just to maintain close relationships with family members, but to interact comfortably with a wide variety of people, to make friends, and to become increasingly independent.

In this task language plays a crucial role. Unable to perceive facial expressions or gestures, the blind child must pay close attention to what other people say, and learn to grasp its implied as well as its expressed meaning. Do blind children become especially skilled at "reading between the lines" of what someone is saying, so that they understand its social significance better than a sighted child would? Apparently not. A recent study by Matsuda (1984) indicates that blind and sighted children are about equal in this respect. The subjects were 33 blind school children, ranging in age from 5 to 12, and an age- and IQ-matched group of sighted children. She played for them a dozen tape-recorded messages, in which speakers implied or conveyed by tone of voice various emotions or attitudes. After each tape the child was asked to describe the speaker, and Matsuda made note of the ability of the children to detect the mood or other "communication-relevant characteristic" of the message. Blind and sighted children turned out to be equivalent in this regard. Moreover, the two groups of children were equally able to respond to each message, in a role-playing way, taking the speaker's point of view into account.

In their ability to understand the social implications of language, then, blind and sighted children are comparable. Is this also true for other aspects of social development? The traditional answer to this question by researchers has been "no," for a number of studies have indicated that blind children and adolescents are somewhat immature in their approach to social situations, compared with sighted children of the same age. Some of these studies have used a behavioral inventory called the Vineland Test of Social Maturity, which is a checklist of items such as "relates experiences" and "goes to bed unassisted." A parent, counselor, or other adult with a first-hand knowledge of the child's day-to-day behavior usually completes the checklist with regard to the child; or the tester may fill it out himself or herself, after interviewing the child and asking a knowledgeable adult to confirm any questionable answers.

Bradway (1937), a researcher at the Vineland, N.J., school where the test was developed, was among the first to apply it to blind children. Her subjects, 73 pupils at a residential school for the blind, ranged in age from 5 to 20. The test showed that the students had an average "social quotient" of 62, very substantially less than the average quotient of 100 for the sighted children on whom the test was standardized. Equally disturbing, the disparity in measured social maturity between sighted and blind children *increased* with age, unlike gaps in language and other areas (to be considered later) that decrease with age.

To what can this appreciable lag in the social development of the blind youngsters be attributed? Part of the answer may be that they were isolated from sighted peers, for a later study (McGuinness, 1970) found that blind children who commuted to a special school scored lower on the Vineland test than other groups who were "mainstreamed," even when IQ and socioeconomic status were taken into account. This isolation is not the only factor involved, however, for McGuinness found that even mainstreamed blind students scored lower on the Vineland test than sighted children of the same age. In fact, mainstreaming itself, while giving blind pupils much-needed exposure to sighted peers, can create stresses not found in a residential school that is specifically tailored to their needs and abilities (Stewart, Van Hasselt, Simon, & Thompson, 1985; Van Hasselt, 1983).

For example, in most public schools there is a heavy emphasis on written homework assignments, rather than on the oral recitations and reports that are characteristic of residential schools. A blind pupil is likely to find the mechanics of completing these written assignments more time consuming than a sighted student would, no matter how he completes them—in braille, in longhand using special tools to keep his pen on the line, on the typewriter, or even by dictating his answers to another person. Thus less time is left for playing and socializing.

Sports constitute another potential problem area (Van Hasselt, 1983). While there are some sports in which blind people can excel, such as wrestling and swimming, there are many others—notably those in which a ball moves rapidly through the air—in which their participation is severely limited, unless the equipment or rules are modified. Thus they are at risk of often being left out of these valuable social interactions.

Furthermore, there is evidence that, even apart from sports, many blind children are not fully accepted by their sighted peers (Havill, 1970). Apparently, the negative attitudes that many adults hold toward disability, discussed in Chapter 5, are common among children as well (Richardson, Goodman, Hastorf, & Dornbusch, 1961; Richardson, Ronald, & Kleck, 1974).

One way to minimize the problem of social isolation is to ensure that the blind child has good social skills, so that he can put his classmates at ease, and interact comfortably with them. Fortunately, the average mainstreamed visually impaired youngster seems to have social skills comparable to those of his sighted classmates. Careful analysis of the behavior of legally blind and sighted adolescents in a series of role-playing situations showed that the two groups performed equally well on a large number of behavioral measures, such as smiling, responding promptly in conversation, absence of stereotyped movements, and friendliness (Van Hasselt, Hersen, & Kazdin, 1985). Only on one measured skill, facility in asking open-ended questions, did the sighted group significantly outperform the visually impaired group. (Visually impaired students at a residential school showed deficiencies in several skill areas, but still scored reasonably well overall.)

There are some visually impaired youngsters, however, who show a marked lack of certain social skills, such as good posture and pleasant tone of voice (Van Hasselt, 1983). To assist such individuals, Van Hasselt, Simon, & Mastantuono (1982) developed a training program, structured around role playing, that focused on the skills in which they were deficient. For example, in one of a number of role-play episodes designed to train assertiveness, the researcher pretended to be another child who wanted to change the channel of a radio the trainee was listening to; the trainee then had to stick up for his rights, but in a nonhostile way. The researcher provided feedback to the trainees on their performance in these hypothetical situations. As a result of training, the children showed clear improvement in the targeted aspects of behavior.

In a particularly noteworthy application of these training methods, Stewart et al. (1985) established a program in which carefully selected, mainstreamed blind teen-agers went for 5 weeks during the summer to a residential school campus, for training in social skills as well as other living skills. The residential school was chosen as a locale for the program because it was ideally equipped for training the children in mobility, food preparation skills, and the like, and because it was available for use during the summer. The social and other skills of the students were carefully analyzed on an individual basis, and training was tailored to their specific needs.

Was the training beneficial? Parents clearly thought so: Asked 6 weeks after the conclusion of the program to rate its effects on their child's skills in several areas, parents gave it an average rating of 5.5 on a scale of 1 ("not improved at all") to 7 ("very much improved"). Students and program teachers likewise felt that the training was worthwhile. An important question remains, however: Did the social skills training allow these blind students to mix more easily with their sighted classmates once regular school began in the fall? Only further research can provide the answer. If it is yes, then this "Community Action Program" would seem to be one that other school systems, in conjunction with residential schools, ought to emulate.

Finally, there is now widespread agreement among educators that sex education ought to be a part of every blind child's upbringing, from an early age (Huebner, 1986). In learning about many aspects of the world, blind children can obtain, through touch, information equivalent to what sighted children obtain through vision. With regard to sex differences, however, social taboos tend to limit a blind child's opportunities to learn by touching. The parents of a blind child therefore need to devote considerable care and thought to ensuring that their child gradually develops a value-oriented understanding of sexual matters that is roughly comparable with that of his or her sighted peers. While a large number of practical suggestions along these lines are available (Schuster, 1986), there is a need for careful research to determine which teaching methods are of the greatest value, and at what age they are most helpful.

## MASTERING THE PHYSICAL ENVIRONMENT

From social development, we turn to the development of the child's ability to interact with her physical environment, by moving within it to locate objects, and by capitalizing on their properties and potential uses. Mastery of the physical environment depends on a combination of motor and cognitive abilities that facilitate one another in complex ways. We will begin this discussion by surveying the early motor development of blind children, which is in some ways delayed compared with that of sighted children; we will then go on to consider reasons for this delay, and ways in which it can be reduced; and finally we will consider the older child's emerging understanding of physical concepts.

### Motor Development

The first extensive study of blind preschool children was carried out by Miriam Norris and her colleagues in the 1940s and 1950s (Norris, Spaulding, & Brodie, 1957). From an exhaustive list of the visually impaired children in the Chicago area, these investigators selected for long-term study 66 individuals who met several criteria, such as that the child be less than 15 months of age, that she have no other serious disabilities, and that she be at least "educationally" blind—that is, that her visual impairment be serious enough to preclude visual reading, given the methods then available. These 66 children were then seen at 3-month intervals by social workers and psychologists, who assessed each child's development and offered advice to parents.

Unfortunately, the Norris study did not include a matched group of sighted children. The investigators were nevertheless able to conclude, by comparing the data they had obtained, with earlier qualitative descriptions of the development of sighted children, that in most respects blind and sighted children developed at similar rates. There were, however, specific abilities, such as walking, for which blind children were often far behind the average sighted child. By observing interactions between blind children and their parents, the researchers became convinced that these developmental lags were in large part the result of parental overprotectiveness. While most parents expressed a willingness to facilitate the development of the child in any way possible, they sometimes behaved in a way which contradicted this verbally expressed attitude—not allowing the child to explore the home freely, for example.

In the 1960s, Selma Fraiberg and her colleagues undertook a more intensive study of the development of blind infants, to which reference has already been made in the section on social development. They selected 10 blind infants for study, using a stricter definition of blindness than the Norris group: Fraiberg's subjects had, at the most, light perception. The researchers saw each infant every 2 weeks, beginning as early as possible in the first year of life.

Throughout the period of the study, the researchers offered suggestions and encouragement to the parents. This advice became more sophisticated as the investigation proceeded, for early observations gave them clues as to how blind babies develop. For example, they urged parents to pay close attention to the infant's expressive hand movements, mentioned earlier.

The Fraiberg group was fortunate in that, during the course of their study, the *Bayley Scales of Infant Development* (1969), which established norms—and normal ranges—for development in sighted infants, were published. Fraiberg (1977) was thus able to compare her data on blind infants with what was, in effect, a large sighted control group, an option that had not been available to Norris and her coworkers. These comparisons turned up a startling discrepancy between two types of motor behaviors. Those behaviors that were initiated and guided by an adult were accomplished, generally speaking, within normal limits. Thus the child's ability to sit alone after being raised to a sitting position by an adult, to stand alone after being lifted to that position, and to walk while an adult held her hands and gently pulled her along, developed nearly on schedule. In contrast, motor behaviors that depended on the child's own initiative, such as raising herself to a sitting position, pulling herself to a standing position, or walking alone, were greatly delayed. For example, the median age for walking with the hands held by an adult was 8.8 months for sighted children, 10.75 months for blind children, a small difference; while for walking across a room unassisted, the median ages were 12.1 and 19.25, a difference of more than 7 months.

Fraiberg concluded that the blind child's delays in motor development have nothing to do with muscular or postural factors, but are instead related to a lack of incentive to interact with the environment, which in turn may be due to a failure to realize that such interaction is possible. As anyone knows who has encouraged a baby to walk by dangling an attractive toy a short distance in front of her, a visual goal helps to bring out these behaviors. Was the self-initiated movement of these blind infants delayed because they had no comparable goals?

At first this sounds implausible, for it can be argued that sounds, such as the noise of a rattle or the speech of another person, should serve as a powerful goal for a blind infant, just as the sight of the rattle or person does for a sighted infant. Fraiberg's observations of the development of reaching, however, showed that auditory goals are not functionally equivalent to visual ones, for while a sighted child will reach for a visible toy by the age of 5 months, a blind infant will typically not reach for a sounding toy until 9 months. Does this mean that a blind infant is less responsive to stimuli in general than the sighted infant? It does not, for even *sighted* infants will not reach for a sounding, out-of-view toy until they are well into the second half of their first year (Freedman, Fox–Kolenda, Margileth, & Miller, 1969).

To explain this marked difference between the development of ear–hand and eye–hand coordination, Fraiberg hypothesizes that infants have a hard time realizing that the sound of an (unseen) object indicates its presence. By intermittently touching a continuously visible object, sighted infants gradually learn that the sight of an object means that the object itself is accessible. Most objects make noise, however, only when they are shaken, struck, or otherwise acted upon. Thus infants, whether sighted or blind, have little opportunity to learn that the *sound* of an object that they are not currently touching indicates that the object is nearby. Only toward the end of their first year do they make this connection.

Fraiberg goes on to suggest that a blind infant may not even realize that out-of-reach objects exist at all, until about the ninth month. Because most objects do not make noise unless she is in contact with them, she has little reason to believe that these objects are permanent things. It may seem to the baby that objects cease to exist when physical contact with them is lost. Thus, Fraiberg speculates, the blind infant may have trouble developing the concept of herself as distinct from her surroundings, for she conceives of the two as forming a single matrix.

While Fraiberg's hypothesis is a powerful and appealing one, further research is needed to establish its validity. And as she herself well understood, to explain developmental lags by attributing them to a conceptual one in no way implies that the lags are unavoidable. Perhaps, if ways could be found to enrich the baby's perceptual experiences, her motor development would be facilitated. In fact, that such acceleration is possible is suggested by the fact that the blind infants in Fraiberg's study, whose parents received considerable guidance in enrichment training from the researchers, showed somewhat faster motor development than did the subjects in the earlier study by Norris et al. (1957). In the following section we will consider these and other methods of enrichment.

## Enhancing Motor Development and Exploratory Behavior

In their study of motor development, Norris et al. (1957) observed that parents unknowingly hindered their children's development by interfering with their attempts to explore their environment. This was typically done out of concern for the child's safety. For example, a 2-year-old might be confined to a playpen while her parent left the room, because of potential dangers such as furniture with corners or sharp edges, a step leading up or down to another room, and so on. Concern for any child's safety is appropriate, but parents should address this concern not by restricting the child unduly, but by attempting to create an environment that is safe to explore. Thus sharp edges can be padded or taped, and a step can be carpeted. In general, the Norris group argued, safety precautions that would be taken with a sighted infant or toddler are also adequate for blind children of the same age.

This view is now widely accepted, and in addition, there is a growing consensus that parents should take active steps to facilitate the motor development that makes exploration possible (Ferrell, 1986a; Fraiberg, 1977; Hart, 1983; Scott et al., 1977). For example, there are several things parents can do to encourage the infant to hold her head up, a prerequisite to sitting. One is to place her face down sometimes, rather than face up, in the crib; this makes it possible for the infant to push herself up. Carrying the infant in a front- or backpack, beginning in the second month, can promote head control, as well as provide social stimulation. To get the child used to sitting, she can by 2 months be placed in a sitting position on the parent's lap facing out; and by 8 months, the infant can be seated in a high chair or doorway swing.

The infant can also be encouraged and trained to use her hands. This can be done by placing a feeding bottle, toys, and other objects in her hands; by playing "patty cake" and other hand games; and by placing a variety of objects of varying size, shape, texture, and sound-producing characteristics within easy reach. Causing an object to make noise steadily for some time before placing it in the infant's hands is a strategy that may in some cases accelerate the reaching response and an understanding of object permanence, although consistently positive results have not been obtained with this procedure (Fraiberg, 1977; Schwartz, 1984).

Once the child has begun to crawl around and explore the environment on her own, however, forcing toys on her attention may be counterproductive, provoking annoyance (Norris et al., 1957), in part because parents may not have a good idea of what the child will find interesting. A quilted ball may be boring to the child, in comparison with pots and pans pulled from a kitchen cabinet. Thus she should be allowed to take the initiative in deciding what to play with and when, to the greatest degree possible.

Walking is a complex motor activity, and a blind child may need considerable adult assistance in learning this skill, given that she cannot see how others walk. To acquaint her with the movements involved in walking, she can stand on the parent's feet, facing the parent, while the parent walks backwards (Scott et al., 1977). Even after she walks consistently, however, the child may be slow to develop a normal gait (Hart, 1983). She may shuffle, not lifting her feet off the ground, or waddle, with the legs held far apart, or slap her feet against the floor to produce sound. These behaviors, which may strike the parent simply as problems in need of correction, are probably ways the child has of preventing a fall or a collision.

At this stage of development it is desirable to have an orientation and mobility instructor begin working with the child. This professional will help the child to develop a "body image"—that is, an understanding of the dimensions and interrelations of the parts of the body—and a working knowledge of spatial concepts; these in turn will make it possible for specific travel skills to be learned (Hill, 1986; Hill, Rosen, Correa, & Langley, 1984). This training must, of course, be appropriate to the child's level of cognitive and social development, and take into account her sensory abilities. Thus the instructor must work closely with parents and teachers in order to stay apprised of her overall level of development, and to provide feedback as to the gradually increasing level of travel activity that the child is able to undertake.

The methods of enriching the child's interactions with the environment that we have discussed may be helpful not only in facilitating normal motor development, but also in reducing undesirable stereotyped behaviors or mannerisms that blind children often show. These include rocking, head banging, eye poking, and repetitive hand movements. Some stereotyped behaviors are physically injurious; all can hinder the child's normal development by putting off other people and interfering with functional, environmentally directed activities. The scientific literature on these behaviors, recently reviewed by Warren (1984), suggests that a number of factors may give rise to and sustain them, including a need for greater sensory stimulation, and a need to block out stressful situations. If parental attempts to reduce stereotyped behaviors by increasing the child's opportunities for alternative activities are not successful, more formal behavior therapy, involving the systematic administration of rewards and mild aversive stimuli, may be indicated (Blasch, 1975).

While there is general agreement among professionals in the blindness field on the procedures described in this section, there is one type of enrichment the value of which is very much in debate. This is the use, with infants and young children, of sensory substitution devices such as the Sonicguide, that were initially developed as mobility aids for blind adults.

The Sonicguide, it will be recalled from Chapter 6, is a travel aid that benefits blind adults by presenting them with audible signals indicating the distance and direction to objects in their path. It works by emitting ultrasound, which reflects from objects and returns to the user, where sensors and electronic circuitry convert the inaudible signals into audible sound. The emitter and detectors are incorporated, for cosmetic reasons, into eyeglass frames, from which thin tubes deliver sounds to the user's ears, without blocking ordinary sounds from the environment.

During the 1970s, a New Zealand research team headed by Leslie Kay, the electrical engineer who invented the Sonicguide, began developing similar instruments that were specifically designed to meet children's needs. A series of studies (Hornby, Kay, Satherley, & Kay, 1985; Strelow, 1983; Strelow & Warren, 1985) have shown that these devices can help school-age children to develop mobility skills, such as avoiding an obstacle in their path, or walking alongside a row of poles. Lessons learned from this behavioral research have helped Kay and his colleagues to improve these sonar instruments further. One long-range goal of this research has been to determine at what age a blind child is first able to benefit from a sonar-type travel aid.

Seeking an alternative to this step-by-step approach to the study of young children, Tom Bower (1977a, 1977b; Aitken & Bower, 1982), a psychologist at Edinburgh University in Scotland, began testing infants with a Sonicguide that was neither designed nor calibrated for infant use (Kay & Strelow, 1977). His testing and training procedures were informal and flexible, in contrast to the prearranged protocols normally used in experiments. He observed that, when wearing the device, an infant frequently would turn her head to face an object that was held up in the sonic field of the instrument. If the object approached the baby, she would typically hold up a hand in front of her face as if to shield herself from it. Most impressive, some infants reached out accurately to seize an object, apparently showing that they were able to interpret the Sonicguide's directional and distance signals. Children more than 13 months old, however, derived little benefit from the Sonicguide in Aitken and Bower's (1982) study; unlike the younger infants, they did not like to be fitted with the instrument, and would not cooperate with the researchers.

Bower concluded from his research that the Sonicguide was of substantial benefit to infants, not only allowing them to develop motor skills on an accelerated timetable, but giving them unprecedented access to environmental information about objects in space. Bower argued that this form of enrichment could greatly increase their understanding of space, early in life when their basic ideas about the world are still being formed; once they are past this "critical period," he speculated, the instrument might be less able to facilitate cognitive development. In his view, electronic aids should be used with infants on a large scale, and as quickly as possible; he criticized as "technomania" Kay's desire to perfect the instrument before advocating its widespread use with blind infants (Bower, 1977b).

Despite Bower's strongly worded assertions, however, his research leaves many questions unanswered and does *not* prove that the Sonicguide would have the profoundly beneficial effects on infants that he claims. More recent studies of infants fitted with a sonar aid help to put Bower's reports in perspective. Were the infants in his studies actually responding to signals from the Sonicguide, rather than to air currents or noises inadvertently made by the experimenter? Probably, for infants who, when wearing the aid, will respond to a looming object by putting up their hand, will not do so on control trials when the instrument is turned off (Muir, Humphrey, Dodwell, & Humphrey, 1985). Can the Sonicguide (or its successors) speed up reaching? Perhaps a little (Ferrell, 1980), but infants who will reach with a sonar aid tend to be those who have already started reaching to sounding objects without the aid (Muir et al., 1985; Strelow, 1983). Thus the instrument can help them to practice reaching, but it has not demonstrated a unique ability to get this behavior started ahead of schedule. Are children between the ages of 1 and 3 too old to benefit from the instrument? Definitely not. Several laboratories have reported (Ferrell, 1980; Humphrey & Humphrey, 1985; Muir et al., 1985; Strelow, 1983) that their reaching, walking and other behaviors can be facilitated by a sonar aid. Some subjects in this age range are unable to use the aid effectively, however, because of problems with posture, stereotyped movements, or unwillingness to wear it (Strelow, 1983). In summary, then, some of Bower's claims have been supported by later work, but others have not.

The central question, however, remains unanswered: Is extended use of sonar aids by blind infants a good idea? While most infants tested have demonstrated some ability to make use of the device's signals, it is unknown whether such use will have a long-term impact. Some of the developmental gains shown by an infant wearing the device may be attributable to the increased attention of parents and teachers as they help her to use it. How would her progress compare with that of another infant who received an equal amount of attention in an enriched natural environment, where sounding objects and echoes can already provide a fair amount of spatial information? On the negative side, would the continuous auditory stimulation provided by the instrument impair the child's hearing, or produce adverse neurological consequences? Would infants grow undesirably dependent on the instrument, so that mobility without it would be impaired (Sonnier, 1985; Strelow & Warren, 1985)?

In view of these negative possibilities, it is prudent to determine the effect of long-term use of the device in young animals, before attempts are made to step up its use with blind human infants. Such a study is now under way, using infant monkeys fitted with Kay-type sensors that are worn over bandages on the upper face, and so prevent visual stimulation (Strelow & Warren, 1985). If this long-term investigation shows ultrasonic sensors to be of substantial benefit to visually deprived monkeys, without producing any ill effects, it will be time to consider a controlled trial of these devices with blind human infants.

## Understanding of the Physical World

Cognitive development during the first few years of life is remarkably fast. During this short span, infants learn how to control their bodies, learn that objects in the environment have a certain amount of permanence and stability, and learn to communicate by means of language. In some ways, toddlers are very mature: They are very skilled at gauging a parent's tolerance for naughty behavior on a particular day, for example. Yet in many other ways, a preschooler's understanding of the world is immature—not just naîve, but qualitatively different from that of an adult.

The cognitive differences between children and adults, and the gradual maturing of the child's understanding of the world, are subjects so fascinating that they occupied Swiss psychologist Jean Piaget for most of his lifetime. Beginning with careful, frequent observations of his own three children, and continuing with the systematic study of many others at his Geneva laboratory, Piaget and his colleagues came to realize that the child's thinking process itself changes in predictable ways as she grows older (Inhelder & Piaget, 1958; Piaget & Inhelder, 1969). He believed that cognitive development occurs in four major stages. In what he called the *sensorimotor stage,* the infant slowly becomes familiar with her environment by means of recurring perceptual experiences, such as the sound of her mother's voice, and through her own simple reflexive actions, such as moving her feet. These elements are gradually combined into more and more elaborate patterns of interaction with the environment, such as walking across the room to reach her mother. The infant's thoughts and behavior are very much under the control of stimuli that are currently present in her environment: She has little conception of past or future. As the second year of life draws to a close, however, the child begins to think symbolically. Words are used not just as a way of summoning her caregiver or obtaining a desired food or toy, but as mental representatives of those things. Her doll becomes an imaginary person, not just a plastic object resembling a person, and the family dog becomes, when she wishes, a horse, a mountain, or a relative. This development of symbolism propels the child into the *pre-operational stage,* according to Piaget. In this stage, children are not yet capable of performing logical operations, such as figuring out that if you go to the zoo on a particular day, there is no time to go also to the playground. Their explanations of physical events show little understanding of cause and effect. At about age 7, however, children enter the *stage of concrete operations,* in which they are able to solve simple problems on the basis of logic. They can do so only when thinking about specific people or objects, however. When asked to puzzle about abstract questions, such as why freedom of the press is good, they tend to respond in very concrete, narrow terms, such as that freedom of the press makes reporters happy. But at about age 12, children typically enter into a mature level of cognitive functioning, the *stage of formal operations,* in which abstract as well as concrete thinking is possible.

Piaget believed that, while cognitive development occurs continuously, transitions from one major stage to the next are somewhat abrupt. His notion was that the child gradually assimilates more and more information from her environment, thinking about it in familiar ways, until these are no longer able to organize the information satisfactorily. When this threshold is reached, a cognitive reorganization occurs, and the child enters a new stage. To some extent the emergence of a new cognitive stage depends on maturation, but also to some extent on the amount of knowledge the child has assimilated. Consider, for example, the child's belief in Santa Claus. The curious 5-year-old asks her parents how many children Santa visits in one night, how he gets down the chimney, and so on, and is satisfied with each answer. But as she gets older and the answers accumulate, there comes a point when she realizes that her previous theory of Santa is no longer adequate. Did this cognitive reorganization occur because her brain had developed sufficiently to allow it, or because she had assimilated so much information about chimneys, time, and other aspects of the world, that she was able to perceive the shortcomings of her previous hypothesis? No doubt both factors are involved.

Piaget's work is valuable from an experimental as well as a theoretical point of view, for he provided numerous ways of testing the child's understanding of physical reality. The ability to solve certain puzzles that he invented does in fact emerge fairly suddenly in individual children, but at an age which varies somewhat from child to child. By comparing the ages at which the puzzles are solved, then, we can compare the rate of cognitive development of individual children, or even groups of children.

Piaget's methods can be used to compare the cognitive development of blind children with that of sighted children. Selma Fraiberg (1977), for example, carefully observed the behavior of a number of blind children to determine when they would first engage in symbolic play, such as using a doll to represent a person. Most of the blind children she studied were considerably delayed in this regard, by more than a year in some cases. On the basis of this lag in symbolic play, combined with delays in motor development (which to her indicated a slowness to understand object permanence),

Fraiberg concluded that the average blind child passes through the sensorimotor stage more slowly than the average sighted child. She advocated early intervention and training as a way to reduce, and perhaps eliminate, the prolongation of this stage.

The greatest amount of experimental attention has been devoted to the transition from the preoperational to the concrete operational stage. This change is especially susceptible to measurement because instructions can be given verbally to the child, who is typically 5 or older in these studies. Hatwell (1966/1985) was the first to compare congenitally blind and sighted children of grammar school age systematically on Piagetian tasks. At the time of this research she was a graduate student at the Sorbonne, and her subjects were schoolchildren living in or near Paris.

Hatwell carried out a variety of studies. In one, children were presented with a board on which were mounted wooden rails meant to resemble railroad tracks. Each track formed a closed loop that went around the platform. Hatwell used different-shaped pegs, which could be inserted in holes in each rail, to represent train cars. Testing each child individually, Hatwell asked her to examine three pegs that represented the different cars of a train that was stopped at a particular station. She then required the subject to use a similar set of three pegs to show how the cars would be arranged when the train got to a different station. Did the children understand that the cars would remain in the same order even though the "train" moved and went around curves? Some did and some did not, but, in general, sighted subjects were able to solve this puzzle several years earlier than blind subjects.

In experiments of this type the researcher always wonders whether to prevent the sighted subjects from using vision, for example, by blindfolding them or requiring them to reach behind a curtain or screen. If the sighted subjects are allowed to use vision, this gives them an advantage in solving the problem, because they can see the apparatus at a glance rather than having to explore it a little at a time. On the other hand, if they are prevented from using vision, then their normal way of doing things will be disrupted, and they may be performing at an unfair disadvantage. In either case, the experimenter may have trouble in isolating cognitive ability from other factors. Perhaps the best way out of this dilemma is to use Hatwell's approach of running separate groups of sighted children, with one group being allowed to use vision, the other not. She found that the sighted children did about equally well whether or not they could see the stimuli. Thus it is a lifetime of vision, rather than vision at the time of testing, that determines the age at which children can solve this problem.

With other types of puzzles Hatwell obtained similar results. In a sorting problem, for example, she gave the child eight pieces of wood: two cubes, two spheres, two flat rectangles, and two disks. One piece of each shape was large, the other small. The experimenter asked subjects to sort the eight objects into two bins, using whatever criterion they wished. If they completed that task successfully, they were asked to sort the same objects again, but using a different criterion; and if they accomplished that also, they were asked to sort in a third way. Whether she examined the subjects' ability to sort with all three criteria (round vs. square, flat vs. solid, large vs. small), or their ability to sort in two ways, or even in only one, she found that the blind subjects lagged about 2 years behind the sighted.

In still another experiment, Hatwell tested the children's understanding of *conservation*—that is, their ability to realize that objects or substances can be rearranged or changed in appearance, without the amount or number of them being altered. For example, a sighted child might be shown two identical balls of clay, and told to roll one into a sausage shape. Then she is asked whether the sausage contains the same amount of clay as the other ball. These conservation tasks are the best known of all the puzzles devised by Piaget, probably because of the striking failure of young children to understand that the amount of a substance remains the same despite changes in shape. For example, a 5-year-old faced with the sausage and ball will typically insist that the sausage contains more clay because it is longer, and will be unpersuaded by a parent's statements to the contrary.

Hatwell's procedure for studying conservation of substance involved a number of steps. After the children examined the two balls of clay and agreed that they were equal, they were asked to roll one into a sausage, and compare this with the remaining ball. Next the children rolled the sausage back into a ball and then flattened it into a pancake, and were asked whether the pancake and the ball contained the same amount of clay. Finally the children rolled the pancake back into a ball, and broke it into several pieces, after which they were asked whether the pieces together contained the same amount of clay as the ball.

Hatwell considered a child to have grasped the idea of conservation of substance only if she answered all these questions correctly. Children of different ages were tested, and within both the blind and sighted groups, the likelihood of demonstrating knowledge of conservation increased with age. But while half of the 7-year-old sighted children answered correctly, it was not until age 9 or 10 that half the blind children did so. Thus blind children, on the average, lagged 2 to 3 years behind sighted children in their ability to solve this puzzle. By age 12, however, about 85% of the blind children were answering all the substance conservation questions correctly. Comparable results were obtained in a similar study of conservation by Gottesman (1973).

In summary, then, Hatwell found that blind children lagged substantially behind sighted children in the development of their ability to compare and quantitatively evaluate objects examined by touch. In contrast, however, she found that there was no lag when the blind children were asked questions about hypothetical objects or people, without the need for physical inspection. For example, the children were given multiple tests of *seriation*, in which they were asked to indicate which of several items was largest or smallest. Some of these tests involved haptic inspection of the items, while others involved the subjects simply being told about them. In a test of the former type, subjects were given a series of wooden sticks varying in length, and were asked to arrange them in order of length; while in a test of the latter type, subjects were asked questions such as "John is shorter than Peter, Peter is taller than Robert; which one of the three is the tallest?"

On the haptic test with the sticks, the blind subjects lagged about 2½ years behind the sighted, but on the verbal test, they were actually somewhat in advance of the sighted children. Thus they were fully equal to the sighted subjects in their ability to draw conclusions from information about linear extent, once they had absorbed it; their problem, instead, was in being able to acquire this information through touch.

As Hatwell concluded in summing up her investigation, these results have complex implications for Piaget's theory of cognitive development. On the one hand, the fact that blind children lag behind their sighted peers on many Piagetian tasks indicates that the amount of environmental stimulation a child receives influences the pace of development of her ability to perform cognitive operations on environmental objects, or, more precisely, on mental representations of those objects. On the other hand, the verbal results indicate that a child can develop the capacity to enter into new ways of thinking even if blindness, and inadequate assimilation of information through touch, have combined to hinder her perception of the physical world.

But is the difficulty in using touch to determine the properties of objects a problem that can be remedied? To address this question, Lopata and Pasnak (1976) undertook to train blind children in those haptic skills that are involved in Piagetian tasks. They gave IQ tests and conservation tests to a large number of blind students, ranging in age from 8 to 13. Only those who failed the conservation tasks were selected for further study. From these, 28 were chosen who could be paired off on the basis of age, degree of blindness and its date of onset, and performance on the IQ test. That is, they chose 14 pairs of subjects in such a way that the two members of each pair were similar on these characteristics. Then Lopata and Pasnak took the crucial step of *randomly* assigning one member of each pair to an experimental group, and the other member to a control group. Such strictly random assignment is an integral part of a controlled study of this type, for it prevents the experimenters from unintentionally but systematically assigning different types of subjects to the two groups—putting the more inquisitive ones into the experimental group, for example.

The researchers then began to train the children in the experimental group on a variety of tasks that brought them into physical contact with everyday objects. For example, subjects were given a "standard" button, and were asked to select, from three others, one that was the same size as the standard. On other trials they were asked to select a larger button, or a smaller one. The same task was carried out repeatedly, using not only buttons but screws, coins, safety pins, and pencils. Any trial on which a child gave a wrong answer was repeated until a correct response was elicited.

Training continued with subjects being asked to arrange three objects in order of size; to choose two short objects which together equaled the length of a longer one; and several similar tasks. Finally they were trained on conservation itself, with a subject being presented with three similar objects or groups of objects. Among the objects used were pieces of clay, cookies, paper clips, rubber bands, and many others. Children were asked about the relative amounts of the three objects—which of three balls of clay was the largest, for example. Then one or more of the stimulus objects were altered, in ways which sometimes caused changes in amount (e.g., removing half a cookie) and sometimes did not (bending a paper clip), and the subjects were asked to re-evaluate them. Subjects were told when they made a mistake, and the task was repeated. One hundred and twenty conservation problems were presented in all.

Each child in the experimental group passed through a fixed series of these training exercises, until all questions had been answered correctly. This training took the form of a series of 1-hour sessions, but some subjects required more sessions to complete all the problems than other subjects did. Control subjects, meanwhile, were given 1-hour enrichment sessions, in which the experimenters played with them using the materials used to train the experimental-group children, chatted with them, and helped them with their homework. Each control subject had the same number of enrichment sessions as the experimental subject with whom she or he had been matched. Thus the two groups did not differ in the amount of attention they received from the experimenters.

Finally, both groups of youngsters were given an IQ test, and a final test of conservation resembling, but not identical to, the one they had been given at the outset. Control subjects had improved only negligibly on their understanding of conservation, but experimental subjects had improved substantially. This difference between the groups in amount of improvement was statistically significant. Thus it is possible for specialized training to improve a blind child's performance on Piagetian tasks, at least if she has reached an age at which most sighted children are able to solve those tasks.

Even more impressive were the results of the IQ test, compared with the scores originally obtained. The average measured IQ of the control subjects had increased from 92.6 to 94, a slight gain that is probably to be explained by the subjects' increased familiarity with the test and the examiner the second time around. The experimental subjects, however, had advanced from 91.2 to 99.7, a marked increase, significantly larger than that of thecontrols. This result shows that training the subjects to think quantitatively about everyday objects had a favorable impact on a wide range of cognitive skills. Apparently these Piagetian tasks are involved, sometimes in an obvious way and sometimes more subtly, in a variety of mental activities.

Why do so many blind children have difficulty (before training) in learning about an object through haptic examination of it? Part of the answer, as Berlá, Butterfield, and Murr (1976) discovered, is that they often examine stimuli in inefficient ways. These researchers studied the strategies used by blind children to explore raised-line drawings, and found marked differences between children who were adept at recognizing shapes they had inspected moments earlier, and children who lacked this skill. The task consisted of examining a card that contained a raised-line outline drawing of a state, and then trying to find the outline of this state on a larger tactile pseudomap containing several states, randomly arranged and connected by additional contours (see Fig. 7.1). Subjects were videotaped so that their hand movements could later be analyzed. The exploratory behavior of those children who performed well at this task was compared with a group who did poorly. The authors found that the more skilled map readers were more systematic in their examination of the embossed drawings: They typically followed a contour until they had gone completely around the enclosed region, lingering at distinctive spots where there were rapid changes in the direction of the contour. The less skilled map readers tended to follow a

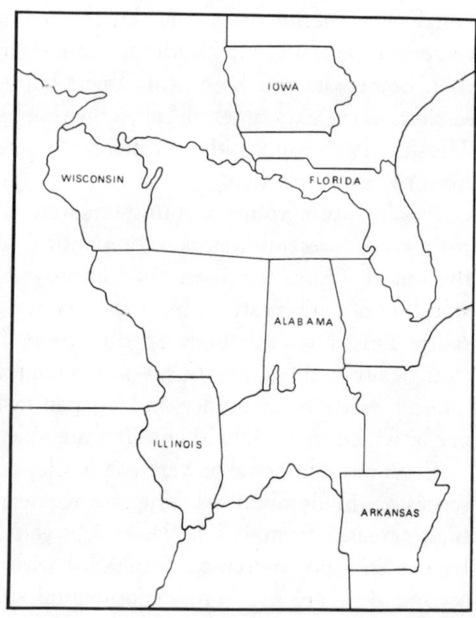


FIGURE 7.1. One of the pseudomaps used by Berlá, Butterfield, and Murr in their study of map-reading skills of blind children. The children first examined a state outline in isolation, and then attempted to locate that same shape on the pseudomap. State names, shown here for clarity, were not included in the embossed version of the pseudomap presented to the children. (From "Tactual Reading of Political Maps by Blind Students: A Videomatic Behavioral Analysis," by E. P. Berlá, L. H. Butterfield, Jr., & M. J. Murr, 1976, *Journal of Special Education, 10,* p. 267. Reprinted by permission of Pro-Ed Inc.)

contour for only a short distance, after which their finger(s) would "lose" it, straying onto uncontoured areas of the map or onto a different contour. Sometimes they skimmed along contours, missing the distinctive twists and turns that the skilled map readers found especially helpful in making their identifications. In a follow-up study, Berlá and Butterfield (1977) trained unskilled map readers to explore contours systematically, by starting at a particular spot and carefully following a contour clockwise or counterclockwise until their finger returned to the point of origin, then repeating the process but with more attention to distinctive features. They found that map-reading skill was greatly improved by this simple training (in comparison with an untrained control group), although less than 2 hours of instruction was involved.

The practical implications of these studies are great. That a few hours of training in the examination and appraisal of objects and embossed drawings can substantially improve performance on Piagetian and map-reading tasks, suggests that such training was more or less absent from the child's previous education; yet clearly it is very valuable training. In recent years, leaders in special education have advocated an increased emphasis on such haptic experiences in the curriculum of visually impaired children (Swallow & Poulsen, 1983). And long before the beginning of formal instruction, parents of a blind child can encourage her not just to name objects, but to make comparisons among them (Ferrell, 1985). If parents and educators work together to strengthen the child's haptic skills, it can confidently be predicted that increased mastery of the physical environment will result.

## SUMMARY

In this chapter we have seen that, although their progress in some areas is often somewhat delayed, blind children can attain levels of social and cognitive development comparable to those of sighted children. To do so, however, it is necessary for them to live in a rich environment, relating closely to other people, and interacting fully with their physical surroundings. Some of the most valuable of such experiences are those that have no explicit educational purpose: playing with siblings, for example, or helping with household tasks. Parents can greatly facilitate their child's development by allowing, and actively encouraging, his or her participation in a wide range of activities.

From a scientific point of view, the most important theme of this chapter is the remarkable extent to which auditory and haptic information can substitute for visual information in fostering a child's development. Again, this substitution can be fully effective only if the child's auditory and haptic experiences are as diverse and stimulating as the visual ones they replace—a requirement that cannot be met without the wisdom and effort of those responsible for the child's upbringing. The fact that such substitution is possible, however, is testament to the power and adaptability of the developing human mind.

Finally, it is important to realize that, while comparisons of blind and sighted children have repeatedly been made in this chapter for heuristic reasons, such comparisons are of limited significance in everyday life, in which every individual, whether sighted or blind, possesses a unique combination of strengths and weaknesses. The goal of a blind child's parents and teachers should be, not for the child to achieve sighted norms, but rather for him or her to attain the fullest development of which he or she is capable.

# CONCLUDING REMARKS

Blindness is an area of study that has attracted psychologists for a century, educators for two centuries, and philosophers for three. The literature on this subject is diverse and voluminous. The present work is only an introduction to the field; it is hoped that readers will have found enough of interest here to encourage them to read further. However, the information reviewed in these seven chapters is sufficient to warrant several important conclusions.

First, blindness is complicated. People can become blind at different ages, for different reasons, and to different degrees, and all of these factors influence the person's later skills and attitudes. Researchers need to take these complexities into account in formulating and testing their hypotheses.

Second, while blindness makes some specific activities impossible, there are no broad areas of human endeavor in which blind people do not participate. This is due to the fact that information about the environment acquired through hearing and touch can to a large degree substitute for visual information. Even spatial principles, of which some congenitally blind people have a poor grasp, are clearly and profoundly understood by others. But knowledge about space, and some other types of information, are more painstakingly acquired by blind people than by the sighted, because of the serial nature of haptic exploration. Thus a blind person must spend more time to read the same book, and concentrate harder to navigate the same unfamiliar neighborhood, than a sighted person would, because information must be taken in bit by bit.

Third, a large proportion of the problems facing a blind person are social in nature. Many sighted people are made uncomfortable by the thought of blindness, and don't know much about it; this tends to strain their interactions with blind people. As a result, many blind people are economically disadvantaged by job discrimination, and socially isolated, moving within a small circle of friends. Research shows that this process of isolation sometimes begins in childhood, and can become self-perpetuating if a blind child loses out on opportunities to practice and develop social skills. A variety of approaches are currently being used to study and deal with these complex issues.

Fourth, more research is needed to answer a wide variety of questions about blindness. Many training methods and electronic devices of potential benefit to blind people need to be systematically evaluated on a large scale, using controlled experimental designs. Because the number of blind people available in any one city is limited, such research will often require a collaborative network of scientists in different universities or other facilities. But small-scale, single-investigator research has produced many of the discoveries and creative insights reported here: More of this type of research is needed too. Two fields of investigation in which only a start has been made are (1) the perceptions, cognitive processes, and spatial skills of people with visual impairment that falls short of total blindness, and (2) the way in which other disabilities combine with blindness to affect the individual's abilities and educational and rehabilitative needs.

Fifth, continued progress in understanding blindness, and in helping blind people to reach their full potential, requires active collaboration among people in several disciplines. For example, studies to determine the practical value of different optical aids for visually impaired people in school and in various lines of work require the collaboration of low-vision specialists, educators, and rehabilitation workers. Similarly, an improved understanding of the ways in which the brain responds to loss of visual input at various ages, and of the behavioral implications of these responses, will require the collaboration of physiologists, physicians, and experimental psychologists. To encourage, in newcomers to the study of blindness, an interest in such interdisciplinary cooperation, is one of the reasons that this book was written.

# REFERENCES


Ackroyd, C., Humphrey, N. K., & Warrington, E. K. (1974). Lasting effects of early blindness. A case study. *Quarterly Journal of Experimental Psychology, 26*, 114–124.

Adorno, T. W., Frenkel-Brunswik, E., Levinson, D. J., & Sanford, R. N. (1950). *The authoritarian personality*. New York: Harper & Row.

Aitken, S., & Bower, T. G. R. (1982). Intersensory substitution in the blind. *Journal of Experimental Child Psychology, 33*, 309–323.

American Foundation for the Blind. (1988). *Directory of services for blind and visually impaired persons in the United States* (23rd ed.). New York: American Foundation for the Blind.

Anderson, D. R. (1987). *Perimetry with and without automation* (2nd ed.). St. Louis: Mosby.

Ashcroft, S. C., & Henderson, F. (1963). *Programmed instruction in braille*. Pittsburgh: Stanwix House.

Ashton, N. (1966). Oxygen and growth and development of retinal vessels. *American Journal of Ophthalmology, 62*, 412–435.

Attneave, F., & Benson, B. (1969). Spatial coding of tactual stimulation. *Journal of Experimental Psychology, 81*, 216–222.

Axelrod, S. (1959). *Effects of early blindness: Performance of blind and sighted children on tactile and auditory tasks*. New York: American Foundation for the Blind.

Bagley, M. (1985). Service providers assessment of the career development needs of blind and visually impaired students and rehabilitation clients and the resources available to meet those needs. *Journal of Visual Impairment & Blindness, 79*, 434–443.

Bauman, M. K. (1972). Research on psychological factors associated with blindness. In R. E. Hardy & J. G. Cull (Eds.), *Social and rehabilitation services for the blind* (pp. 153–173). Springfield, IL: Charles C. Thomas.

Bayley, N. (1969). *Bayley scales of infant development*. New York: The Psychological Corporation.

Benedetti, F. (1985). Processing of tactile spatial information with crossed fingers. *Journal of Experimental Psychology: Human Perception and Performance, 11*, 517–525.

Benedetti, F. (1986). Tactile diplopia (diplesthesia) on the human fingers. *Perception, 15*, 83–91.

Benedetti, L. H., & Loeb, M. (1972). A comparison of auditory monitoring performance in blind subjects with that of sighted subjects in light and dark. *Perception & Psychophysics, 11,* 10–16.

Berger, R. J., Olley, P., & Oswald, I. (1962). The EEG, eye-movements and dreams of the blind. *Quarterly Journal of Experimental Psychology, 14,* 183–186.

Berlá, E. P. (1982). Haptic perception of tangible graphic displays. In W. Schiff & E. Foulke (Eds.), *Tactual perception: A sourcebook* (pp. 364–386). Cambridge, England: Cambridge University Press.

Berlá, E. P., & Butterfield, L. H., Jr. (1977). Tactual distinctive features analysis: Training blind students in shape recognition and in locating shapes on a map. *Journal of Special Education, 11,* 335–346.

Berlá, E. P., Butterfield, L. H., Jr., & Murr, M. J. (1976). The actual reading of political maps by blind students: A videomatic behavioral analysis. *Journal of Special Education, 10,* 265–276.

Bertelson, P., Mousty, P., & D'Alimonte, G. (1985). A study of Braille reading: 2. Patterns of hand activity in one-handed and two-handed reading. *Quarterly Journal of Experimental Psychology, 37A,* 235–256.

Blank, H. R. (1957). Psychoanalysis and blindness. *Psychoanalytic Quarterly, 26,* 1–24.

Blasch, B. B. (1975). A study of the treatment of blindisms using punishment and positive reinforcement in laboratory and natural settings. *Dissertation Abstracts International, 36,* 3558A. (University Microfilms No. 75–27,236).

Bledsoe, C. W. (1980). Originators of orientation and mobility training. In R. L. Welsh & B. B. Blasch (Eds.), *Foundations of orientation and mobility* (pp. 581–624). New York: American Foundation for the Blind.

Bower, T. (1977a). Blind babies see with their ears. *New Scientist, 73,* 255–257.

Bower, T. (1977b). Babies are more important than machines. *New Scientist, 74,* 712–714.

Bradway, K. P. (1937). Social competence of exceptional children. III. The deaf, the blind, and the crippled. *Journal of Exceptional Children, 4,* 64–69.

Brady, J. P., & Lind, D. L. (1961). Experimental analysis of hysterical blindness. *Archives of General Psychiatry, 4,* 331–339.

Brazelton, T. B., Koslowski, B., & Main, M. (1974) The origins of reciprocity: The early mother–infant interaction. In M. Lewis & L. A. Rosenblum (Eds.), *The effect of the infant on its caregiver* (pp. 49–76). New York: Wiley.

Bridgeman, B., & Staggs, D. (1982). Plasticity in human blindsight. *Vision Research, 22,* 1199–1203.

Brindley, G. S. (1973). Sensory effects of electrical stimulation of the visual and paravisual cortex in man. In R. Jung (Ed.), *Handbook of sensory physiology: Vol. VII/3* (pp. 583–594). New York: Springer–Verlag.

Brindley, G. S., Gautier–Smith, P. C., & Lewin, W. (1969). Cortical blindness and the functions of the non-geniculate fibers of the optic tracts. *Journal of Neurology, Neurosurgery and Psychiatry, 32,* 259–264.

Brindley, G. S., & Lewin, W. S. (1968). The sensations produced by electrical stimulation of the visual cortex. *Journal of Physiology, 196,* 479–493.

Brontë, C. (1945). *Jane Eyre.* New York: Literary Classics. (First published in 1847).

Buck, A. A. (Ed.). (1974). *Onchocerciasis: Symptomatology, pathology, diagnosis.* Geneva: World Health Organization.

Bull, R., Rathborn, H., & Clifford, B. R. (1983). The voice-recognition accuracy of blind listeners. *Perception, 12,* 223–226.

Burlingham, D. (1961). Some notes on the development of the blind. *Psychoanalytic Study of the Child, 16,* 121–145.

Campion, J., Latto, R., & Smith, Y. M. (1983). Is blindsight an effect of scattered light, spared cortex, and near-threshold vision? *Behavioral and Brain Sciences, 6,* 423–448.

Carpenter, P. A., & Eisenberg, P. (1978). Mental rotation and the frame of reference in blind and sighted individuals. *Perception & Psychophysics, 23,* 117–124.

Carroll, T. J. (1961). *Blindness: What it is, what it does, and how to live with it.* Boston: Little, Brown.

Cashdan, S. (1968). Visual and haptic form discrimination under conditions of successive stimulation. *Journal of Experimental Psychology, 76,* 215–218.

Chevigny, H. (1946). *My eyes have a cold nose.* New Haven, CT: Yale University Press.

Chevigny, H., & Braverman, S. (1950). *The adjustment of the blind.* New Haven, CT: Yale University Press.

Cholden, L. S. (1958). *A psychiatrist works with blindness.* New York: American Foundation for the Blind.

Chow, K. L., Riesen, A. H., & Newell, F. W. (1957). Degeneration of retinal ganglion cells in infant chimpanzees reared in darkness. *Journal of Comparative Neurology, 107,* 27–42.

Clark, Martire, & Bartolomeo, Inc. (1984). *A study of attitudes toward blindness and blindness prevention: Overview.* (Report of a public opinion poll conducted for the National Society to Prevent Blindness).

Clarke-Stewart, A., & Koch, J. B. (1983). *Children: Development through adolescence.* New York: Wiley.

Cole, D. F. (1978). Ciliary processes. In K. Heilmann & K. T. Richardson (Eds.), *Glaucoma: Conceptions of a disease.* Philadelphia: W. B. Saunders.

Cole, F. C. (1971). Contact as a determinant of sighted persons' attitudes toward the blind (Doctoral dissertation, Florida State University, 1970). *Dissertation Abstracts International, 31,* 6892B–6893B.

Colenbrander, A. (1976). Low vision: Definition and classification. In E. E. Faye, *Clinical low vision* (pp. 3–6). Boston: Little, Brown.

Collins, C. C. (1985). On mobility aids for the blind. In D. H. Warren & E. R. Strelow (Eds.), *Electronic spatial sensing for the blind: Contributions from perception, rehabilitation, and computer vision* (pp. 35–64). Dordrecht, The Netherlands: Martinus Nijhoff.

Coren, S., Porac, C., & Ward, L. M. (1984). *Sensation and perception* (2nd ed.). Orlando, FL: Academic Press.

Cotzin, M., & Dallenbach, K. M. (1950). "Facial vision": The role of pitch and loudness in the perception of obstacles by the blind. *American Journal of Psychology, 63,* 485–515.

Cowen, E. L., Underberg, R. P., & Verrillo, R. T. (1958). The development and testing of an attitude to blindness scale. *Journal of Social Psychology, 48,* 297–304.

Craig, J. C. (1977). Vibrotactile pattern perception: Extraordinary observers. *Science, 196,* 450–452.

Cratty, B. J. (1967). The perception of gradient and the veering tendency while walking without vision. *American Foundation for the Blind Research Bulletin, 14,* 31–51.

Cratty, B. J. (1971). *Movement and spatial awareness in blind children and youth.* Springfield, IL: Charles C. Thomas.

Cupp, E. W., Bernardo, M. J., Kiszewski, A. E., Collins, R. C., Taylor, H. R., Aziz, M. A., & Greene, B. M. (1986). The effects of ivermectin on transmission of *Onchocerca volvulus. Science, 231,* 740–742.

Cutsforth, T. D. (1980). *The blind in school and society: A psychological study* (2nd ed., reprint). New York: American Foundation for the Blind. (This edition first published 1951; original work published 1933.)

Dante Alighieri. (1961). *The purgatorio* (J. Ciardi, Trans.). New York: New American Library. (Original work completed 1321.)

Dante Alighieri. (1970). *The paradiso* (J. Ciardi, Trans.). New York: New American Library. (Original work completed 1321.)

Davidson, P. W. (1972). Haptic judgments of curvature by blind and sighted humans. *Journal of Experimental Psychology, 93,* 43–55.

Davidson, P. W., Wiles-Kettenmann, M., Haber, R. N., & Appelle, S. (1980). Relationship between hand movements, reading competence and passage difficulty in braille reading. *Neuropsychologia, 18,* 629–635.

Davis, C. J. (1980). *Perkins–Binet Tests of Intelligence for the Blind.* Watertown, MA: Perkins School for the Blind.

Davis, F. (1961). Deviance disavowal: The management of strained interaction by the visibly handicapped. *Social Problems, 9*, 120–132.

Dawson, C. R., Jones, B. R., & Tarizzo, M. L. (1981). *Guide to trachoma control in programmes for the prevention of blindness.* Geneva: World Health Organization.

Deering, M. F. (1985). Computer vision requirements in blind mobility aids. In D. H. Warren & E. R. Strelow (Eds.), *Electronic spatial sensing for the blind: Contributions from perception, rehabilitation, and computer vision* (pp. 65–82). Dordrecht, The Netherlands: Martinus Nijhoff.

Dobelle, W. H. (1977). Current status of research on providing sight to the blind by electrical stimulation of the brain. *Jorunal of Visual Impairment & Blindness, 71*, 290–297.

Dobelle, W. H., & Mladejovsky, M. G. (1974). Phosphenes produced by electrical stimulation of human occipital cortex, and their application to the development of a prosthesis for the blind. *Journal of Physiology, 243*, 553–576.

Dobelle, W. H., Mladejovsky, M. G., Evans, J. R., Roberts, T. S., & Girvin, J. P. (1976). "Braille" reading by a blind volunteer by visual cortex stimulation. *Nature, 259*, 111–112.

Dobelle, W. H., Mladejovsky, M. G., & Girvin, J. P. (1974). Artificial vision for the blind: Electrical stimulation of visual cortex offers hope for a functional prosthesis. *Science, 183*, 440–444.

Donovan, A. (Producer), & Benton, R. (Writer & Director). (1984). *Places in the heart* [Film]. New York: Tri-Star Pictures.

Dowling, J. L., & Bahr, R. L. (1985). A survey of current cataract surgical techniques. *American Journal of Ophthalmology, 99*, 35–39.

Eco, U. (1984). *The name of the rose* (W. Weaver, Trans.). New York: Warner Books. (Original work published 1980.)

Ellis, D. (Ed.). (1986). *Sensory impairments in mentally handicapped people.* London: Croom Helm.

Erickson, P. A., Fisher, S. K., Anderson, D. H., Stern, W. H., & Borgula, G. A. (1983). Retinal detachment in the cat: The outer nuclear and outer plexiform layers. *Investigative Ophthalmology & Visual Science, 24*, 927–942.

Farmer, L. W. (1980). Mobility devices. In R. L. Welsh & B. B. Blasch (Eds.), *Foundations of orientation and mobility* (pp. 357–412). New York: American Foundation for the Blind.

Favazza, A. R., & Favazza, B. (1987). *Bodies under siege: Self-mutilation in culture and psychiatry.* Baltimore: Johns Hopkins University Press.

Faye, E. E. (1976). *Clinical low vision.* Boston: Little, Brown.

Ferrell, K. A. (1980). Can infants use the Sonicguide? Two years experience of Project VIEW! *Journal of Visual Impairment & Blindness, 74*, 209–220.

Ferrell, K. A. (1984). The editors talk. . . . [guest editorial]. *Education of the Visually Handicapped, 16*, 43–46.

Ferrell, K. A. (1985). *Reach out and teach: Meeting the training needs of parents of visually and multiply handicapped young children* (2 vols.). New York: American Foundation for the Blind.

Ferrell, K. A. (1986a). Infancy and early childhood. In G. T. Scholl (Ed.), *Foundations of education for blind and visually handicapped children and youth: Theory and practice* (pp. 119–135). New York: American Foundation for the Blind.

Ferrell, K. A. (1986b). Working with parents. In G. T. Scholl (Ed.), *Foundations of education for blind and visually handicapped children and youth: Theory and practice* (pp. 265–274). New York: American Foundation for the Blind.

Foulke, E. (1971). The perceptual basis for mobility. *American Foundation for the Blind Research Bulletin*, No. 23, 1–8.

Foulke, E., & Berlá, E. P. (1978). Visual impairment and the development of perceptual ability. In R. D. Walk & H. L. Pick, Jr. (Eds.), *Perception and experience* (pp. 213–240). New York: Plenum Press.

Foulke, E., & Sticht, T. G. (1969). Review of research on the intelligibility and comprehension of accelerated speech. *Psychological Bulletin, 72,* 50–62.

Fraiberg, S. (1977). *Insights from the blind: Comparative studies of blind and sighted infants.* New York: Basic Books.

Fraiberg, S. (1979). Blind infants and their mothers: An examination of the sign system. In M. Bullowa (Ed.), *Before speech: The beginning of interpersonal communication* (pp. 149–169). Cambridge, England: Cambridge University Press.

Freedman, D. A., Fox-Kolenda, B. J., Margileth, D. A., & Miller, D. H. (1969). The development of the use of sound as a guide to affective and cognitive behavior—A two-phase process. *Child Development, 40,* 1099–1105.

Gallup, G. (1976). Cancer is most feared affliction. *The Gallup Poll.* News release of December 2.

Gelbart, S. S., Hoyt, C. S., Jastrebski, G., & Marg, E. (1982). Long-term visual results in bilateral congenital cataracts. *American Journal of Ophthalmology, 93,* 615–621.

Gershe, L. (1969). *Butterflies are free.* New York: Samuel French.

Gibson, E. J., & Levin, H. (1975). *The psychology of reading.* Cambridge, MA: M.I.T. Press.

Glass, P., Avery, G. B., Subramanian, K. N. S., Keys, M. P., Sostek, A. M., & Friendly, D. S. (1985). Effect of bright light in the hospital nursery on the incidence of retinopathy of prematurity. *New England Journal of Medicine, 313,* 401–404.

Glickstein, M. (1988). The discovery of the visual cortex. *Scientific American, 259, #3,* 118–127.

Goffman, E. (1963). *Stigma: Notes on the management of spoiled identity.* Englewood Cliffs, NJ: Prentice-Hall.

Goldie, D. (1977). Use of the C-5 Laser Cane by school age children. *Journal of Visual Impairment & Blindness, 71,* 346–348.

Gorham, D. R. (1956). A proverbs test for clinical and experimental use. *Psychological Reports, 2,* 1–12 (Monograph Supplement 1).

Gottesman, M. (1973). Conservation development in blind children. *Child Development, 44,* 824–827.

Gowman, A. G. (1957). *The war blind in American social structure.* New York: American Foundation for the Blind.

Greenacre, P. (1926). The eye motif in delusion and fantasy. *American Journal of Psychiatry, 5,* (new series), 553–579.

Greene, B. M., Taylor, H. R., Cupp, E. W., Murphy, R. P., White, A. T., Aziz, M. A., Schulz-Key, H., D'Anna, S. A., Newland, H. S., Goldschmidt, L. P., Auer, C., Hanson, A. P., Freeman, S. V., Reber, E. W., & Williams, P. N. (1985). Comparison of ivermectin and diethylcarbamazine in the treatment of onchocerciasis. New England Journal of Medicine, *313,* 133–138.

Gregory, R. L., & Wallace, J. G. (1963). *Recovery from early blindness: A case study* (Experimental Psychology Society Monograph No. 2). Cambridge, England: Heffer.

Guarniero, G. (1974). Experience of tactile vision. *Perception, 3,* 101–104.

Hanford, J. H. (1949). *John Milton, Englishman.* New York: Crown.

Hart, H. H. (1949). The eye in symbol and symptom. *Psychoanalytic Review, 36,* 1–21.

Hart, V. (1983). Motor development in blind children. In M. E. Mulholland & M. V. Wurster (Eds.), *"Help me become everything I can be": Proceedings, North American Conference on Visually Handicapped Infants and Preschool Children* (pp. 74–79). New York: American Foundation for the Blind.

Hartlage, L. C. (1969). Verbal tests of spatial conceptualization. *Journal of Experimental Psychology, 80,* 180–182.

Hastorf, A. H., Northcraft, G. B., & Picciotto, S. R. (1979). Helping the handicapped: How realistic is the performance feedback received by the physically handicapped? *Personality and Social Psychology Bulletin, 5,* 373–376.

Hatwell, Y. (1985). *Piagetian reasoning and the blind* (P. Verdet, Trans.). New York: American Foundation for the Blind. (Original work published 1966.)

Havill, S. J. (1970). The sociometric status of visually handicapped students in public school classes. *American Foundation for the Blind Research Bulletin*, No. 20, 57–90.

Hayes, S. P. (1941). *Contributions to a psychology of blindness.* New York: American Foundation for the Blind.

Heath, P. (1950). Retrolental fibroplasia as a syndrome. *Archives of Ophthalmology, 44*, 245–274.

Heinrichs, R. W., & Moorhouse, J. A. (1969). Touch-perception thresholds in blind diabetic subjects in relation to the reading of Braille type. *New England Journal of Medicine, 280*, 72–75.

Heller, M. A. (1983). Haptic dominance in form perception with blurred vision. *Perception, 12*, 607–613.

Heller, M. A. (1986). Central and peripheral influences on tactual reading. *Perception & Psychophysics, 39*, 197–204.

Hendrickson, A., & Boothe, R. (1976). Morphology of the retina and dorsal lateral geniculate nucleus in dark-reared monkeys (*Macaca nemestrina*). *Vision Research, 16*, 517–521.

Hess, C. W., Meienberg, O., & Ludin, H. P. (1982). Visual evoked potentials in acute occipital blindness. Diagnostic and prognostic value. *Journal of Neurology, 227*, 193–200.

Hill, E. W. (1986). Orientation and mobility. In G. T. Scholl (Ed.), *Foundations of education for blind and visually handicapped children and youth: Theory and practice* (pp. 315–340). New York: American Foundation for the Blind.

Hill, E. W., Rosen, S., Correa, V. I., & Langley, M. B. (1984). Preschool orientation and mobility: An expanded definition. *Education of the Visually Handicapped, 16*, 58–72.

Hollins, M. (1985). Styles of mental imagery in blind adults. *Neuropsychologia, 23*, 561–566.

Hollins, M. (1986). Haptic mental rotation: More consistent in blind subjects? *Journal of Visual Impairment & Blindness, 80*, 950–952.

Hollyfield, R. L., & Foulke, E. (1983). The spatial cognition of blind pedestrians. *Journal of Visual Impairment & Blindness, 77*, 204–210.

Holmes, G. (1919). The cortical localization of vision. *British Medical Journal, 2*, 193–199.

Hoover, R. E. (1950). The cane as a travel aid. In P. A. Zahl (Ed.), *Blindness: Modern approaches to the unseen environment* (pp. 353–365). Princeton, NJ: Princeton University Press.

Hornby, G., Kay, L., Satherley, M., & Kay, N. (1985). Spatial awareness training of blind children using the Trisensor. In D. H. Warren & E. R. Strelow (Eds.), *Electronic spatial sensing for the blind: Contributions from perception, rehabilitation, and computer vision* (pp. 257–272). Dordrecht, The Netherlands: Martinus Nijhoff.

Hubel, D. H. (1963). The visual cortex of the brain. *Scientific American, 209*(5) 54–62.

Hubel, D. H., & Wiesel, T. N. (1962). Receptive fields, binocular interaction and functional architecture in the cat's visual cortex. *Journal of Physiology, 160*, 106–154.

Huebner, K. M. (1986). Social skills. In G. T. Scholl (Ed.), *Foundations of education for blind and visually handicapped children and youth: Theory and practice* (pp. 341–362). New York: American Foundation for the Blind.

Humphrey, G. K., & Humphrey, D. E. (1985). The use of binaural sensory aids by blind infants and children: Theoretical and applied issues. In F. J. Morrison, C. Lord, & D. P. Keating (Eds.), *Applied developmental psychology* (Vol. 2, pp. 59–97). Orlando, FL: Academic Press.

Hunter, I. M. L. (1954). Tactile-kinaesthetic perception of straightness in blind and sighted humans. *Quarterly Journal of Experimental Psychology*, 6, 149–154.

Hyvärinen, J., Carlson, S., & Hyvärinen, L. (1981). Early visual deprivation alters modality of neuronal responses in area 19 of monkey cortex. *Neuroscience Letters, 26*, 239–243.

Inhelder, B., & Piaget, J. (1958). *The growth of logical thinking from childhood to adolescence.* New York: Basic Books.

Jacquy, J., Piraux, A., Jocquet, P., Lhoas, J. P., & Noel, G. (1977). Cerebral blood flow in the adult blind: A rheoencephalographic study of cerebral blood flow changes during Braille reading. *Electroencephalography and Clinical Neurophysiology, 43*, 325–329.

James, W. (1961). *The varieties of religious experience.* New York: Collier Books. (First published in 1902).

Jastrow, J. (1888). The dreams of the blind. *New Princeton Review, 5,* 18–34.

Jose, R. T. (Ed.). (1983). *Understanding low vision.* New York: American Foundation for the Blind.

Josephson, E. (1964). A report on blind readers. *New Outlook for the Blind, 58,* 97–101.

Judd, D. B., & Wyszecki, G. (1963). *Color in business, science, and industry* (2nd ed.). New York: Wiley.

Kahn, H. A., & Moorhead, H. B. (1973). *Statistics on blindness in the Model Reporting Area, 1969–1970.* DHEW Publication No. (NIH)73-427.

Kahn, T. C. (1956). Kahn test of symbol arrangement: Administration and scoring. *Perceptual and Motor Skills, 6,* 299–334. (Monograph Supplement 4).

Kastein, S., Spaulding, I., & Scharf, B. (1980). *Raising the young blind child: A guide for parents and educators.* New York: Human Sciences Press.

Kay, L., & Strelow, E. (1977). Blind babies need specially-designed aids. *New Scientist, 74,* 709-712.

Kekelis, L. S., & Andersen, E. S. (1984). Family communication styles and language development. *Journal of Visual Impairment & Blindness, 78,* 54–65.

Keller, H. (1905). *The story of my life* (J. A. Macy, Ed.). New York: Grosset & Dunlap.

Keller, H. (1929). *Midstream: My later life.* Garden City, NY: Doubleday, Doran.

Kellogg, W. N. (1962). Sonar system of the blind. *Science, 137,* 399–404.

Kennedy, J. M. (1983). What can we learn about pictures from the blind? *American Scientist, 71,* 19–26.

Kennedy, J. M., & Fox, N. (1977). Pictures to see and pictures to touch. In D. Perkins & B. Leondar (Eds.), *The arts and cognition* (pp. 118–135). Baltimore: Johns Hopkins University Press.

Kerr, N. H., Foulkes, D., & Schmidt, M. (1982). The structure of laboratory dream reports in blind and sighted subjects. *Journal of Nervous and Mental Disease, 170,* 286–294.

Kessler, J. (1984). Accessible computers in the university. *Journal of Visual Impairment & Blindness, 78,* 414–417.

Kinsey, V. E. (1956). Retrolental fibroplasia: Cooperative study of retrolental fibroplasia and the use of oxygen. *A. M. A. Archives of Ophthalmology, 56,* 481–543.

Kipling, R. (1899). *The light that failed.* Garden City, NY: Doubleday.

Kirchner, C., & Peterson, R. (1980). Statistical brief No. 7: Multiple impairments among non-institutionalized blind and visually impaired persons. *Journal of Visual Impairment & Blindness, 74,* 42–44.

Kirchner, C., & Peterson, R. (1982). Statistical brief No. 21: Vocational and rehabilitation placements of blind and visually impaired clients: U.S. 1980. *Journal of Visual Impairment & Blindness, 76,* 426–429.

Kirtley, D. D. (1975). *The psychology of blindness.* Chicago: Nelson–Hall.

Klatzky, R. L., Lederman, S. J., & Metzger, V. A. (1985). Identifying objects by touch: An "expert system". *Perception & Psychophysics, 37,* 299–302.

Klatzky, R. L., Lederman, S., & Reed, C. (1987). There's more to touch than meets the eye: The salience of object attributes for haptics with and without vision. *Journal of Experimental Psychology: General, 116,* 356–369.

Kleck, R. (1968). Physical stigma and nonverbal cues emitted in face-to-face interaction. *Human Relations, 21,* 19–28.

Kleck, R., Ono, H., & Hastorf, A. H. (1966). The effects of physical deviance upon face-to-face interaction. *Human Relations, 19,* 425–436.

Koestler, F. A. (1976). *The unseen minority: A social history of blindness in the United States.* New York: David McKay.

Kolata, G. (1986). Blindness of prematurity unexplained. *Science, 231*, 20–22.

Kosslyn, S. M. (1980). *Image and mind.* Cambridge, MA: Harvard University Press.

Kuder, G. F. (1966). *Kuder Occupational Interest Survey. General manual.* Chicago: Science Research Associates.

Landau, B., & Gleitman, L. R. (1985). *Language and experience: Evidence from the blind child.* Cambridge, MA: Harvard University Press.

Landau, B., Spelke, E., & Gleitman, H. (1984). Spatial knowledge in a young blind child. *Cognition, 16*, 225–260.

Langer, E. J., Fiske, S., Taylor, S. E., & Chanowitz, B. (1976). Stigma, staring and discomfort: A novel-stimulus hypothesis. *Journal of Experimental Social Psychology, 12*, 451–463.

Lashley, K. S. (1943). Studies of cerebral function in learning. XII. Loss of the maze habit after occipital lesions in blind rats. *Journal of Comparative Neurology, 79*, 431–462.

Lederman, S. J., & Klatzky, R. L. (1987). Hand movements: A window into haptic object recognition. *Cognitive Psychology, 19*, 342–368.

Lederman, S. J., Thorne, G., & Jones, B. (1986). Perception of texture by vision and touch: Multidimensionality and intersensory integration. *Journal of Experimental Psychology: Human Perception and Performance, 12*, 169–180.

Lerman, S. (1959). Glaucoma. *Scientific American, 201*(2), 110–117.

Livingstone, M. S., & Hubel, D. H. (1987). Psychophysical evidence for separate channels for the perception of form, color, movement, and depth. *Journal of Neuroscience, 7*, 3416–3468.

Loomis, J. M. (1981). On the tangibility of letters and braille. *Perception & Psychophysics, 29*, 37–46.

Lopata, D. J., & Pasnak, R. (1976). Accelerated conservation acquisition and IQ gains by blind children. *Genetic Psychology Monographs, 93*, 3–25.

Lowenfeld, B. (1981). *Berthold Lowenfeld on blindness and blind people: Selected papers.* New York: American Foundation for the Blind.

Lukoff, I. F. (1972). Attitudes toward the blind. In *Attitudes toward blind persons.* New York: American Foundation for the Blind.

Lukoff, I. F., & Whiteman, M. (1961). Attitudes toward blindness—Some preliminary findings. *New Outlook for the Blind, 55*, (2), 39–44.

Marmor, G. S., & Zaback, L. A. (1976). Mental rotation by the blind: Does mental rotation depend on visual imagery? *Journal of Experimental Psychology: Human Perception and Performance, 2*, 515–521.

Marmor, M. F. (1982). Aging and the retina. In R. Sekuler, D. Kline, & K. Dismukes (Eds.), *Aging and human visual function* (pp. 59–78). New York: Alan R. Liss.

Matsuda, M. M. (1984). A comparative analysis of blind and sighted children's communication skills. *Journal of Visual Impairment & Blindness, 78*, 1–5.

McAuley, D. L., & Russell, R. W. R. (1979). Correlation of CAT scan and visual field defects in vascular lesions of the posterior visual pathways. *Journal of Neurology, Neurosurgery and Psychiatry, 42*, 298–311.

McConkie, G. W. (1983). Eye movements and perception during reading. In K. Rayner (Ed.), *Eye movements in reading: Perceptual and language processes* (pp. 65–96). New York: Academic Press.

McCormick, A. (1977). The retinopathy of prematurity in the newborn. *Current Problems in Pediatrics, 7*(11).

McGuinness, R. M. (1970). A descriptive study of blind children educated in the itinerant teacher, resource room, and special school settings. *American Foundation for the Blind Research Bulletin*, No. 20, 1–56.

McInnes, J. M., & Treffry, J. A. (1982). *Deaf-blind infants and children: A developmental guide.* Toronto: University of Toronto Press.

McKinney, J. P. (1964). Hand schema in children. *Psychonomic Science, 1*, 99–100.

Meadows, J. C. (1974). Disturbed perception of colours associated with localized cerebral lesions. *Brain, 97,* 615–632.

Merzenich, M. M. (1987). Dynamic neocortical processes and the origins of higher brain functions. In J.-P. Changeux & M. Konishi (Eds.), *The neural and molecular bases of learning* (pp. 337–358). Chichester, England: Wiley.

Meshcheryakov, A. (1979). *Awakening to life: Forming behaviour and the mind in deaf-blind children* (K. Judelson, Trans.). Moscow: Progress Publishers. (Original work published 1974).

Metzler, J., & Shepard, R. N. (1974). Transformational studies of the internal representation of three-dimensional objects. In R. L. Solso (Ed.), *Theories of cognitive psychology: The Loyola symposium* (pp. 147–201). Potomac, MD: Erlbaum.

Millar, S. (1978). Short-term serial tactual recall: Effects of grouping on tactually probed recall of Braille letters and nonsense shapes by blind children. *British Journal of Psychology, 69,* 17–24.

Monbeck, M. E. (1973). *The meaning of blindness: Attitudes toward blindness and blind people.* Bloomington: Indiana University Press.

Muir, D. W., Humphrey, G. K., Dodwell, P. C., & Humphrey, D. E. (1985). Use of sonar sensors with human infants. In D. H. Warren & E. R. Strelow (Eds.), *Electronic spatial sensing for the blind: Contributions from perception, rehabilitation, and computer vision* (pp. 299–324). Dordrecht, The Netherlands: Martinus Nijhoff.

Muldoon, J. F. (1986). Carroll revisited: Innovations in rehabilitation, 1938–1971. *Journal of Visual Impairment & Blindness, 80,* 617–626.

National Society to Prevent Blindness. (1980). *Vision problems in the U.S.* New York: National Society to Prevent Blindness.

Newport, E. L., Gleitman, H., & Gleitman, L. R. (1977). Mother, I'd rather do it myself: Some effects and non-effects of maternal speech style. In C. E. Snow & C. A. Ferguson (Eds.), *Talking to children: Language input and acquisition* (pp. 109–149). Cambridge, England: Cambridge University Press.

Nolan, C. Y., & Kederis, C. J. (1969). *Perceptual factors in braille word recognition.* New York: American Foundation for the Blind.

Norris, M., Spaulding, P. J., & Brodie, F. H. (1957). *Blindness in children.* Chicago: University of Chicago Press.

Novikova, L. A. (1974). *Blindness and the electrical activity of the brain: Electroencephalographic studies of the effects of sensory impairment* (B. Sznycer & L. Zielinski, Trans.; Z. S. Jastrzembska, Ed.). New York: American Foundation for the Blind. (Original work published 1967).

Omwake, E. B., & Solnit, A. J. (1961). "It isn't fair": The treatment of a blind child. *Psychoanalytic Study of the Child, 16,* 352–404.

Orbach, J. (1959). "Functions" of striate cortex and the problem of mass action. *Psychological Bulletin, 56,* 271–292.

Parks, M. M. (1982). Visual results in aphakic children. *American Journal of Ophthalmology, 94,* 441–449.

Partos, F., & Kirchner, C. (1986). Statistical brief No. 32: The Randolph–Sheppard business enterprise program: Program characteristics. *Journal of Visual Impairment & Blindness, 80,* 685–689.

Pearlman, A. L., Birch, J., & Meadows, J. C. (1979). Cerebral color blindness: An acquired defect in hue discrimination. *Annals of Neurology, 5,* 253–261.

Perenin, M. T., & Jeannerod, M. (1978). Visual function within the hemianopic field following early cerebral hemidecortication in man. I. Spatial localisation. *Neuropsychologia, 16,* 1–13.

Perenin, M. T., Ruel, J., & Hecaen, H. (1980). Residual visual capacities in a case of cortical blindness. *Cortex, 16,* 605–612.

Peterson, M. (1985). Vocational evaluation of blind and visually impaired persons for technical, professional, and managerial positions. *Journal of Visual Impairment & Blindness, 79,* 478–480.

Phillips, J. R., Johnson, K. O., & Browne, H. M. (1983). A comparison of visual and two modes of tactual letter resolution. *Perception & Psychophysics, 34,* 243–249.

Piaget, J., & Inhelder, B. (1969). *The psychology of the child.* New York: Basic Books.

Platt, P. S. (1950). Additional factors affecting the blind. In P. A. Zahl (Ed.), *Blindness: Modern approaches to the unseen environment* (pp. 57–68). Princeton, NJ: Princeton University Press.

Pogorelc, R. L. (1972). Developing special programs for subprofessionals and volunteers. In R. E. Hardy & J. G. Cull (Eds.), *Social and rehabilitation services for the blind* (pp. 108–114). Springfield, IL: Charles C. Thomas.

Polyak, S. (1957). *The vertebrate visual system.* Chicago: University of Chicago Press.

Ponchillia, P. E., & Kaarlela, R. (1986). *Post-rehabilitation use of adaptive skills. Journal of Visual Impairment & Blindness, 80,* 665–669.

Pöppel, E., Held, R., & Frost, D. (1973). Residual visual function after brain wounds involving the central visual pathways in man. *Nature, 243,* 295–296.

Potok, A. (1980). *Ordinary daylight.* New York: Holt, Rinehart, & Winston.

Reivich, M., Cobbs, W., Rosenquist, A., Stein, A., Schatz, N., Savino, P., Alavi, A., & Greenberg, J. (1981). Abnormalities in local cerebral glucose metabolism in patients with visual field defects. *Journal of Cerebral Blood Flow and Metabolism, 1* (Suppl. 1), S471–S472.

Révész, G. (1950). *Psychology and art of the blind* (H. A. Wolff, Trans.). London: Longmans, Green.

Rice, C. E. (1967). Human echo perception. *Science, 155,* 656–664.

Richardson, S. A., Goodman, N., Hastorf, A. H., & Dornbusch, S. M. (1961). Cultural uniformity in reaction to physical disabilities. *American Sociological Review, 26,* 241–247.

Richardson, S. A., Ronald, L., & Kleck, R. E. (1974). The social status of handicapped and nonhandicapped boys in a camp setting. *Journal of Special Education, 8,* 143–152.

Riesen, A. H. (1947). The development of visual perception in man and chimpanzee. *Science, 106,* 107–108.

Rieser, J. J., Guth, D. A., & Hill, E. W. (1982). Mental processes mediating independent travel: Implications for orientation and mobility. *Journal of Visual Impairment & Blindness, 76,* 213–218.

Rieser, J. J., Guth, D. A., & Hill, E. W. (1986). Sensitivity to perspective structure while walking without vision. *Perception, 15,* 173–188.

Rieser, J. J., Lockman, J. J., & Pick, H. L. (1980). The role of visual experience in knowledge of spatial layout. *Perception & Psychophysics, 28,* 185–190.

Riggs, L. A. (1985). Sensory processes: Vision. In G. A. Kimble & K. Schlesinger (Eds.), *Topics in the history of psychology* (Vol. 1, pp. 165–219). Hillsdale, NJ: Lawrence Erlbaum Associates.

Ripps, H. (1981). Rods, rhodopsin, and the visual response. In L. M. Proenza, J. M. Enoch, & A. Jampolsky (Eds.), *Clinical applications of visual psychophysics* (pp. 152–169). Cambridge, England: Cambridge University Press.

Rives, L. H., Jr. (1972). History of federal vocational rehabilitation as it affects the blind. In R. E. Hardy & J. G. Cull (Eds.), *Social and rehabilitation services for the blind* (pp. 69–87). Springfield, IL: Charles C. Thomas.

Roberts, F. K. (1986). Education for the visually handicapped: A social and educational history. In G. T. Scholl (Ed.), *Foundations of education for blind and visually handicapped children and youth: Theory and practice* (pp. 1–18). New York: American Foundation for the Blind.

Rock, I., & Victor, J. (1964). Vision and touch: An experimentally created conflict between the two senses. *Science, 143,* 594–596.

Rowland, C. (1984). Preverbal communication of blind infants and their mothers. *Journal of Visual Impairment & Blindness, 78,* 297–302.

Rubin, E. J. (1964). *Abstract functioning in the blind.* New York: American Foundation for the Blind.

Schauer, G. (1951). Motivation of attitudes toward blindness. *New Outlook for the Blind, 45,* 39–42.

Schlaegel, T. F., Jr. (1953). The dominant method of imagery in blind as compared to sighted adolescents. *Journal of Genetic Psychology, 83*, 265–277.

Schneider, G. E. (1969). Two visual systems. *Science, 163*, 895–902.

Scholl, G. T. (Ed.). (1986). *Foundations of education for blind and visually handicapped children and youth: Theory and practice.* New York: American Foundation for the Blind.

Schulz, P. J. (1980). *How does it feel to be blind?* Los Angeles: Muse–Ed Co.

Schuster, C. S. (1986). Sex education of the visually impaired child: The role of parents. *Journal of Visual Impairment & Blindness, 80*, 675–680.

Schwartz, M. (1984). The role of sound for space and object perception in the congenitally blind infant. *Advances in Infancy Research, 3*, 23–56.

Scott, E. P., Jan, J. E., & Freeman, R. D. (1977). *Can't your child see?* Baltimore: University Park Press.

Seashore, C. E., & Ling, T. L. (1918). The comparative sensitiveness of blind and seeing persons. In C. E. Seashore (Ed.), University of Iowa Studies in Psychology, No. 7. *Psychological Monographs, 25*(2), (Whole No. 108), 148–158.

Senden, M. von. (1960). *Space and sight* (P. Heath, Trans.). Glencoe, IL: Free Press. (Original work published 1932).

Shepard, R. N. (1978). The mental image. *American Psychologist, 33*, 125–137.

Sherman, S. M. (1973). Visual field defects in monocularly and binocularly deprived cats. *Brain Research, 49*, 25–45.

Sherman, S. M. (1977). The effect of cortical and tectal lesions on the visual fields of binocularly deprived cats. *Journal of Comparative Neurology, 172*, 231–245.

Sherman, S. M., & Spear, P. D. (1982). Organization of visual pathways in normal and visually deprived cats. *Physiological Reviews, 62*, 738–855.

Siller, J. (1970). Generality of attitudes toward the physically disabled. *American Psychological Association Convention Proceedings, 5*, 697–698.

Silverman, W. A. (1980). *Retrolental fibroplasia: A modern parable.* New York: Grune & Stratton.

Simeonsson, R. J. (1986). *Psychological and developmental assessment of special children.* Boston: Allyn and Bacon.

Singer, W., & Tretter, F. (1976). Receptive-field properties and neuronal connectivity in striate and parastriate cortex of contour-deprived cats. *Journal of Neurophysiology, 39*, 613–630.

Skrtic, T. M., Clark, F. L., & White, W. J. (1982). Modification of attitudes of regular education preservice teachers toward visually impaired students. *Journal of Visual Impairment & Blindness, 76*, 49–52.

Smith, V. C., Pokorny, J., & Ernest, J. T. (1977). Primary hereditary optic atrophies. In A. E. Krill, *Krill's hereditary retinal and choroidal diseases: Vol. II. Clinical characteristics* (pp. 1109–1135). Hagerstown, MD: Harper & Row.

Snyder, M. L., Kleck, R. E., Strenta, A., & Mentzer, S. J. (1979). Avoidance of the handicapped: An attributional ambiguity analysis. *Journal of Personality and Social Psychology, 37*, 2297–2306.

Sommer, A. (1982). *Nutritional blindness.* New York: Oxford University Press.

Sonnier, B. J. (1985). Animal models of plasticity and sensory substitution. In D. H. Warren & E. R. Strelow (Eds.), *Electronic spatial sensing for the blind: Contributions from perception, rehabilitation, and computer vision* (pp. 359–364). Dordrecht, The Netherlands: Martinus Nijhoff.

Starlinger, I., & Niemeyer, W. (1981). Do the blind hear better? Investigations on auditory processing in congenital or early acquired blindness. I. Peripheral functions. *Audiology, 20*, 503–509.

Stern, D. N. (1974). Mother and infant at play: The dyadic interaction involving facial, vocal, and gaze behaviors. In M. Lewis & L. A. Rosenblum (Eds.), *The effect of the infant on its caregiver* (pp. 187–213). New York: Wiley.

Stewart, I. W., Van Hasselt, V. B., Simon, J., & Thompson, W. B. (1985). The Community

Adjustment Program (CAP) for visually impaired adolescents. *Journal of Visual Impairment & Blindness, 79,* 49–54.

Stotland, J. (1984). Relationship of parents to professionals: A challenge to professionals. *Journal of Visual Impairment & Blindness, 78,* 69–74.

Strelow, E. R. (1983). Use of the Binaural Sensory Aid by young children. *Journal of Visual Impairment & Blindness, 77,* 429–438.

Strelow, E. R., & Warren, D. H. (1985). Sensory substitution in blind children and neonates. In D. H. Warren & E. R. Strelow (Eds.), *Electronic spatial sensing for the blind: Contributions from perception, rehabilitation, and computer vision* (pp. 273–298). Dordrecht, The Netherlands: Martinus Nijhoff.

Strenta, A., & Kleck, R. E. (1982). Perceptions of task feedback: Investigating "kind" treatment of the handicapped. *Personality and Social Psychology Bulletin, 8,* 706–711.

Supa, M., Cotzin, M., & Dallenbach, K. M. (1944). "Facial vision:" The perception of obstacles by the blind. *American Journal of Psychology, 57,* 133–183.

Swallow, R.-M., & Poulsen, M. K. (1983). Cognitive development of young visually handicapped children. In M. E. Mulholland & M. V. Wurster (Eds.), *"Help me become everything I can be": Proceedings, North American Conference on Visually Handicapped Infants and Preschool Children* (pp. 36–46). New York: American Foundation for the Blind.

Teuber, H.-L., Battersby, W. S., & Bender, M. B. (1960). *Visual field defects after penetrating missile wounds of the brain.* Cambridge, MA: Harvard University Press.

Thornton, W. (1975). Four years' use of the binaural sensory aid. *New Outlook for the Blind, 69,* 7–10.

Tou, J. T., & Adjouadi, M. (1985). Computer vision for the blind. In D. H. Warren & E. R. Strelow (Eds.), *Electronic spatial sensing for the blind: Contributions from perception, rehabilitation, and computer vision* (pp. 83–124). Dordrecht, The Netherlands: Martinus Nijhoff.

Twersky, J. (1953). *The face of the deep.* Cleveland: World Publishing Co.

Twersky, J. (1955). *Blindness in literature: Examples of depictions and attitudes.* New York: American Foundation for the Blind.

Twersky, J. (1959). *The sound of the walls.* Garden City, NY: Doubleday.

U.S. Bureau of the Census. (1984). *Statistical abstract of the United States: 1985* (105th ed.). Washington, DC.

Urwin, C. (1983). Dialogue and cognitive functioning in the early language development of three blind children. In A. E. Mills (Ed.), *Language acquisition in the blind child: Normal and deficient* (pp. 142–161). London: Croom Helm.

Urwin, C. (1984). Communication in infancy and the emergence of language in blind children. In R. L. Schiefelbusch & J. Pickar (Eds.), *The acquisition of communicative competence* (pp. 479–524). Baltimore: University Park Press.

Valvo, A. (1971). *Sight restoration after long-term blindness: The problems and behavior patterns of visual rehabilitation* (L. L. Clark and Z. Z. Jastrzembska, Eds.). New York: American Foundation for the Blind.

Vander Kolk, C. J. (1981). *Assessment and planning with the visually impaired.* Baltimore: University Park Press.

Van Hasselt, V. B. (1983). Social adaptation in the blind. *Clinical Psychology Review, 3,* 87–102.

Van Hasselt, V. B., Hersen, M., & Kazdin, A. E. (1985). Assessment of social skills in visually-handicapped adolescents. *Behaviour Research and Therapy, 23,* 53–63.

Van Hasselt, V. B., Simon, J., & Mastantuono, A. K. (1982). Social skills training for blind children and adolescents. *Education of the Visually Handicapped, 14,* 34–40.

Wallsten, T. S., & Lambert, R. M. (1981). Visual braille and print reading as a function of display field size. *Bulletin of the Psychonomic Society, 17,* 15–18.

Walsh, J. (1986). River blindness: A gamble pays off. *Science, 232,* 922–925.

Walsh, J. (1987). Merck donates drug for river blindness. *Science, 238,* 610.

Walsh, S. R., & Holzberg, R. (Eds.). (1981). *Understanding and educating the deaf-blind/severely and profoundly handicapped: An international perspective.* Springfield, IL: Charles C. Thomas.

Ward, A. L. (1973). The response of individuals beginning work with blind persons. *New Outlook for the Blind, 67*(1), 1–5.

Warren, D. H. (1970). Intermodality interactions in spatial localization. *Cognitive Psychology, 1*, 114–133.

Warren, D. H. (1982). The development of haptic perception. In W. Schiff & E. Foulke (Eds.), *Tactual perception: A sourcebook* (pp. 82–129). Cambridge, England: Cambridge University Press.

Warren, D. H. (1984). *Blindness and early childhood development* (2nd ed., rev.). New York: American Foundation for the Blind.

Warren, D. H., Anooshian, L. J., & Bollinger, J. G. (1973). Early vs. late blindness: The role of early vision in spatial behavior. *American Foundation for the Blind Research Bulletin, 26*, 151–170.

Warren, D. H., & Strelow, E. R. (1985). Training the use of artificial spatial displays. In D. H. Warren & E. R. Strelow (Eds.), *Electronic spatial sensing for the blind: Contributions from perception, rehabilitation, and computer vision* (pp. 201–216). Dordrecht, The Netherlands: Martinus Nijhoff.

Watkins, D. W., Wilson, J. R., & Sherman, S. M. (1978). Receptive-field properties of neurons in binocular and monocular segments of striate cortex in cats raised with binocular lid suture. *Journal of Neurophysiology, 41*, 322–337.

Weiskrantz, L. (1980). Varieties of residual experience. *Quarterly Journal of Experimental Psychology, 32*, 365–386.

Weiskrantz, L. (1987). Residual vision in a scotoma: A follow-up study of "form" discrimination. *Brain, 110*, 77–92.

Weiskrantz, L., Warrington, E. K., Sanders, M. D., & Marshall, J. (1974). Visual capacity in the hemianopic field following a restricted occipital ablation. *Brain, 97*, 709–728.

Weiter, J. J., Delori, F. C., Wing, G. L., & Fitch, K. A. (1985). Relationship of senile macular degeneration to ocular pigmentation. *American Journal of Ophthalmology, 99*, 185–187.

Welch, R. B., & Warren, D. H. (1980). Immediate perceptual response to intersensory discrepancy. *Psychological Bulletin, 88*, 638–667.

White, B. W., Saunders, F. A., Scadden, L., Bach-y-Rita, P., & Collins, C. C. (1970). Seeing with the skin. *Perception & Psychophysics, 7*, 23–27.

Whitsel, B. L., Favorov, O., Tommerdahl, M., Diamond, M., Juliano, S., & Kelly, D. (1989). Dynamic processes govern the somatosensory cortical response to natural stimulation. In J. S. Lund (Ed.), *Sensory processing in the mammalian brain: Neural substrates and experimental strategies* (pp. 84–116). New York: Oxford University Press.

Whitstock, R. H. (1980). Dog guides. In R. L. Welsh & B. B. Blasch (Eds.), *Foundations of orientation and mobility* (pp. 565–580). New York: American Foundation for the Blind.

Wiesel, T. N., & Hubel, D. H. (1963). Single cell responses in striate cortex of kittens deprived of vision in one eye. *Journal of Neurophysiology, 26*, 1003–1017.

Wiesel, T. N., & Hubel, D. H. (1965a). Comparison of the effects of unilateral and bilateral eye closure on cortical unit responses in kittens. *Journal of Neurophysiology, 28*, 1029–1040.

Wiesel, T. N., & Hubel, D. H. (1965b). Extent of recovery from the effects of visual deprivation in kittens. *Journal of Neurophysiology, 28*, 1060–1072.

Wiesel, T. N., & Hubel, D. H. (1974). Ordered arrangement of orientation columns in monkeys lacking visual experience. *Journal of Comparative Neurology, 158*, 307–318.

Williams, R. C. (1972). Orientation and mobility: A symposium. Background discourse. In R. E. Hardy & J. G. Cull (Eds.), *Social and rehabilitation services for the blind* (pp. 226–241). Springfield, IL: Charles C. Thomas.

Worchel, P. (1951). Space perception and orientation in the blind. *Psychological Monographs: General and Applied, 65*(15), (Whole No. 332).

Worchel, P., & Dallenbach, K. M. (1947). "Facial vision:" Perception of obstacles by the deaf-blind. *American Journal of Psychology, 60*, 502–553.

World Health Organization Programme Advisory Group on the Prevention of Blindness. (1980).

Report, Sect. 5 and Annex II (Unpublished WHO document PBL/79.1, 1979). Reprinted in International Agency for the Prevention of Blindness under the direction of Sir J. Wilson (Ed.), *World Blindness and its prevention* (pp. 73–84). New York: Oxford University Press.

Yoken, C. (1979). *Living with deaf-blindness: Nine profiles.* Washington, DC: National Academy of Gallaudet College.

Young, R. W. (1976). Visual cells and the concept of renewal. *Investigative Ophthalmology, 15,* 700–725.

Zeki, S. M. (1978). Functional specialization in the visual cortex of the rhesus monkey. *Nature, 274,* 423–428.

Zimler, J., & Keenan, J. M. (1983). Imagery in the congenitally blind: How visual are visual images? *Journal of Experimental Psychology: Learning, Memory, and Cognition,* 9, 269–282.

# AUTHOR INDEX

C



D



E



F



G

W



Y Z

# SUBJECT INDEX